The Ponzi Princess

The Ponzi Princess

—ᴟ—

Mark Morewitz

Author's photo by Bill Pirkel Photography

ISBN: 150779018X
ISBN 13: 9781507790182
Library of Congress Control Number: 2015901738
CreateSpace Independent Publishing Platform
North Charleston, South Carolina

For Myron and Kim
Thank you for your unwavering love and support

Author's Note

In this book, I recount relevant events and interactions related to my relationship with Laurie Schneider. I include details she told me about her personal life so that readers can best understand how powerful her deceit was in all spheres of her life and how extensively she manipulated people to further her illegal activities. As with everyone who has come into contact with her, there was no line between our "personal" and our "professional" relationship. Everything about our "friendship" related to her victimization of me, my family, and my friends. I do not repeat things Laurie Schneider told me because I believe they are true. In fact, as this story makes clear, most of what she told me turned out to be false. Therefore, within the context of this book, the reader should not construe my recounting of her stories as an indication that anything she told me was based in reality, particularly when it comes to things she told me about others.

I have changed most of the other people's names to respect her victims' privacy. I have reconstructed conversations in order to describe the gestalt of my interactions with Laurie Schneider as accurately as possible. Where written records exist that I have access to, I use text from actual correspondence, journal entries, emails, and court documents to reconstruct conversations.

Introduction

"I love you more today than yesterday" was the way Laurie ended many of our in-person and text conversations. She reached out to me whenever I was on her mind, regardless of the time of day or if I was out of town. Her face lit up when I walked into a room. She'd always sashay over, offering a cheek for me to kiss. "I like having that handsome face and your brilliant mind as close to me as possible" she gave as the reason why I sat only a foot away from her in the 10,000 square-foot warehouse rented for her entertainment and janitorial supply companies. Her husband Vince was annoyed at our close connection and several of her other business partners seemed to wonder what I had to offer Laurie that made her love me so much.

The truth is that I honestly enjoyed being with my eccentric friend and valued our connection right up until the end. She showed incredible loyalty and support during happy and sad times. Laurie was also a ton of fun, two tons if you count each of her enormous breasts, which she wielded like seductive weapons. Her innate playfulness was a beacon to the kid in me. We bonded over huge amounts of food as we shared stories about our mashugana families and the many men in her life. The fact that she was helping me and my family earn enormous amounts of money often seemed like icing on the cake.

Most of the others were just using her and she knew it. "They're all just greedy assholes. No one loves me the way you do," she'd say with sadness in her eyes. At the time, I felt it was her own fault because she presented herself as an alchemist and therefore became a pied piper to many who only saw her as a source of unlimited income. Helping people acquire and exponentially increase their wealth through her homegrown high-yield investments was a magnetic attraction that brought most people to their knees in front of her. She had an instinctive talent to create an environment where she was queen bee, and anyone who came in contact became her drone. It turns out that I was no exception.

At the time I met Laurie, greed was a popular, if unspoken, trend in the United States. The financial industry's many divisions seemed to be working independently to create a perfect storm of instability. Home appraisers padded the value of properties. Mortgage companies gave out high-interest loans, based on inflated property values, to people without the ability to pay the long-term debt. Banks packaged these less-than-stable subprime mortgages in bulk and sold them to international financial firms, claiming they were solid investments. Main Street individuals bought stock in these international financial firms, trusting the judgment of brokers who made a commission on the sale. Regulators seemed to look the other way while the entire Western world was being hoodwinked. The economy soared and average American consumers maxed out their credit cards instead of saving up for what they wanted to buy.

At the end of 2008, when the world found out about the far-reaching impact of Bernie Madoff's $65 billion Ponzi scheme, irregularities in other financial institutions came to light. The international monetary picture quickly turned solemn. Huge fiduciary institutions like Bear Stearns collapsed, banks stopped lending, and the U.S. government began planning a large scale bailout. The global financial crisis forced most individuals to pull money out of short-term investments in preparation for a possible economic depression.

We now understand that this sudden change in the economy caused an abrupt halt to the thousands of Ponzi and pyramid schemes being run by charismatic charlatans all across the country. There was no way to pay the existing investors without new money coming in. Hundreds of thousands of people across the United States soon found out they were victims of fraud. Many lost everything.

In January 2009, I discovered that I too had been duped. Laurie's "deals" that I had invested in and introduced as a sure thing to almost all of my family and friends turned out to be a total scam. Most of us saw our life savings disappear. People who were very close to me were unsure if I was in on the con. I lost the respect and trust from the people I loved most, and my life totally fell apart. My relationship with Laurie Schneider would forever be altered as I came to realize her true nature.

This is the story of the Ponzi Princess and me.

Every Story Has a Beginning

Like a child's fairy tale, everything started out easy and fun. In December 2005, my husband, Nate, and I met Laurie Schneider and she asked us if we wanted to invest in an exciting real estate deal.

At the time, I was thirty-five and ripe to make a major life change. The grueling daily grind I was living in New York City was the complete opposite of what I wanted my life to be. I was bored with my administrative job in social services and had been looking for a way out of nonprofit work. Nate and I had gotten married a year before, and along with my good friend Joe had scraped enough money to buy a large dilapidated Victorian house in Ditmas Park, Brooklyn, that needed substantial renovation. The neighborhood was filled with lovely late-nineteenth-century Victorian homes and was only twenty minutes outside of Manhattan by way of the Q subway line. Much of my time and all of our cash went into the house, which added constant stress to our marriage. I had also been terribly lonely since we left San Francisco, where I had developed a strong community of friends. In Brooklyn, I simply didn't seem to fit in, no matter how hard I tried.

Privately, I had begun to long for greater financial freedom that would allow me to quit my job, renovate our house, support my mom, and eventually have kids. It was my version of the American dream. My silent prayers were answered when a Long Island Mary Poppins showed up at my door.

We first heard of the mythical Laurie through Troy and Gregory, a gay couple who lived next door. They credited her with helping them make enough money to allow Gregory to be full-time parent to their daughter, Jamie, and renovate their 4,000-square-foot home. With Laurie and her husband Vince, Troy had cofounded Party Hearty, an entertainment company that provided music, dancers, and other amusements for family and corporate events. Although Gregory, who reminded me of the shy elf from *The Year without a Santa,* tended to be a quiet observer. His partner was a born storyteller; Troy was stout with caramel skin and loved to regale us with scandalous tales of corporate events or the indulgent life of Long Island Jewish families.

"The Bat Mitzvah girl demanded to be brought into the party on the shoulders of four muscle men, like fucking Cleopatra!" he'd say, then pause for dramatic effect. "And lemme tell ya, this twelve-year-old bitch was a fat butterball who had a face that could stop a *clock*!" The last few words were delivered in an affected scream. Everything Troy said came out in a raspy yell that sounded like a hybrid of Carol Channing and Louie Armstrong. I don't think he knew how to speak in a normal voice.

While the entertainment world sounded exciting, it was their other business venture with Laurie that caught our attention. Troy told us that through her charm and persuasiveness, Laurie had coaxed her way into the exclusive world of the Brooklyn docks, which were run by Hasidic Jews. It was a coup that such a male-dominated religious community would work with a woman. She had accompanied her uncle on some of his business runs when she was a teenager, and later Laurie turned the introduction into a small enterprise of buying goods that came into the docks but were never claimed. She called these deals "closeouts" and focused mainly on janitorial supplies, including toilet paper and paper towels.

Troy told us that she used investors' money to buy cargo containers of irregular or slightly damaged supplies, then sold them to wholesalers with a huge markup. The wholesaler would then pay Laurie the profit over a period of three to twelve months, depending on the size of the container. Investors who put up the capital for the buy were given a hefty share of the profits.

Laurie kept the minimum investment at $25,000 but made exceptions for friends (and friends of friends) who didn't have that amount of money. It was the tiny but lucrative world of bottom feeders in the capitalist market. Troy and Gregory had consistently earned 15 to 30 percent profit on their investments throughout the previous four years.

"Why wouldn't Laurie just put up the capital herself?" I asked the boys next door after hearing them brag, yet again, about how much money they were making.

Shaking his head, Troy said, "Most of her money's tied up in two big real estate investments."

Gregory chimed in, telling us that Laurie loved giving extravagant gifts. "Remember a few months ago, we got that oversized hot tub installed in our backyard? It was a present from her, out of the blue."

"Is there a way for us to get in on the action?" I finally asked them one day in October. If they were going to dangle their good fortune in our face, I wanted to at least try to get involved.

"She's gotta invite you in. It's her exclusive club," Troy responded. "But you guys can meet her at my birthday party next month. We definitely want you two to make more money so you can get that ugly-ass house looking better!"

Ever since we had moved in next door, Troy and Gregory had taken on the role of being our financial mentors. Neither Nate nor I had prioritized making a lot of money. I was a social worker who wanted to help people to have better lives. I'd been on my own since I was in college and only made enough money to cover my expenses—no more. The only luxury I afforded myself was eating out at diners or Mexican restaurants whenever I felt like it. Nate was an actor in his late twenties who wanted to own a theater company. He came from a wealthy family but supported himself through working several jobs. We realized that if we wanted to obtain our life goals we needed to make more money and eagerly listened to our neighbors' advice.

They encouraged us to read the *Rich Dad, Poor Dad* books in which the author uses events from his life to teach average people the tricks of earning and maintaining wealth. Troy and Gregory said they followed the author's advice to the letter. However, as Nate and I diligently studied the books and took related seminars over the course of the next six months, we quickly realized that they knew very little about the author's philosophy and were actually relying on Laurie's investments as their sole source of wealth.

On the subway ride to Troy's birthday party, we saw the Statue of Liberty far off in the distance. "Okay, Marky, put on the Morewitz family charm tonight," Nate joked. He knew that my gregarious parents had trained my brothers and me to be socially affable.

I put my arm around him and kissed his cheek. "Trust me, everything I've ever learned will be used to woo and flatter the goddess Laurie."

The birthday party was at a Manhattan club called Lips where pretty boys dressed in drag and lip-synched songs between serving food and drinks. It wasn't a regular hangout for any of us but was a fun sex-in-the-gay-city thing to do. We thanked our lucky stars when we were seated across from Laurie and her assistant Betty.

Laurie's appearance didn't match the glamorous image that I had built up in my mind through months of hearing Troy and Gregory's stories. I had expected a cross between Mae West and Barbara Streisand, but instead I saw a plain-looking woman who resembled Bette Midler from her 1980s blockbuster movies. I anticipated the zaftig body but was very surprised at how disheveled Laurie looked. She kept her khaki floor-length raincoat on when she sat down. Her shoulder-length mousy brown hair had obviously gotten wet during an afternoon rain shower, but she'd made no attempt to tame it. She wore minimal makeup, a little mascara, and lots of lip gloss. Her button nose looked too small for her wide, almond-shaped face, and her lips were too plump. I suspected both were a gift from a plastic surgeon.

It was clear she had no interest in looking good for the crowd that night. In fact, both she and Betty were quiet and seemed out of place. I did my best to make her feel at ease.

"Troy and Gregory told us about the hot tub you bought for them. That was an incredibly sweet gesture," I said, attempting to make conversation.

Laurie looked up from typing a message on her phone. "I bawtered with a client for a pawty we did," she said in a heavy Long Island accent. "He got a kickass pawty, and I got two Jacuzzis. One's in my back yawd, and Troy got the other because he emcee'd the event."

Under the table, Nate tapped me on the knee as a signal to keep the conversation going.

"So, uh, how did you get started in the party-planning business? My mom's a caterer, so I worked in that world for most of my life as a kid."

Laurie's eyes lit up. "Your mom caters in New Yawk?"

"No, I just moved to New York a few years ago," I said, leaning across the table to make myself heard over the music. "How long have you been doing event planning?" I did my best to maintain eye contact and not seem desperate.

Betty was twirling a finger in her blonde hair. "Laurie's da best pawty plannah there is—no doubt!" she managed to say through her gum chewing.

Laurie seemed bored again. "I stawded at my parents' pawty-supply business in Long Island." She dug in her purse for a compact then looked back up at me. "And then met my handsome and talented husband. When I started managing his band, I ended up planning the events he played." She shrugged her shoulders as she checked her phone. "Go figya."

Now Nate leaned into the conversation. "Is he gonna come tonight? I mean your husband . . ." He was trying to be chill, but I could see he was excited to be interacting with Laurie.

"No offense to you two, but my husband doesn't do anything gay, so he'd nevah step foot in a place like *this*." She turned her gaze to the middle of the room where two drag queens with huge neon wigs lip-synched a Cher song. Even though Betty appeared to be in her late forties, she giggled like a schoolgirl as she watched the show.

Laurie peered at Nate and me. "Do you two like this stuff?"

"This is our first time here . . . it's kinda cheesy," I said turning to Nate. "Whaddaya think?"

"Not exactly my thing either. But it's harmless fun."

"So how do you two know Troy again?" Laurie stopped playing with her phone and seemed genuinely interested.

"We're neighbors," Nate said. "We moved in about six months ago."

"Oh, you're *those* gay boys. Troy told me about you."

"But he didn't say nothing 'bout how sweet you both are," Betty interjected with a big toothy grin.

"So, what do you two cuties do?" Laurie asked.

"He's an actor, and I work at a nonprofit that provides services to homeless people."

Laurie looked pleased. "You evah heard of OneSheltah?" she asked. "It's the biggest homeless charity in the City. I provide all their janitorial and paper supplies."

"Wow, that must be huge business," I said, genuinely interested.

"Yeah, the thousands of homeless bums staying in their sheltahs are wiping their asses with my toilet paper." She laughed. "They do about a million dollahs of business with me each year, and their main office is just a few blocks from you, on Church Street, across from the train station."

"I'll keep that in mind. I'm kinda bored right now with what I'm doing and am beginning to look around for other jobs."

"I see that house of yours when I drop off checks for Troy . . . it needs *a lotta* work," Laurie said as she put the compact back into her purse. "If you don't mind me asking, are your families helping with the cost of fixing it up?"

I looked at Nate. "His family lives in Manhattan and is pretty wealthy, but he wants to be independent, so we don't really get any help."

After applying another coat of gloss to her lips, Laurie pointed at Nate. "Lemme guess, your fathah's a lawyah or a doctah."

Nate nodded. "Yep, my dad's an attorney."

"A very successful, big-time corporate attorney," I interjected.

"How'd you guess?" Nate said eagerly.

"It's obvious you went to good schools with the way you tawk with no New Yawk accent," she said. "And you're too polite to be some asshole businessman's kid."

Nate and I looked at each other, wide-eyed.

"Wow, that's incredible, and you make it look so effortless," I said.

"Dawling, you ain't seen nothin' yet!" Laurie said with a smile. "I'm like an X-ray with people. I see right through them." Just then, her phone began to vibrate and she answered it. We tried not to eavesdrop as she talked six-figure deals with someone on the other end of the line.

On the subway ride home, Nate turned to me. "How'd you think it went?"

"We were pleasant and focused on her as much as we could." I rubbed my hands back and forth on my thighs and gritted my teeth. "But Jesus, I so wanted to confront her when she made that ridiculous comment about her homophobic husband."

"That *was* a little awkward. I wasn't sure what you were gonna do."

"But the thing that surprised me most was that she and Troy didn't say a word to each other the entire evening. He's always made it seem like she *loves* the two of them, but I wasn't seeing any of that tonight."

Nate looked straight ahead, then back at me. "You always see things that I never notice."

Nevertheless, a few weeks later, the boys from next door told us that they had good news. We were all watching TV at our house.

"Laurie's got a new real estate deal, and she specifically asked if you two want to hear about it," Gregory said.

"Yeeeessss!" Nate yelled. We gave each other a high five.

"I'm glad we made a good impression," I said. "Tell us more about the deal?" I was ecstatic at the thought of making even a fraction of the money Troy and Gregory earned with her each month.

"It's something about flipping property in fucking Mississippi or Alabama or something," Troy said with his usual dramatic flair. Buying properties at a low price, doing a few hasty renovations, and selling them for a nice profit was a popular trend.

We decided to invite the boys and Laurie to meet at our place. From the outside, the house, which we had named Hazel after the peppy character from the 1960s television show, looked like a decaying castle. It was a three-story Victorian built in the late 1890s with a full, unfinished basement. The crumbling gray siding, installed in 1957, was made of asphalt panels that had a faux cinderblock pattern. Inside, the original ornate parquet floors and woodwork were almost destroyed by renovations made in the late '50s to early '60s. We laughed at some of the kitschy changes, including the mirrored parlor walls that were straight out of Studio 54 and the plastic ceiling tiles in the first floor bathroom that looked like red velvet.

The previous owners had raised a large family in the house and left us their eight-foot Formica dining table, which turned our huge kitchen into a gathering place. The walls were covered with butter-yellow plastic panels that were favored by 1960s-era diners all around New York City, and many of the smoked-stained ceiling tiles sagged like ripe fruit on a tree. Even though the house was tacky and run down, it was cavernous and exuded elegance beneath the schmaltz. Nate and I wanted to restore it to its former glory.

Laurie may have been quiet at Troy's birthday party, but she was in full superstar mode on the night we met at our house. She arrived dressed to impress in a flowing cocoa pantsuit with an over-the-top matching velveteen cape. As she sauntered into the house, I couldn't help but notice her plunging neckline, which revealed her Dolly Parton–sized breasts. Her hair was now a honey blonde and had been professionally styled, and her face was heavily made up. She sashayed down the long hallway toward the kitchen as if a camera crew were following her every step. It only felt natural to seat her at the head of the table.

Her eyes widened at the spread of pesto pizza, hummus, veggie dip, chocolate cookies, and brownies on the table. "Look at *awl* of this food!" She exclaimed. "Oh, the brownies look so yummy, I'll just have a bite . . . mmm, they're delicious! You gay men make such happy homemakahs!"

It was clearly the Laurie Show and we were her adoring audience. As she took out some brochures and put them on the table, she asked,

"Evah heard of the brilliant Floyd Durgin who made millions in real estate? He's a dear friend and he's letting me in on a deal to flip property in Myrtle Beach, Carolina—I forget is it North or South?"

Like a teacher's pet, I studious chimed in. "Myrtle Beach's in South Carolina. I'm from Virginia and know that area."

"A Jewish boy from Virginia? I didn't know our people existed down there!" she said, taking another bite of pizza.

"We're everywhere but down South: we Jews say 'y'all' a lot." I smiled.

"Very cute, Mr. Southern Jewish Man. Okay, this is how the deal works. Floyd has done this a hundred times, and it's guaranteed to triple your money. There's a huge construction company named Beazah Properties that is developing communities in Myrtle Beach." She took a bite of the pizza, chewed a bit, then continued. "If you read the papers, you'll see that millions of Northerners are retiring and moving South, where it's much cheapah."

"I heard somethin' 'bout that, too," Troy said, nodding.

"My aunt and uncle just moved from Jersey to Virginia for that reason," Nate added.

"We're gonna buy huge chunks of these properties in predevelopment and then sell them before construction is complete," Laurie said. Floyd was purchasing entire neighborhoods and allowing her to buy a small block; she in turn was offering to let us buy some of her parcels of land.

"The turnaround is only about nine to twelve months!" she said with a Vanna White smile. She passed out maps of the Beazer development with blueprints of the condos slated for construction. I was impressed.

As she stood up from the table and moved a few chairs down toward Gregory and Troy, her flowing cape made a rustling noise. "I'm giving one of the properties to you as a gift for your lovely dawter because you two are my favorite gay men." She turned toward Nate and me. "No offense, you two." She put her hand on Troy's shoulder. "The money you make from the sale can go into her college fund," she said. She gave each of them an air-kiss.

"Wow, what an amazing gift!" I said as Nate and I gave each other a wide-eyed look. Strangely, Gregory and Troy didn't seem especially grateful for Laurie's present.

After a thorough discussion of the deal, I asked if I could call my two college friends Tracey and Derek, who lived in Los Angeles. Before the meeting, I had told them about Laurie and they also wanted to get in on the deals. As I gave them a quick update over the phone, Derek went online to check out Beazer and the real estate market in Myrtle Beach.

Without looking up from checking email on her phone, Laurie said knowingly, "People always feel like they have to verify the details, but then they learn that Mother Laurie *always* knows best!"

It only took a few minutes for Derek to find information on Beazer and the lucrative predevelopment real estate trend in the South. Nate also looked online. By nature, he was cautious and studied things at length before making decisions. This included spending months researching the best air conditioner for our apartment or a new laptop. He seemed to interact with life with a certain level of fear that I had never understood. I tended to trust my gut in addition to reviewing relevant facts. Laurie's spiel appealed to both of us. As part of our financial education, we'd looked into flipping property and buying mortgages. But the factor that weighed heaviest in our decision to participate in the deal was our neighbors' constant testimony about Laurie's Midas touch.

By the end of the meeting, all six of us agreed to put down payments on several townhouses at $8,000 each. While that amount was a bargain on the real estate market, it was a substantial sum to each of us. Within the week, we had all signed power-of-attorney statements authorizing Laurie to buy on our behalf and had wired money to her bank account. I had extra pep in my step as I fantasized about how Nate and I would improve our home and our lives.

A few weeks later, Troy invited me to his house to discuss a new business opportunity. He told me that Laurie had been very impressed that I was polite, Jewish, and had a master's degree. It didn't matter that my degree was in social work and that I'd worked for nonprofits for fifteen years.

She thought I could help her develop Scrub-A-Dub-Dub, her janitorial supply company, and I took her offer seriously. I found out the number of medium-sized nonprofits in New York City and the names of the companies that provided their janitorial and paper supplies. The information helped me develop a viable and potentially lucrative business proposal.

Troy and Gregory's house had the same footprint as ours but had not been gutted like Hazel had. Their home had a traditional Victorian design with many smaller rooms linked together to create a cozy feel. On the day we met at their dining room table, Gregory and Troy seemed to be actors on a stage with Laurie, all three performing to impress me.

"You owe us three thousand for the deal that closed last month, and here's a check for four hundred for what we owe you from November," Troy said to Laurie.

"Don't forget you owe me a thousand from the closeout that I advanced you two months ago, and I'm taking out another thousand for what you owe me from the property we flipped," Laurie said, writing out a check and handing it to Gregory.

"We know this must seem confusing to you, but we'll be done in a minute," Gregory said with a patronizing smile.

This cryptic jargon and swapping of checks went on for fifteen minutes as I sat silently like a good boy. They may as well have been speaking Greek to each other. I knew they could have completed these transactions before my arrival but assumed Laurie wanted me to witness the excitement. It was also another opportunity for Troy to brag about his success. Their behavior seemed silly to me, but still, if Nate and I were going to enter this world, we had to play by Laurie's rules.

When they finished, I pitched my idea to increase Laurie's nonprofit business by returning 5 percent of the amount an organization paid her annually. The give-back would be a tax-deductible donation for Laurie and more money for the nonprofit. It was a win-win situation for all involved. I suggested she contact two companies that served as brokers for local nonprofits by negotiating lower rates for organizations that collectively ordered common supplies like toilet paper. If Laurie could get on the brokers' vendor list, I told her, she could increase her business tenfold.

Putting out her arms as though she wanted to hug me from across the table, she called out, "This man is brilliant! I love these ideas!" Her excitement was palpable and contagious. "Listen, Handsome, you get 10 percent of any business I sell on your plan."

Laurie's excitement was quickly interrupted by Troy.

"*Hold on,* Miss Thang. I brought him to the table, so I get a cut of *whatever* he brings in." Troy stared bug-eyed at Laurie. I was shocked at his greed. There was no appreciation for the work I had put into developing my idea. My heart pounded with anger.

"Okay, Mr. Smarty-pants, I'll give you 5 percent of what I make, and will keep Mark at 10 percent," Laurie retorted. I took her defense of my interest as an indication of her confidence in my skills and a general air of protectiveness, but I was acutely aware that they were also doing some sort of preening together.

"Whatever you think is best, Laurie. Your offer's really generous," I said as politely as possible. I was disgusted by the primal way Troy spoke to Laurie. My motivation for being there was to impress her so that Nate and I could deepen our stake in her investments. We were ambitious, I told myself. Troy was just greedy.

In the weeks that followed, I wrote up a formal sales pitch and sent Laurie research on the nonprofits I thought she should approach. I even went on a few sales appointments with her. We were a good team; she was a visionary who spoke about broad ideas, and I filled in the minute details and made pleasantries that smoothed the conversation. We were both expert schmoozers. Even though we didn't make a sale, she begged me to come work for her.

"I need someone like you to help me get organized and run my businesses. You could make more money with me in two years than you could evah make at that social work job."

My current job felt stale and unchallenging. I worked at a community center that served housing projects in Chelsea. As director of program development and evaluation, I helped to develop new programs and monitored their success. Ten years earlier, I'd gotten a master's in social work with the hope of becoming a therapist. Although my current job helped others, I was bored with the world of nonprofits. I also was exhausted by the hour-long subway commute. In one of her many emails, Laurie offered to let me work three days a week for more money than I made at my full-time job.

"A man as capable as you should be making no less than $180,000 a year. I promise, you'll make that much for at least the next two years, between your salary and investments."

As I lifted weights at the gym that night, I mulled over her offer. At the time, I was earning $75,000 a year and struggled to make ends meet. I had a large house to renovate, a mother in poor health who needed financial support, and plans to have children with Nate one day. As I moved through my weight-training routine, one thought kept repeating in my head: "Money could help in every area of my life."

At home, I found Nate in the den watching *Friends* and sat down next to him.

"I'm seriously thinking about taking Laurie's job offer."

He slowly turned to look me in the eye. In a parental tone, he spoke slowly and deliberately. "She's a little crazy, Mark. I know you're unhappy at work, but do you really think this is a good idea?"

I put my hand on his knee. "I know, but I can handle her. I would only be working three days a week. With the extra money we'd make through the investments, I can get outta there in three years."

Nate kept his eyes on my face and said coolly, "It sounds exciting. I just hope it's gonna be a good fit."

I ignored his hesitancy because I was so excited. "Oh, I forgot to mention that she wants to pay me three months in advance so we'll have more money to invest with her."

"Damn she's good!" Nate let out a laugh. "She knew exactly what you needed to hear."

After seeing Troy's aggressive greed at our meeting, I didn't tell him or Gregory about Laurie's offer. I worried that Troy would demand a cut of my salary.

Leaving the world of social work didn't seem like a stretch to me. I'd grown up in a family where both my mother and father owned businesses. Dad ran a furniture store that his grandfather opened in the 1900s. Located in my hometown of Newport News, Virginia, Greenspon Furniture catered to residents who were mostly poor or working-class African Americans. The space was previously a supermarket, and the vast sea of furniture never seemed to end. I fondly remember the heavy smell of cigarette and pipe smoke and the handful of old salesmen sitting on the couches watching television. When we walked in, they'd all raise their hands in greeting, but their eyes didn't veer far from their soap operas.

My dad was usually in his office smoking a cigarette or putting one out in the ashtray on his desk. "Hi, Son," he'd say as he got up to kiss me on the head. He never seemed to be busy, and although he was sometimes preoccupied, I never observed my father stressed about work. As a child, I liked going into his office because it felt like a smoky womb, but I hated the back warehouse, which was filthy and had walls filled with calendars of nude women in suggestive poses.

When I was eleven, my mother turned her natural gift for baking into a company called Judy's Catering. She primarily cooked in our home and turned the playroom into her work area. The floor was covered in red, white, and blue parquet vinyl laid in 1976 to match the bicentennial craze. She installed stainless steel shelves and a commercial refrigerator. Her employees were often in our kitchen, and she sometimes enlisted my brothers and me to help her with small tasks. By the time I was a teenager, I was routinely baking and preparing food, as well as working parties. I loved the camaraderie of being part of a team.

As one of four Morewitz brothers, I often felt lost in the mix of kids. It was far more common for us to fight than to work together. More than once, I was left behind as our station wagon pulled away from a store. But at my mother's catering company, I was valued for specific skills that contributed to an event's success. My natural leadership ability, coupled with the fact I was the boss's son, ensured that I was never invisible. When we were at work, Mom and I could relate to each other as two people instead of just mother and son. This was especially helpful during my adolescent years when we were at each other's throats from sunrise to sunset. Catering gave me experience in event planning, crisis manage-ment, supervision, budgeting, and customer relations. I also learned how to work with a boss who had a huge personality but could be very quirky.

In considering Laurie's offer, I reflected on my parents' work. Dad's furniture store was similar to Laurie's janitorial supply warehouse, and her entertainment company had similarities with Mom's catering company. Adding in my fifteen years' experience running public health programs, budgeting, and supervising employees, I thought that Laurie's business-es could be the perfect place to use all my skills. Beyond the excitement of making more money, I felt that accepting the job would be a kind of coming home for me. She shared my mother's strength and vibrancy and also had my father's flirtatiousness and generosity. I decided to go for it.

Before I quit my nonprofit job, I wanted to make sure there was a signed contract in place. I sensed that Laurie's was a world of deals made on a handshake, but I told her that I required a one-year written agree-ment. During my first year living in New York, I continued to work as a consultant for my San Francisco employer and used a contract template from that job to include all the things Laurie had promised me. The spe-cifics seemed to throw Laurie for a loop. She didn't respond for several days to the email I'd sent containing a draft of the consulting agreement. This perplexed me, given how vigorously she'd pursued me. I emailed a few days later to give her a nudge.

"Crazy busy with a huge amount of entertainment parties to plan. Remind me why I'm paying you in advance?" she responded.

I told her that she had suggested that perk herself. The salary she offered me was just $5,000 more than what I was making, but I had built in a three-day workweek as Laurie had suggested. She was still very enthusiastic about my joining her but made it clear that the three-month advance was a one-time deal.

"This is what I meant about working with her," Nate said when I told him how the contract negotiations were going. "Doesn't it worry you that she's so inconsistent?"

An unfamiliar tightness gripped my chest. "I know, honey, I know. That's why I am having her sign an agreement—because it protects me and guarantees me a year of salary. I don't think there is a way I can lose on this."

The episode gave me my first taste of what it would be like to work for her. The rules changed as her moods shifted. It was a 180-degree difference from the work culture I'd known for the previous fifteen years.

Once she signed the agreement, we set a start date for mid-May 2006. I gave four weeks' notice to my job and formally accepted the offer to enter the magical world of Laurieland.

A Fragile Balance at Home

"Rise and shine," I said to Nate as I got out of the shower. It was my first day of the new job with Laurie, and I woke up energized even though I hadn't slept well. My mind had raced with excitement throughout the night. Nate had worked late preparing for an audition and was still sleeping when I got up.

"Shhhh, I'm still sleeping," Nate growled as he put the pillow over his head.

I climbed back into bed and snuggled with him for a minute before giving him a kiss and putting on my clothes.

As I watched him sleep, I thought about how Nate had initially been wary of my plan to work with Laurie. But over the past month, he'd become increasing excited. His ego still seemed to be a bit bruised because Laurie had been impressed with me and not him. Nate had a powerful competitive streak, and it sometimes impacted our dynamic. We were both silently aware that there was a delicate balance to our relationship. This big change would not only affect my career but could alter our lives in ways we could not imagine.

As I got into our 1997 Honda Accord to make my first trip to Laurie's office, I noticed the first cream-colored blossoms on the dogwood tree that Nate had planted in the front yard the year before. I smiled, picturing him working diligently in the garden. I also felt sad and lonely thinking about how a stale fragility had crept into our year-old marriage.

I met Nate in the fall of 1999, while living in San Francisco. I had recently turned thirty and was single. My six-year relationship with my previous boyfriend, Ira, had ended the December before.

There was love, affection, and a shared sense of humor with Ira, but in our relationship I was clearly the caretaker. Even though he was nine years older than I, Ira needed someone to look after him, and that seemed to be easy for me. In our last year together when I heard Ira repeatedly say, "I can't give you what you need," I got the message that it was time to move on, and we ended the relationship. By the time he moved out, I was ready to be free and breathe in new life.

Around the time of our breakup, I stopped being a vegetarian and gained about fifteen pounds of muscle. I used this newfound physical change to explore sex and romance with new people, and for the first time in many years I simply had fun. Along the way, I had a smoldering, sensual summer love affair that I mistook for an actual relationship. When the beautiful man with Tom Cruise looks abruptly ended it to go back to a previous lover, I was heartbroken in a way that didn't seem appropriate for the short time we had been together. I spiraled into a very hurt place, and when I met Nate several months later, he seemed so bright-eyed, bushy-tailed . . . and safe.

He was twenty-two, just out of college, and was working at a local store called Harvest Market that was around the corner from my gym. At the time, I had a habit of getting a fresh banana after my workout each day to make a protein smoothie. Harvest was the most convenient place to buy organic fruit, and it was there that I first saw the cute new checkout guy.

Nate was six-two, my height, with a lean body, strong nose, black curly hair, and beautiful blue eyes that seemed to gaze into mine longer than necessary when I'd pay for my banana. Although usually extroverted, I'm shy when I like someone and often do not make the first move. The result is that although I saw Nate every day, the only thing we'd said to each other for months was "Hi."

In December, two months after meeting, I was riding on the above-ground vintage 1940s streetcar through San Francisco when I noticed a blur of an image come from the back of the train and then saw his face a few inches from mine.

"Hey there." He let a long pause go by before speaking again. "I see you a lot at work. I'm Nate." Then another pause and those huge pools of blue were gazing into my eyes. He was wearing baggy overalls and a tight, red long-sleeved shirt that showed his taut upper body; it was the fashion at the turn of the new millennium.

"I'm performing in a friend's play next month—maybe you'd like to come see it?" And with this overture, Nate had moved us from silent gazes to interacting. A week later, I offered to drive him home from work, and we ended up making out in my car, which led to him spending the night.

From the first time we were sexual together, I noticed something different about our connection. Even though Ira and I had been incompatible on a heart level, our sex had been passionate and robust until the day we split. My summer love affair had been built on sensual passion, as had been all my other dating. Sex before Nate was full of fire and air. It had no bounds and could expand as high as the sky. With Nate, sex was like an underground spring. While another, more astute individual may have understood that the fire was of elemental importance to an adult romantic relationship, I was simply taken by the sweet tenderness of my love connection with him. He was very young in the ways of the world but had a depth that my thirty-year-old self related to and enjoyed.

Previous to our meeting, I had always dated older guys, so it was a huge switch for me to connect with someone who had just graduated from college six months before. He had grown up in Manhattan with well-to-do Jewish parents so had been exposed to culture and had an urban sensibility that meshed well with my personality and experience. It was our varying levels of skill and style in communicating that was the greatest chasm to bridge. I was very present with my feelings and comfortable communicating them. Nate tended to take time to figure out how he felt and was not as comfortable sharing deep emotions that might cause conflict.

Within six months, Nate moved into my cozy apartment. He worked three jobs to support his passion for acting and was frequently very tired when he came home. His work schedule didn't leave much room for close friendships. I had a small group of intimate friends I'd made during my eight years in San Francisco, and these folks had become my family of choice. Nate never seemed to click with any of them. The result was that we maintained separate lives within our relationship, and I appreciated the autonomy.

Those years were full of sweet surprises as our hearts opened up to one another. In a picture Nate took of me at this time, I am on the floor in cargo shorts and a white tank top, looking up at him. My tanned face shows total openness, and it's obvious I'm in love.

Although we both enjoyed living in San Francisco, around the summer of 2001, we grew restless and decided to explore relocating to New York City, where Nate might have a better chance at making it as an actor. He had a large extensive family in Manhattan who were very supportive of our making the move.

It took a year for us to make arrangements to move. During this time, I had gotten accepted to a Ph.D. program at New York University in clinical social work, which would move me closer to my life dream of becoming a therapist. Although I deeply loved the nine years I had lived in San Francisco, I felt excited about making the move with Nate and starting on a new career path.

We bought a 1985 Volkswagen campervan to drive across the country. Nate had only five days between his last day at his San Francisco jobs and his start date for his new acting school gig in New York, so the trip involved long days of driving. Away from the daily grind, our passion for one another heightened. The close quarters of our cozy van enabled us to hibernate from the world. This added to the feeling that we were doing a major move together and that solidified us as a couple. I recall feeling like we had gotten married along the many miles between the coasts.

I had flown out to New York the month before to find us an apartment so we were able to pull right up to our new home and unpack. A truck with our furniture arrived the next day and soon our apartment felt like home. Unfortunately, at my first day of school orientation, I was told that the program had completely been redesigned over the summer to focus on research. Because my interest had been in training to be a therapist, I quit the program and quickly lost all sense of purpose.

In addition to working, Nate was also taking lots of acting classes and auditioning. As in San Francisco, he didn't connect with individuals or make new friends. I felt lost and very alone. I had hoped to make friends through school and without a job felt like it was very difficult to meet new people. Luckily, prior to moving I agreed to continue consulting with my previous San Francisco employer and had enough public health work to support myself for a year. This meant that I traveled back to San Francisco about once a month for a few days.

I am unsure who initiated the idea, but within the first six months of our arrival in New York, Nate and I decided to open up our relationship because our sexual spark was dwindling in all the busyness. We were also influenced by the masses of gorgeous gay men all over the city. For us, this openness meant that each of us had permission to "play" with others as long as it was safe sex. As soon as we opened this gate, Nate was constantly on the laptop looking for guys. By seeing him online, I learned about the social networking sites that catered to gay men, and I joined in. We shared a computer and therefore were aware when the other was online cruising, which became a norm.

This new outlet took the pressure off of our sexual relationship and introduced new obstacles to intimacy. Although our lives were intertwined as partners, we began to function more as cuddling roommates than lovers. In January 2004, Nate uncharacteristically initiated a discussion about our relationship.

"I'm worried about our sexual connection," he said one day while we were in bed getting ready to go to sleep.

"You mean that it's not what you want," I offered back.

"No, it's not what either of us wants, Mark, but I love you so much and I'm confused and sad."

"I am, too. I don't want to be without you, but it seems we lack some important heat in the sex department."

We proceeded to have an open and honest discussion about our relationship and feelings toward one another. As part of that process, we began seeing a therapist and made some attempts to work on our relationship. Although I felt we had deep incompatibilities, I also had strong competing feelings that we belonged together. It was very difficult to imagine life without Nate by my side, and for several weepy weeks we considered breaking up. One morning I woke myself up crying from a dream, and in that sadness I decided to do all I could to keep us together.

At the same time, murmurs of legalizing gay marriage were beginning in San Francisco and Massachusetts. Since college, I had been an activist for equal rights and was exhilarated by the wave of change that seemed to be coming. The timing of my grief over the possibility of our breaking up and the excitement of this huge social shift pushed me to continue efforts to save our relationship. Nate was confused about how he wanted to proceed, and when I was so intent on staying together, he acquiesced. The result was that we had a brief honeymoon period of a few months. During this time, I proposed to him.

"Will you marry me?" I asked quietly one morning as he opened his eyes from a long night sleep of our bodies intertwined.

"I just woke up, Mark. Let's talk about this another time," he said quietly.

A few days later, I tried again when we were going to bed.

"Sweetie, I love you."

"I love you too, Mark," and he reached over to give me a kiss and took my hand.

"Will you marry me?" I asked again with my heart open and vulnerable.

"What would that mean?" he said shyly.

"Uh, it would mean that we would be legally married."

He lay silently holding my hand then murmured, "Let's think about it."

Our conversation continued over the next few weeks, and we finally scheduled our ceremony for June 2004. In that decision, we also completely put aside the sexual issues we had been experiencing and instead replaced them with a huge sense of hope about a happy future together. We soon told our families and began planning the big event. Nate's parents generously threw us a beautiful party for all our family and friends the day before the ceremony. While socializing with the guests, I glanced over at the neighbor's yard and saw two magnificent stags gazing right at me. I stopped for a moment and took in their grace and beauty as a sign of our union.

Only our closest family and friends were invited to the actual ceremony, which was held the next day on a state park's grassy knoll with all of us in a circle. Even with all the knowledge about the issues in our relationship, our wedding was the happiest day of my life. The bright sun and clear skies matched how I felt throughout the ceremony and lunch afterward. There was such an outpouring of love among our family and between Nate and me. Our friend Joe, whom I had met during my college years, officiated the wedding and a justice of the peace legally pronounced us married using a glittery fairy wand that we gave her to use. The day was pure magic and joy until Nate and I drove back to his family's country home where we planned on staying the night.

We had taken separate cars because each of us had given rides to friends who had traveled by train from New York City. As he drove ahead of me, I saw his head begin to droop and I realized he was asleep at the wheel as the car began to swerve off the road. I frantically sped up and honked while yelling at him out the window. He woke up just in time to miss a telephone pole. At the same moment, the clear skies began to sprinkle rain, and I realized that the majesty of the day was over. We were back to reality. Pulling into his parents' driveway, I saw one lone stag gallop ahead of my car and turn around to stare at me. My heart felt heavy with the realization that this one magical day wouldn't erase all the issues we had to face in our relationship.

Within six months, we decided to purchase a condo but instead found an incredible, huge run-down house and asked Joe, a physician who worked at the local VA, if he wanted to buy it with us. Through a combination of our meager savings, our wedding present money, and Joe's bank account, we were able to buy the property. Nate and I lived on the first floor, Joe lived on the second floor, and we rented the third floor to some of Nate's actor friends.

Prior to working for Laurie, my life seemed settled. I had a husband, a house, a few local friends, and a sense of knowing who I was even though I felt that I was not living up to my full potential. I was bored and lonely, but I lived in a world that seemed familiar and matched my sense of values and history. I always felt that I had control over my life and made decisions based on my sense of who I was in the world. I was aware there was a certain risk in putting my future in the hands of Laurie.

As I pulled into the small parking lot of Laurie's office, I took a deep breath. I didn't want to keep on thinking sad thoughts about Nate as I walked into my new job. I wiped the tears from my eyes and took in another deep breath. I had no idea how radically and rapidly my life would change the minute I walked into that door.

Down the Rabbit Hole

Walking from my car to the building ahead, I remembered how Laurie had described the new office when she was still wooing me.

"It's so sick, you won't believe it!" She licked her lips in anticipation of what she was going to say next. "I turned this crappy warehouse into the hottest pawty space in all of Long Island." She told me it had a fully equipped stage and dance floor and a huge lounge area; she had painted it a sexy red so everyone would be in a party mood when they walked through the door. Swaying back and forth, she finished with a wave of her arms in the air as if she were at a disco: "It's gonna make your head spin!"

Based on what I saw from the small parking lot, I lowered my expectations as I walked in the door. I quickly saw that Laurie hadn't technically lied, but she had just seriously stretched the truth. There was a ten-foot stage with a row of colored lights above it. And across the room, I saw several pieces of white Ikea furniture including a large round ottoman that could seat six or seven people and a few wooden stools that I assumed comprised the lounge area. My first thought was that the space was not much bigger than my living room, which was quite large for a house, but puny for anything considered a party space. At most, fifty people could comfortably fit inside.

The smell of stale cigarettes and smoke filled my nostrils, and although there was no one to see me, I made a face showing my disgust. I followed the sound of muffled voices and walked up a short staircase that led to a tiny white office lit by a single bulb. It was cozy at best but felt claustrophobic.

Laurie stood up from the cheap glass desk and kept texting as she said, "Hi, dawling, welcome to your first day at work!" She somehow managed to give me a kiss on the cheek without taking her eyes and hands off her cell phone.

"I'm so excited," I beamed back at her trying to get her attention and at the same time giving her space. As she finished her text, she glanced up at me smiling and then scanned my body. She quickly averted her eyes and said flatly, "Don't feel like you have to dress up for work like *that*. Just wear comfortable clothes like the rest of us." I was wearing gray Banana Republic pants and a maroon argyle sweater. The three other people in the room, including Laurie, were in various types of designer tracksuits.

Although it was unspoken, what Laurie had said to me was, "Don't come in here looking so gay tomorrow. Fit in with the rest of us." The underlying meaning of her comment was jarring to me on several levels. I am not a particularly well-dressed man, so to be called out on overdressing was not something that had occurred in my life. And no one had ever insinuated that I dressed "gay." I had always worked in gay-positive environments, and although I had lived through a fair amount of harassment in my personal life, I never had experienced problems in my professional life. With her statement, Laurie opened the door to her racist and homophobic world that was full of closed-minded Jewish and Italian Long Islanders who only had interest in their own local clans.

Betty gave me a big smile and said, "Hiya, Mawk." As she twirled her fingers through her shiny blonde hair while sitting in one of the chairs, she looked like a bored little girl.

Laurie introduced me to Miguel, a good-looking Latino guy dressed in a baggy white designer tracksuit sitting at the other desk. She called out to both of us, "I expect great things from both of my brand-new employees!"

Although Laurie owned several businesses, she had decided that I would focus my efforts on expanding Scrub-A-Dub-Dub and had hired Miguel to help run Party Hearty. Betty was her "assistant," which I soon found out meant she delivered food and beer to Vince several times a day, and ran errands with Laurie from the wee hours of the morning to well past midnight when necessary. A computer screen sat at each of the desks. Piles of folders and papers were scattered throughout the space. Boxes of janitorial supplies filled up every inch of the room where there were no people sitting.

"So Mister Smarty Pants. Get started on making my company a million dollahs!" Laurie quipped to me with a big smile on her face.

I laughed and asked, "Well, the first thing I need to do is see a list of current clients so I can get a sense of your market."

"I knew you would help me get organized. Isn't he amazing?" she called out to no one in particular. She was on as though a camera was capturing her every move like a successful reality-series celebrity. She swiveled toward Miguel's desk and clicked the mouse connected to the computer on that desk, which opened a database. "Everything's in here. I know how to see the last order but have no idea how to make it show me what you're asking. I usually keep everything in my head."

I scanned the computer screen, which showed one invoice per page. I could scroll up or down to see previous invoices and click into the invoice to see all the contract information for the customer. "Okay, I can probably figure out the database. Where's the stock of supplies kept?" I asked.

"We use the pawty space downstairs. When something comes in, we move it fast. And remember, the closeouts are always delivered directly to the buyer, so we don't use warehouse space."

"I never heard of that before. What's a closeout?" Miguel asked, slouching and staring at the computer screen. I could tell he was curious but wanted to seem too cool to care.

Laurie turned her head toward Miguel but kept her hands on the keyboard. "I work with the religious Jews who run the Brooklyn Docks—you wouldn't know them 'cause you're just a handsome Puerto Rican from the Bronx. They call me when a shipment of paper products is rejected by the company that ordered it, and I buy it cheap. I use investors to put the money up and split the profit. I never buy unless I have already arranged another wholesaler to be the end buyer and then have the product shipped directly there. It's where I make most of my big money." Miguel sat stupefied, taking it all in. I was salivating at the thought of getting in on some of those deals.

A few minutes later, she turned to me, and in a high-pitched voice that betrayed the chutzpah she was attempting to exhibit, said, "I know we agreed that you'd only be working three days a week, but for the next few months I need you here Monday through Friday until everything gets organized." The fear in her eyes showed that she was waiting for a reaction, but I was willing to go with the flow. I had always been a hard worker, and there seemed to be a lot to do to strengthen her businesses. If I could become part of Laurie's machine, then maybe Nate and I would be guaranteed a slot in one of her deals.

Calmly and with a smile I said, "No worries, I see there's a lot of work to do. I can come in tomorrow and Thursday, too, but we'll have to revisit the discussion of my schedule in a few months—*agreed*?"

A big smile came across her face. "Wow, you're such a southern gentleman, unlike the assholes around here!" Without a pause, she stood up and as she was walking out the door looking down reading a text, she said, "Okay, I'm going to meet with a very rich client to book his son's bar mitzvah for Party Hearty. I am expecting a check from Sterling for twenty-two thousand, and if Frank from Eastern Paper calls, tell him I'll get back to him." As she pulled keys out of her huge Chanel purse, she continued with her litany of items. "When Rhonda Starks calls about her upcoming pawty, get the numbah of kids for the event without letting her know that I forgot. And find out the cost of gold-colored paper plates and bubblegum-flavored ice cream. Make sure the ice cream is pink, which is our theme for this event. I'll be back in an hour." And in a flash she was gone down the stairs.

Miguel and I looked over at each other and said nothing. We didn't yet trust each other but our eyes both said the same thing: "Oh shit, what did I get myself into?"

The list Laurie had spouted off was incomprehensible to me. What were Sterling and Eastern Paper? What if Rhonda Starks had questions that I couldn't answer? How many gold-colored paper plates and how much bubblegum ice cream? Laurie had given me no orientation or training of any kind. She seemed to not know what to do with me and yet seemed confident I would be a savior and get her organized. She didn't come back for four hours and ignored our phone calls and texts while she was gone. She did call one time to ask us to read the phone number scrawled "on a yellow piece of papah somewhere downstairs near the stage." We never found that piece of paper but spent an hour scouring the building. Hours later when Laurie returned, she nonchalantly mentioned, "Oh that? Betty found it in my house earlier." I learned quickly that her whims took a lot of time and patience.

Miguel had previously worked at another entertainment company and thankfully knew the database enough to show me how to pull out basic information. I found a way to look up Sterling, which was a janitorial supply company, and Eastern Paper on the system to get their history and contact information so I had context if I had to deal with either in her absence. It wasn't difficult to find ice cream wholesalers in the area by looking online.

A stream of people came into the office looking for Laurie. Some people worked for her entertainment company as dancers or were in a band and wanted to be paid. Some were vendors who wanted money; others were clients who came to pay her. Miguel and I had no idea what to do with anyone, but we found a way to wing it.

I was shocked by the lack of poise and polish in every person whom I spoke to in person or on the phone. I had often berated my father for calling waitresses or other women "Sweetheart" or "Honey," but I found myself employed in a place where that kind of talk seemed to be the rule.

It was as if I had dropped in on a different universe from the one I had been living in for almost forty years.

By six o'clock, my first day was done and I was exhausted. On my drive home, my head was spinning and I had a headache. I hadn't left the tiny office the whole day. Laurie had ordered in food for us while she was still out. Miguel and another warehouse worker kept smoking inside the building, and the smell drove me nuts. The work environment was incredibly chaotic but enthralling at the same time.

I knew Nate would be working late that night, so I stopped at a diner on the way home. I was too tired to follow through with my plan to go to the gym. By the time I walked in the door at eight-thirty, I was exhausted but excited. The day had been stressful, and yet it was exhilarating to be around Laurie and begin to learn what was behind the curtain of her secret world. Of course, I was interested in learning everything I could about her investments and somehow trying to get Nate and me in so that we could start making money in that realm, but I first needed to master my job with her. When I told Nate of my unexpected schedule change, he was angry.

"If she does this to you on the first day, think about what she'll do in a year!" he said sternly. "I don't trust her."

"I know she's erratic and inconsistent, honey, but remember, I'm making more money than I ever have before. I'll make sure I get my three-day work week in a few months."

Nate crossed his arms. "You say that now, but we'll see."

For the first few weeks, I did my best to get nonprofits and synagogues to buy their janitorial supplies from Laurie but found that people were extremely loyal to their current suppliers. The businesses didn't care that we would refund them 5 percent of the amount they spent during the year. The economy was booming in those days, so that amount of money was not a concern. Because the small office we shared also had a lot of Party Hearty traffic, I ended up answering phones and dealing with clients when they stopped by and Laurie was not around. It took a month, but just when I thought I had acclimated to the craziness of the work pace, Laurie had an announcement.

"I'm switching you two. Miguel is gonna take control of Scrub-A-Dub-Dub and Marky is going to help me on Pawty Hearty. You're so great with your southern charm with all the spoiled cunts, and you'll be much better working with me on that business. I shoulda known that the janitorial ass-holes wouldn't respond to you because you sound so gay."

"What's that supposed to mean?" I yelled. I had quickly learned that everyone yelled in Laurieland.

"Let's just try it out, cutie-pie. I think you'll have way more fun plan-ning parties than organizing a warehouse." At that I shut up. My early work experience with my mom made planning parties second nature to me, although I still had a lot to learn.

Laurie was right to switch me over to the entertainment business. Within a week, I had designed a new system for her to use to organize each party and created a database of dancers, musicians, singers, and people who provided other kinds of amusements for the Long Island wealthy. The boss lady was very pleased with my performance and had me sit in on consultations with potential clients. She was always impressed with my social skills and felt that somehow I complemented her working style. In her mind, having a manager accompany her at client meetings made her look more professional.

I had quickly found out that Laurie took notes on whatever paper she could find in her purse. She usually lost the paper and forgot the details of the meeting by the time she sat down to create a proposal or contract, so she was very pleased that I had the capacity to send out an email with details of the meeting within a day. She also found a way to slip in that I was gay, as though that was somehow helpful in the party planning business. I continued to be shocked and appalled to be the token gay wherever we went.

The people who came to her to plan their bar mitzvahs, weddings, anniversaries, and other events were all Long Islanders. As a southern Jew who had lived in San Francisco for the previous ten years, I was a foreigner to this culture and so had to adjust to a new set of social rules. Generally speaking, southern Jews are respectful, polite, and rarely talk publicly about money. For the six years that I dated Ira, I often visited his family in Syosset, a town in Long Island, and found them to be lovely and the town charming. Ira's family was frugal and shunned anything ostentatious. However, my experience with Laurie's clients was that they were ignorant of anything other than their incredibly materialistic world. Almost everyone was brash, entitled, and bragged about all aspects of their monotonous lives. Conversations quickly moved to money, plastic surgery, social status, and who knew various influential or popular people. Money was always a primary topic of conversation, from how much the outfit a person was wearing cost to the expenses of their houses or cars. Every piece of clothing was embossed with huge logos ensuring that anyone from fifty feet away knew they were designer brands. I often felt disgusted during these meetings because people were so gauche and seemed ill at ease with themselves. Laurie was always a redeeming factor because she seemed to only pretend to be fitting in. In private, she was clear that most of the people we met were "spoiled douche bags."

Laurie's role was to make people want to spend money on her businesses. To help with that goal, she found a way to fit in with the social norms of the Long Islanders in her world. Her huge double-E breasts and thick build created an obstacle for her looking glamorous and successful, so she wore stirrup pants every day along with a simple tank top. This outfit accentuated her curves and kept her cleavage as the primary visual people would focus on instead of her huge legs. When there were wealthy clients to meet, she borrowed gaudy diamond jewelry from friends to fit the part. "Look at this seven-carat ring that Mary lent me! Isn't it gorgeous?" she said as she waved her hand in front of my face quickly before doing the same thing to everyone else in the room. When I first started working with her, she drove a big black Ford Explorer but soon switched to a Nissan Murano, and then finally a black super-long special extended Cadillac Escalade that was probably bigger than some trailer homes. Image was key to success in Laurieland.

Laurie had a way of talking Jewish Geography with many of the clients who came in to plan their events. Once she knew where they lived and their synagogue, she could throw out a list of names: "Do you know Lil Shoenbaum, Beth Schwartz, or how about the Goldmans who have the twins? We threw the best party for them at the science museum last year." Status was everything to these people, and Laurie having worked with other families in their circle helped in the wooing process. I soon observed that every interaction was a chance for Laurie to prove her power and influence over others. When she was not able to convince someone to use her company, she took it as a personal failure and lay blame on the people who rejected her. "That *stupid* ugly cunt has her head up her ass. Her children are miserable assholes, and you know the husband cheats on her with cheap whores. Who wouldn't, with a wife as hideous as her? Oh well, fuck them all," she spewed out in one angry breath. When these tirades would happen, it was best to let her vent and not argue in any way. It never took very long for her to let it all go and get back to the happy person that we knew to be her core.

Although everyone wanted something distinct and different, Laurie always gave the same spiel: "My band is the hottest in all of New Yawk. We've got Toni Braxton's drummer, Earth Wind and Fire's horn section, singers who have backed all the best in the business, and of course my husband, Vince, who is pure magic on the guitar. My photo booths make everyone look like Andy Warhol paintings. I also have the classic Coney Island photo booths that print out in strips, and the best emcee and dancers to motivate your guests to boogie all night long!" There was a range of other kinds of services offered, but these were the most commonly chosen. A DVD compilation of her parties showed new clients the kinds of exciting events she had successfully planned. Although utterly disorganized, she was an excellent saleswoman. Her strength was in being able to convince people to add on many fun items that they had no intention of getting when they walked in the room. There was a persuasive energy that formed a vortex most people had difficulty resisting. The result was that most event-planning clients agreed to upgrade their parties to much more expensive packages. Repeatedly, Laurie accomplished these up-grades by making the clients feel overly comfortable with her and open-ing up a pseudo-friendship with them in a matter of minutes. She also was a master at quickly figuring out who the person was who actually made decisions, who had power over that person, and how malleable the family was with their vision of the party.

I was always amazed how easily she could sway people and felt glad that I was outside of her sphere of influence. I could sense when she was trying to sweet-talk me into doing something and would call her out on it. "Cut the crap, sweetie, and just tell me what you want me to do. I'll see if it's the right thing for me," I'd say. She would always smile, as though happy someone could see through her. "Even when you are being mean to me, you still have that southern charm, and I love that you never bullshit me for one second."

Coming from a culture where children are taught to say, "Yes, ma'am" or "sir" and called adults "Mr." and "Ms.," I was shocked to encounter kids who were completely spoiled and entitled. Jewish kids celebrating bat/bar mitzvahs, who were thirteen, or Italian kids who were fifteen celebrat-ing their quinceañera wore more jewelry than most of my adult friends in California had ever owned. These teenagers had traveled extensively and were jaded from having attending so many extravagant parties at such a young age. There seemed to be no innocence and genuine excitement. The few times early on that I asked the clients how they wanted to include sedaka, the Yiddish word for charity, as a way to balance the hundreds of thousands being spent on a party for a teenager, I was met with hostile silence. I was most appalled when the Party Hearty staff told me tales of thirteen-year-old girls giving blowjobs to boys under the table at bar mitzvah parties. In every way, I felt like a visitor on a new planet in the Long Island world Laurie ruled.

Regardless of the level of disdain I felt for the clients, I was in awe of how talented Laurie was at was making people feel like their party would outdo everyone else's.

"You're so good at making people happy. I've been watching you and its incredible how you get people excited," I said as we noshed on some bagels and cream cheese in the office one morning.

"Look, everyone works hard, and I want them to have the best paw-ty ever. The only thing that makes me happier than putting a smile on other people's face is making men cum and putting money in my bank account!" With that we both laughed together.

"My husband can always make me orgasm, but every morning I'd rather go in the shower and use my adjustable shower head to pleasure myself. What always brings me over the edge is looking at my bank statement and seeing that I have a million dollars."

Without a pause she said, "So when did you discover that you liked penis more than vaginas?"

Conversations with her were a whirlwind of brain activity all at once. "Hold on, how far away are you from that million dollars?" I asked.

"All my money is tied up in a long-term real estate investment deal in Amityville, and that's why I use investors' money for the closeouts," she immediately responded without giving it a thought.

"Oh, I see. Well, back to your question. I've always known I am gay so never did anything with women.'"

Her eyes lit up. "You mean you've nevah even been inside a woman?" She was picking out the raisins from a bagel and popping them in her mouth. "So, how do you know you won't like us better?"

I had to focus on swallowing my food so I wouldn't choke as I attempted to suppress a laugh. "Trust me, I know what I like and enjoy it very much, thank you."

"I think you just need to find the right woman." With both hands, she pulled back the tank top to reveal even more cleavage. "Do you like my tits? Touch them, and see how you like it."

I broke out laughing. "Laurie, sexual orientation is not a choice. It is just part of me. Just like I'm assuming you never thought about women in a sexual way?"

She let go of her top, stared at me for a second too long, and said with a smile, "Okay, handsome. We will continue this conversation later."

She had an uncanny ability to read people—including me. On a stinking hot afternoon during the first summer, I was incredibly stressed. The sun turned the office into an oven. I tend to drip sweat when I get overheated: there is nothing on my bald head to stop the sweat from pouring down my face. Laurie was in overdrive that day. She went out on several sales appointments and left several of us in the office with a huge amount of work organizing upcoming events. In addition, she kept calling, emailing, and texting every so often to ask for a number on a piece of paper somewhere in the office. It was a day in which I felt like I was following her around and scooping up an unending pile of dog poop. When she finally came back in the late afternoon, she took one look at me and announced to everyone else, "Marky is coming with me. Finish whatever he was doing." She turned to me and said, "Get in the car. I'm driving you to my house." The drive was only ten minutes. I was surprised when we pulled up to a simple ranch-style house. With all of her business savvy, I had assumed that she lived in a mansion.

"I know it's smawhla than your huge house, but we're on the waddah and the property values and taxes are much highah out in Long Island." She had read my mind and had addressed my internal comment without my saying a word. I was finding out that she had a wicked sense of intuition.

Two huge German shepherds came barreling out to meet her. The kisses and hugs she gave the dogs showed the intensity of her love. She picked up a toy and threw it energetically, and all of a sudden Laurie was transformed into a little girl playing with her favorite friends. In all my interactions with and observations of her, I never saw Laurie in love with anything more than those dogs. She may have used words to indicate excitement and love for others, but it was always clear to me that her dogs were the priority in her life.

The interior of the house was a strange combination of ostentatious and bland. The floors and counters were all marble, but the furniture was from Z-Gallery and JC Penny. She had turned her garage into a professional recording studio so Vince could stay at home and make music with others. The house reminded me of the simple cottages my family rented at Virginia Beach for vacations when I was a kid. The smell of cleaning supplies filled the air. She told me that her two maids cleaned the small space three or four times a week. Even though she brought clutter wherever she went, she wanted a tidy house and especially a clean toilet that she didn't like sharing with others. I had already observed that Laurie was a fanatic about the cleanliness of the bathrooms at work.

She seemed disgusted that people of color were using the same toilet she sat on. "I hate thinking that some nasty black ass was on the seat. It makes me sick to think about." I always assumed that she likely said the same things about having to share a bathroom with me behind my back.

Laurie walked into her bedroom and came out with a pair of blue Hawaiian-style swim trunks and a big smile. Her husband and I were the same height and weight so I could easily fit into his clothes. "Here, put these on, cutie." I went into the bathroom for privacy and did what I was told. Then we walked to her backyard and then down ten feet to the canal. Long Island had numerous manmade canals, which allowed an exponential amount of obnoxious residents to claim that they too "live on the waddah."

She took me out to a pier where two jet skis were on the dock. Although I was much stronger, she pushed each jet ski into the water on her own and then instructed me how to drive. We had to go very slowly so that our wake wouldn't upset docked boats. Soon the waterway opened up to a large bay, and it seemed as if there were miles and miles of beautiful tall green grass growing in the placid water. My heart rate immediately dropped and all stress left my body as a gentle breeze kissed my face. Laurie noticed immediately even though she was several feet ahead of me.

With a big smile on her face, she called out, "I knew you needed to get out of that office. I saw it on your face the second I walked in."

"This is paradise," I said in a voice that was surprisingly calm and meditative. All the anger and frustration I had been experiencing an hour before were completely gone. As soon as the waters opened up a bit more, she sped up and stood as the jet-ski bounced on the waves. Of course she called out for me to follow her, but when we reached thirty miles an hour and the jet-ski was hitting the wave with such a hard bounce, I slowed down. I glanced over to Laurie and saw, not surprisingly, that she was thrilled with the excitement of the risk.

Being read so well by her that day increased my sense of trust in this quirky new person in my life. By inviting me into her home to do something she so enjoyed brought us closer together and gave me a sense that I was making an exhilarating new friend.

Laurieland had finally begun to be fun.

Our First Deal

A few months later, Laurie offered us a chance to participate in one of her investment deals.

She called out to me as I walked in the office. "How would you like to make twenty-five hundred dollahs in three months' time? I went to the docks yesterday and have a small closeout available in a few days if you want it." She told me Nate and I would have to put up $20,000 to get in on the deal.

I felt elated that she offered us a deal. "Yes, we can scrape together that much, and we're definitely interested." I pulled up a chair at her desk. She spooned fruit salad into her mouth while typing with one hand on the computer. "What's the product and who will you sell it to?"

She stopped typing, continued eating a few bites of ripe cantaloupe, and turned toward me to respond to my inquiry. "It's toilet papah and papah towels. I'm still working on finding a buyah. That's why it will take a few days, but don't worry your handsome face, I'll find someone and you'll make your money." She looked down at her cleavage, set down her food, and reached into her bra to adjust herself. "Don't tell the boys next door to you that I'm letting you do this because that greedy asshole Troy will want a cut of your profit." She turned her attention to a text that had just come in.

"Of course! I'll keep this between me and Nate." Since I had begun to work for Laurie, Troy had become suspicious of me. And I think Laurie was right that he would make a big deal out of us starting to invest. "Can I write you a check?" I asked. "I'm not sure how this works."

Laurie looked up from texting and said, "Yeah, bring the check tomorrow."

That night when I drove home, I was on cloud nine. I was excited to have the door opened to these lucrative investments and imagined earning enough money to completely renovate Hazel and begin saving for a future that included children.

I told Nate about the opportunity and together we decided to go for it. We had to transfer money from other accounts to get the funds together. We definitely were not people who had $20,000 sitting in our checking account. The next day I gave Laurie the check.

She scolded me while giving me a harsh look. "Don't you want a contract?"

"Sure," I shrugged. "Tell me what I need to do." I was a complete novice in her world.

She asked me to open up an email from her account that contained a contract used for another investor. She instructed me to change the names, dates, and amounts. It was a simple half-page document that stated that her company Scrub-A-Dub-Dub was brokering a purchase of paper goods and that Nate and I were putting up the capital for the purchase. The capital plus the profit would be paid within three months. As I signed the contract, I was jumping for joy inside. Making that much money in just a short time felt amazing.

The next day Laurie stormed into the office. "The check you gave me bounced!" She still had her Jackie O sunglasses on and her couture purse in the crook of her arm. "I can't ruin my reputation with the people at the docks with checks that are no good!"

My heart sank. "Oh shit! We had to move money to cover the check. I guess we didn't do it fast enough. What can I do to make this right?"

"Get a cashier's check. Go now please so I can deposit it." And with that she turned around and started looking in her purse for something. I had been dismissed.

"How much did the check bounce fee cost you? I want to pay that, too."

"That would be nifty. It is thirty dollars." Laurie said with a smile. She was happy that I was willing to do all I could to make this error go away. I went to the bank and obtained a cashier's check and added sixty dollars to show Laurie how sorry I truly was.

In a few months' time I reminded Laurie about our payment being due, and the next week she showed me the invoice from the wholesale supply company she had sold the product to and wrote me a check for $22,500. Nate and I did a happy dance that night. We were finally in.

As I was immersing myself more into Laurieland, I spent less time with my husband. I had acclimated to the stress of the office and usually went to the gym after work and then stopped at a diner on my way home. When I walked in at nine o'clock, Nate was usually not home yet. I got into the habit of watching TV by myself, and when he came in, I had lots of stories to tell about the hilarious characters of my day, like Joey the ex-mobster who went to prison for hanging a movie producer out the window by his ankles and bragged that his brother had run for Congress in 1988. Their mother, Mary, co-owned Party Hearty and often loaned her eye-popping jewelry to Laurie. Keith, another ex-con who spent eight years in prison for selling hard drugs, now partnered with Laurie on real estate deals. There was also Marvin, Laurie's former accountant; Floyd, a real estate mogul; and Steven, the corporate event planner—all of whom had been making money through Laurie's investments for years. Nate showed interest, but I could tell my new world was not one where he felt he belonged. As my friendship with Laurie strengthened, he seemed to drift further and further away.

Laurie and I were becoming fast friends. I enjoyed her fun spirit and outrageous attitude. She liked that I was both bluntly honest and yet professional. I asked questions about her life and wanted to get to know her, which I saw was unusual in her world of people who used one another to make money. We both also loved food and sex and while eating copious amounts at lunch would share stories of men and our dreams for the future. I told her that I wanted kids and to become a therapist with a neighborhood practice so I could be a stay-at-home dad.

"My dream is to find a rich man to impregnate me," she blurted out.

"What about your husband?" I asked shocked.

"Vince is a miserable mean drug addict, who is hateful to me most of the time. He's beautiful to look at and has a big penis, but he is a mean mutha fuckah."

I could see she was both angry and disappointed about her marriage. "I'm so sad to hear that. I had no idea that you weren't happy," I said with empathy and concern.

With a mouth full of pastrami, she said, "I'd be happy with a million dollars! I'd love to be Anna Nichole and have a rich old man supporting me while I get to still fuck my hot husband." Taking a sip of Diet Coke, she quickly asked, "So are you the girl or the boy when you and Nate have sex?" She paused, then looked back at me. "Vince said he thought you were the woman, but I bet you're the man, right?" Laurie had a way of saying a million things in one second and then steering the conversation where she wanted it to go. Luckily I had grown up with a mother with similar tangential tendencies so knew how to volley the conversation back and forth.

I laughed out loud. If someone else had said the same thing to me, I may have been offended, but Laurie had both the curiosity and ignorance of a child. "It's not like that with us or most gay men that I know. We're versatile and don't have just one role." Knowing that this was an area where she was likely to not want to hear any details, I quickly changed the subject.

I had chosen to place myself in a world where the only reference people had to gay people were their designers, hairdressers, and the characters from the movie *The Bird Cage*. I found myself describing my wedding to Laurie and other people at work and showing the video of us jumping the broom, something we borrowed from the African American tradition where the leap signifies going into a new life together. The images I was putting out in the world were different from what I was living. Not only were Nate and I having very little sexual contact, in May 2006, the month I began working for Laurie, he began what I call "his period of silence." He would talk when it had to do with a task like buying groceries or the house, but otherwise he stopped initiating conversation and barely responded when I asked him questions about his day. A pall had crept over us again, but this time I was too involved with my new exciting work life with Laurie to overtly register it inside myself.

When we had met, Nate had been a lean young man just out of college. He was now in his late twenties and had gotten into bulking up. The guy who used to voice disdain for gay men who sculpted their bodies at the gym had transformed himself into an Adonis. My job with Laurie had sidetracked me from devoting myself to fitness, and although I was still lean, I was definitely not toned and tight as I had been when Nate and I first met.

One day as she was driving us to a business appointment, Laurie blurted out, "Don't you just love making Nate orgasm? I love the powah of making a man cum in my mouth," Laurie said with a passionate laugh.

"Yeah, I know what you mean. It's a rush to know I'm making someone feel that good, but I also like when a guy does the same for me. Don't you like that?"

"I just want my husband to be happy so he doesn't go anywhere else for sex."

Laurie was a self-described "whore to the core," and prior to meeting me had no one to share that part of herself. From her perspective, I was a wonderful combination of a guy to flirt with and a girlfriend to tell all of her secrets. The straight girl–gay male friend dynamic was nothing new to me, but it seemed to rock Laurie's world. I appreciated that she was a badass and made up her own rules every day even if her morals and ethics were very different from mine. Her recognition of my skills and integrity put me at ease and allowed me to open up to her as someone special in my life. She was one of only a tiny handful of people I could call friend during the time I lived in New York.

Saving Laurie's Ass

In June 2006, about six weeks after I started working for Laurie, I stayed home to go to a dentist appointment. Sitting in the comfort of my den with a rerun of *Will and Grace* on television, I called to check in. I was surprised to find her more upset and panicked than I'd observed since we met six months before. Her voice was shrill with fear.

"My investors pulled out at the last minute, and Dick is expecting two hundred thousand by the end of the week. I've never had this happen. He's gonna be *so* angry with me!"

I took my feet off the coffee table and started walking around the house, "Hold on, sweetie, slow down. Who is Dick and what's this money for?" I asked.

Laurie rambled on about Dick being a multimillionaire who made his fortune in real estate but on the side put together "China Deals," which were investments in which he identified construction equipment that an end buyer wanted to purchase and had it manufactured in Chinese factories, thereby cutting out all middlemen.

"After getting to know me, he finally let me start putting in some money in these deals because he wants to mentor me. His kids are worthless assholes, and he wants me to take over after he dies."

"How old is he now?" I asked as I looked out the window at my neighbor washing his car in the driveway across the street.

"He's seventy-seven and very cute. When I told him I had $200,000 to invest, I made it clear I was 100 percent in. He doesn't know it isn't my money because I want him to think I have this kind of cash available so he will keep letting me in on these deals."

"Okay, I get it now. This is a new break for you and you don't want to fuck it up," I chimed in. I noticed the paintings on my walls had a layer of dust on their frames and needed cleaning.

"Exactly, this is my ticket to being a multimillionaire. The deal will pay me 50 percent profit."

I closed my eyes and stopped pacing my hallway. "Holy shit! That's amazing. I may be able to help. How long is the deal for?"

"Listen, I appreciate you trying, but you could barely scrape up the $20,000 for the closeout last month."

"Yeah, I understand, but I have a few close friends in mind who have the kind of money you're looking for and are in the market to make some good investments. Tell me the terms and I'll check with them."

Laurie got very excited, and although her voice remained high, it was with hope and excitement this time. "You're such an amazing man! I need $200,000 just for ten days until I get a real investor. I'll pay 5 percent to the lucky people who can help me out. Nowhere can anyone make this kind of money." She had quickly switched into sales mode.

My heart was racing. "Jesus, this is amazing! I'll give everyone I know a call and get back to you as soon as possible!" I spent the next hour speaking to my friends Tracey and Derek, who were already investing in the Myrtle Beach properties with Laurie. After a long discussion, they both decided to get a home equity line of credit and to pull together $100,000 to invest. I also called another college friend and her husband who had recently sold their house to simplify their life and had a pile of money in the bank. They were risk-averse but trusted me implicitly that if I vouched for Laurie they would invest. Within a few days, everyone wired their share of the $200,000, and she was able to cover her investment with Dick. That night I received an email from Laurie that gushed her appreciation to me:

You're so special, so incredible, such a blessing. I am going to share everything I earn with you for the rest of my life. I am putting you in my will next week, and making you the beneficiary of my million-dollar life insurance policy tomorrow. I am giving you 10 percent of the sale of Party Hearty, and 15 percent of Scrub-A-Dub-Dub. I will have stock certificates made in your name before Monday. You'll not have to wait until I sell the businesses to begin earning this money. Starting this quarter you are a partner in both companies. I truly love you with all of my heart. I'm crying right now I am so thankful.

I knew Laurie enough to doubt everything she swore to in the email, but I was excited that I had done something to gain her trust. My friends made their money two weeks later, and I was shocked when Laurie gave me $5,000 for helping her out in the bind. Handing me the check, she declared loudly, "You're so trustworthy and reliable, not like the other muther fuckahs that constantly suck me dry."

"I mean it was a win-win for everyone, right?" I said with a big smile.

"Listen to you with the 'win-win' like you're a newscaster or politician. You are brilliant, and I'm going to make you a rich man. From now on everything I plan for in my future includes you."

"Sounds great to me because everything you touch turns to gold!" I was ecstatic. I hadn't at all planned on the outcome being so good for all of us. I simply saw that Laurie was in trouble and thought it was a good way to help my friends make some money. But this one act of coming to Laurie's rescue put me first in line for future deals and would provide me with a place dear to her heart for the next few years. She was correct; I had mostly spoken to my friends out of altruism and had been very surprised to find that I had been rewarded so generously. I had been working in public health and social work so long that I just expected to always be of service without any extra reward. Laurieland seemed like paradise in comparison.

Later in June, Derek called to tell me that he wanted to visit the property in Myrtle Beach that he had bought with Laurie back in December. He was driving across the country looking at several other houses that he had purchased during the past year. I decided I would meet him there and told Laurie of our plans in the office the next day.

Laurie had ordered breakfast for the office and per usual had seriously overordered the amount of food. It was always jarring to see that for someone who ate voluminous amounts of crap each day she got sheer pleasure starting her day with a large container of healthy fruit. She then usually moved on to eggs, bagels, and maybe some Danish dipped into jelly or cottage cheese. Laurie could eat for hours.

I sat at my desk and was making my way through a wheat bagel as I said, "Hey, Derek and I want to go to Myrtle Beach to see how our properties are doing. You said by December of this year we could flip the property and make triple our money. We're antsy to see the progress of our investments."

Laurie paused for a millisecond as she took a bite and checked her phone for texts before answering. "Of course, that sounds great." She didn't turn around to look at me as she spoke.

"So we'll need to know exactly where to go and which lots are the ones we bought."

Without a beat Laurie said, "Sure, dawling. I'll have that information for you in a few days. I have to call South Carolina and speak to the agent I worked with down there."

That night after we both got home from work, I told Nate that Derek and I would be meeting in Myrtle Beach and asked if he wanted to join us. He was pleased we were going but was too busy with work and rehearsals to go. It was the first time that I felt he and I engaged in a real conversation in months. That night as he slept next to me, he kept his foot pressed against mine. It was a small gesture but still reminded me of the intimacy between us.

I once had heard an acquaintance describe his first boy-crush when he was fourteen years old. They never had sex but used to hold hands while sleeping in separate twin beds during sleepovers. For someone like me who had been closeted until college, it seemed incredibly romantic and full of love. Nate and I possessed that quality. I'd never shared such tenderness with another man. His silence over the past few months was deeply worrying to me, and I didn't sleep well that night not being able to let go of the feeling that something irreparable had happened to us.

Surprisingly in the morning, we woke each other up with passionate kissing and caressing before Nate got out of bed and walked into the kitchen. I was relieved and a bit elated that we had reconnected that way, but my heart sank when I got up and saw that Nate had gone directly to his laptop to cruise for sex. The sensual interaction we had just enjoyed all of a sudden felt empty and somehow dirty. He was completely in a zone where he was almost unaware that I existed. I silently ate breakfast, showered, and as I left the house was aware of feeling very lonely.

On the forty-five-minute ride to Long Island, I listened to an Annie Lennox CD that I could always count on to match my mood when I was feeling both powerfully sad and full of angst. Although work was going well, I felt as though my personal life was falling apart. Our families assumed we were still in our honeymoon phase, and we didn't have any friends to dilute the strange feeling between us. In addition, Nate had begun to explore the gay club scene on his own. While I had enjoyed that world in college and in my first years in San Francisco, Nate never had the chance to sow his wild oats. Often, as I got ready for bed, he was leaving to go dancing. He also had Michael, a new gay friend whom he met clubbing. I assumed the two were interested in each other, but that was within our rules. The more he hung out with Michael, the more I could sense that he felt I was boring and that our life together was stagnant.

I was incredibly angry with Nate for not communicating with me or fully participating in our household. I initiated most of the house projects and did tasks like food shopping and cleaning. In many ways, I felt as if we had transitioned into the roles of parent and teenager, landlord and tenant.

I had a strategy that when I left my car and walked into the office, I put my personal woes behind me so that I kept my worlds separate. I didn't trust Laurie or anyone I worked with to understand or empathize with my relationship problems because they all seemed so ignorant of anything gay. All of this heightened my feeling that I was very alone.

Laurie was out of the office all the next day and didn't call in to ask me to check her email or give her messages. When I saw her the next afternoon, she surprised me with an announcement. With her eyes glued on the computer screen as she read emails, she said, "Hi, lovey. I've decided that Betty and I will be joining you in Myrtle Beach to check out the properties, too."

Although her desire to join us seemed out of the blue, I thought it could be a fun way for her to meet Derek. "That's great! But won't you be anxious missing all the action in Long Island the whole time we're gone?"

"You know me so well, my gay friend. We'll fly in and out the same day and will hopefully only be gone five or six hours. I'll have my phone to stay on top of things back home."

I worked to find a date when Laurie was available and that would work within Derek's travel schedule. I had become a glorified assistant to Laurie and was used to making flight arrangements for some of the musicians she used for her entertainment company who also worked in Las Vegas. Since I covered her ass on the $200,000 deal with Dick, she completely trusted me with her credit card numbers and access to her emails.

A week later, I met Laurie and Betty at the airport early in the morning to catch the flight to Myrtle Beach. Both had their hair up in ponytails and were dressed very casually with no makeup.

"You look so beautiful without all that crap on your face!" I said enthusiastically to both Laurie and Betty.

"Yeah, right. I'm hideous and she looks like an old hag. Don't be retawded." she said as she texted.

"No, I'm serious, you have such great skin, Laurie."

Looking up briefly from her phone, her face brightened. "This is why I love having a gay man in my life. Only you would look at this disgusting face and say that."

Laurie sat in between Betty and me on the plane. After takeoff, she turned to me, touched my arm, and said meekly, "It is important for you and Derek *not* to go to the real estate office to ask about the properties, because there's nothing in your name." I felt the veins in my temples begin to throb.

"What? I don't understand. Then where did our money go, and why the hell are we on a plane to go see the properties?"

"Calm down, love. Remember when I explained the investment to you, I told you that Floyd Durgin is a real estate mogul who was letting me in on the deal. I wanted Floyd to think that I had come up with the investment money myself."

"So it's like the deal with Dick where you needed help so he wouldn't find out you didn't have that kind of money available?"

"Exactly. All these rich old men need to see me as a young woman who they can mentor so they will eventually turn over these lucrative business opportunities to me when they retire."

"I see the brilliance in that long-term plan for you, but it's fucked up that you didn't mention any of this to us when you pitched the deal, and I'm especially pissed you didn't tell me until now."

As I'd seen her do when she was trying to appease unhappy customers, she began a long breathless statement that had nothing to do with our conversation. "I know Floyd through Mary Romano, whose husband was friends and partners with Floyd before he died. Mary just bought into Party Hearty and is now a partner, so she and her son Joey will be in the office more to check on things and discuss business with me. Mary also has a lot of the property in Myrtle Beach, so I called Floyd and told him I would like to come down on behalf of the two of them and take a look at the property to see how it's doing. Floyd called down to the real estate office and found our parcels of land. Because it's all lumped together with theirs, I won't know the exact houses that are yours but can show you the block they're on."

I knew her well enough to realize she understood what she had done was not right, but after hearing the rationale I was comfortable with the situation in terms of my own investment. I was not as confident that my friend would feel the same way.

After the plane touched down, we went to the rental car office where Laurie rented the most expensive red convertible she could find. Unless she was with her husband, Laurie rarely let anyone drive so she took the wheel. With the top down and me in the passenger seat, it felt like summer vacation. The sun beat down on us as I waved my hand out the window to catch the air thick with humidity.

We stopped at a typical southern pancake house for breakfast, and Laurie was enamored of all the southern accents. Her world was so seeped with Long Island culture that she was shocked to see that people lived differently. When the waitress asked, "Do y'all want anything else?" Laurie sweetly turned to her and said, "I'm fine but thanks for asking yuawol." In her Long Island accent, she had added a few syllables to the word, but it was endearing to see her trying to relate to the Southerners in their own jargon.

While we waited for Derek to arrive, we went shopping at a store that catered to tourists. The place was huge and was lined with wall-to-wall tacky T-shirts, towels, bathing suits, and bumper stickers. Besides making money and eating a ridiculous amount of food, Laurie liked nothing better than shopping for crap. We routinely visited TJ Maxx, Bed Bath and Beyond, and the Home Store so she could buy things on impulse. It was clear she didn't understand the concept of delayed gratification, and that day was no different. We spent an hour picking out towels, hats, T-shirts, and other crap to give as gifts that no one would ever use. By the time Derek arrived, we had a trunkful of goodies to take back with us.

I knew from living with him in college that Derek is a very organized guy. He had a map and directions all ready for our excursion to look at the properties. During the ride, Laurie again explained that the property would not be in our names. Like me, Derek was surprised and gave me a quick intense look that said, "What the fuck?" He was also acutely aware that in the previous month he made several thousand dollars with Laurie, so he went with the flow.

The neighborhood with "our" parcels of land was a huge new development with several subdivisions. When Laurie had pitched the idea to us, she told us the properties would be in the Glendale subdivision, and so we tried to find our way there. The developers had cleared all the land so there were no trees and acres of cheap-looking empty houses with nondescript vinyl siding. Every so often, we'd see a car in a driveway and some visual indication that someone was living in one of the houses, but otherwise it seemed pretty desolate. Because we were not going to the realty office, we were reliant on Laurie to show us our property.

"Floyd said that the properties are almost completed," Laurie said eagerly looking out the window.

"Did he give you the name of the street?" I asked.

"No, he gave me a range of property numbers to check because he owns a huge amount, too. It should be coming up soon," she said as she tilted her head to see out of the windshield from the backseat. Laurie had graciously acquiesced control over driving when Derek showed us the huge SUV he had rented for his trip. A few minutes later, we passed a street that had several vacant lots and then eight or ten completed and vacant houses. She pointed to a house several plots over. The house number was 785. "Yes, these next five are the ones all of you bought together."

Betty chimed in. "Yeah, I remember when I was with you twos, him saying that house numba, cuz the houses I bought were next to yours."

We stopped the car and walked around the property. We had purchased two- and three-bedroom townhouses, and there in front of us were the finished buildings. Although barely completed and definitely not appealing to us, it was exciting to see that our money, which had been invested only six months before, had helped make this happen. It was doubly exciting that we would be tripling our investment in the next three to six months. I could see the quality of building materials was not the highest, but the important things to us were that the project was on time and we would have our money by the end of the year.

We were all in a jovial mood as we left the development and decided to have lunch before saying good-bye to Derek. We found a touristy sandwich joint on the strip at the beach and had a pleasant meal together. Because she was so used to the chauvinistic and narcissistic assholes who made up the male contingent of her life, Laurie was amazed that Derek and I were both polite and so easy to talk to. "You southern boys are amazing! Are you all like this?"

"She means that we know how to listen as well as talk. Most of the men in her world are Archie Bunker types . . . seriously, like from 1965," I told Derek.

"We're generally raised to be affable gentlemen," Derek said, looking Laurie directly into her eyes.

Turning to me, Laurie shouted out, "I don't know what affable means, but I think you're both adorable and very handsome." Giving her attention back to Derek, Laurie focused on her favorite topic. "Are you like your friend Mark and nevah had any girlfriends?"

"I did have one girlfriend briefly before coming out," Derek said.

"So women's bodies were not as sexually fulfilling as men's?"

"Yeah, I guess that's one way of putting it." Derek wore a poker face. I had told him how crazy Laurie could be, and I wasn't sure if he was amused or offended.

"Well, at least you tried. Your old friend is missing out on at least knowing what it's like to put his penis inside of a woman."

I put my hand up in a stop sign motion. "Okay, enough of that line of talk, Laurie!" I said laughing but also seriously. It was one thing to deal with her joking sexual harassment in private, but I didn't want that to taint Derek's perception of her. Thankfully, we moved on to discussing other topics besides where my penis had been.

After saying good-bye to Derek, we headed to the airport where we found out the flight was substantially delayed. Up until that moment,

Laurie had been relaxed, and although she frequently checked her phone for emails and texts, she was staying present with us. This all changed when she realized she wouldn't be getting home until late that night.

"Please figah out another way to get me on a plane," she ordered and sat down while frantically texting. I spent the next hour working with various airlines trying to come up with an alternative flight plan but to no avail. We sat for hours in the crowded airport. There weren't enough seats and many people were lying on the floor. I could see the situation was making Laurie anxious as she became increasingly quiet. She really thrived in her Long Island world, and without it she seemed to shrink away.

Around nine at night I found out our flight had been canceled and that we'd be on the first one out in the morning. This meant we'd have to spend the night. It was high season in a tourist town, and the only hotel I could scrounge up was a Motel 6, which was well below the four-star variety that Laurie was accustomed to. As we walked into the hotel, Laurie was horrified at what a dump it was.

The room was actually not so bad and reminded me of the kinds of places my family stayed at on our childhood vacations. The walls were painted salmon, and the pile on the gray carpet was very low and obviously there for utility and not luxury. Just big enough for two double beds, the room felt small for three people, and the bathroom smelled subtly of bleach and mildew.

"Don't touch anything in here, *especially* the sheets or the bedspread! It's probably covered with microscopic sperm and feces," said Laurie.

I could see from her face that she was serious. We had no change of clothes or toiletries, so we all took our turn in the bathroom, where Laurie made it clear that she squatted over the toilet instead of sitting, and went to bed. Both Laurie and Betty climbed into bed fully clothed except for their shoes. Each rolled themselves in one of the towels that we had bought earlier, hoping it would provide protection from whatever cooties lived in the bed. I shared none of their paranoia and stripped down to my underwear and T-shirt.

"You know they don't change the sheets in a dump like this!" Laurie yelled with maternal concern.

"I'll take my chances and risk scabies and other parasitic diseases," I said with a big smile on my face.

"Suit yourself, Mr. Smarty Pants," Laurie said as she put her phone into her cleavage and turned on her side.

"Oh my God. Are you really going to sleep with your phone between your breasts?" I said as I pointed to her cleavage and laughed out loud.

"I nevah need to worry about where the phone is when I get a call or text in the middle of the night," she said matter-of-factly.

Several times during the night I was awoken by the sound of Laurie typing on her phone's keyboard. She had not exaggerated: texts and emails came in all night long. I assumed it was the guys from the Brooklyn docks, who opened shop before the sun was up. The next morning we flew out and Laurie seemed rejuvenated the minute we landed back in New York, where in some magical way she gained strength.

The Beginning of the End of a Marriage

About a month after our trip to Myrtle Beach, Laurie came into the office one afternoon with a smile and a faraway gaze. She was in a trance.

"What's up, Laurie? You look like you're on ecstasy."

"Oh my Gawd, I don't know what to say. I think I may have just had a date with my next husband."

"What are you talking about?" I asked.

"Remembah I told you my dear friend Joy died in a terrible jet ski accident?"

"Oh right, it was when their family was on vacation last January, right? I had barely met you."

"I've been devastated evah since and can't stop crying when I think of her." Laurie turned her gaze to meet mine, and I noticed her eyes were dry. "She was my best friend . . . even more obese than me. I see her beautiful kids as much as I can."

I knew that Laurie had made special play dates with Joy's teenage children and witnessed how maternal she could be with them. "But how does this figure into you finding a new husband?" I paused and then said sarcastically, "And by the way, I didn't know you were looking."

Laurie explained that Stuart had been in such terrible grief the last time she saw him so she suggested the two go to lunch.

"He's so sad without his loving wife, who used to make such a lovely home and give him sex every day."

"You talked about how much sex they had?" I said, a bit shocked.

"She's the only woman he's evah slept with in his whole life!" she said with a pure look of admiration.

My voice lowered in disdain. "So his wife, your best friend, died a few months ago, and you two had a date today?"

She shook her head. "Don't be ridiculous. It wasn't a date."

"I'm curious what happened. You look so happy right now."

She explained that Stuart had no one to talk to about his amazing love for Joy. "Even with a disgusting fat wife, he still wanted to make love at least once a day." With a twinkle in her eye, she went on about how Stuart was a dedicated father and had done all he could to make up for the loss of the children's mother. She wrapped her arms around her chest with a self-hug. "At the end of lunch we looked into each other's eyes and he said that he really enjoyed the time together. He's been texting me nonstop ever since."

"Wow . . . I'm not sure what to say to all that." I paused thinking to myself how ridiculous the situation sounded to me. "What about your husband?"

She shouted, "He's a violent drug addict who makes my life *miserable*! I'd leave him in a second!"

"What are you gonna do now?" I said with neutrality. I had learned that the rules changed with her moods, so it was best to see how she was feeling about the situation instead of offering a judgment she hadn't asked for. Internally, I thought the whole thing sounded crazy.

"I'm going to have dinner with Mr. Stuart Silverman tomorrow night."

All the next day, Laurie had that disassociated look in her eyes and a huge smile. She and Stuart must have texted a hundred times. Each time she looked down at her phone, she flashed a big grin and would pause to think about how to craft a response.

"Is adorable spelled 'a-d-o-r-a-b-l-e'?" she'd ask me, and "Is phenomenal the right word to compliment him on his parenting?" She showed me several of his texts to her that were all lovely comments about what a special person she was and how his kids adore her already. Although she still went to appointments and made the motions of doing work, her mind and heart were with Stuart. It was as if she had taken a love potion and had lost all sense of herself.

She texted me late that night after they had finished dinner and he'd dropped her back off at the office: "He's handsome and a multimillionaire. His beard felt nice when he kissed me good night."

It seemed clear to me that both Stuart and Laurie were in various stages of grieving the loss of Joy and that they were substituting each other for the actual feelings of loss they were experiencing. However, I was just the court jester and had no say in what the queen did with her playmates.

In the next few days as their courtship grew into a budding relationship, Laurie lost all interest in the businesses except the closeouts and real estate deals. She missed Party Hearty appointments, forgot to return phone calls, and seemed to procrastinate even more than normal.

As Laurie's love life heated up, my marriage was on life support. Nate and I were at an all-time low. He had barely spoken to me about anything meaningful for months.

My younger brother Paul and his wife, Hannah, had their first son in July of that year. Nate and I planned on going to the bris in Los Angeles where they lived. My mother flew up to New York and spent a night with us before we flew out the next day.

Because I lived in Nate's hometown, we spent considerable time with his lovely family, all of whom openly embraced me as part of their clan. At the countless dinners and weekends at their country home, no one seemed to notice our drifting apart. It took my Mom all of two hours to take me aside.

"What's going on with you two? He's totally shutdown and you're seething with anger." Mom is a foot shorter than I am and has a good sixty pounds on me. Standing next to each other, we are like Laurel and Hardy. We have the same color hazel eyes; as I looked into hers, I could no longer hide what I had been trying so hard to avoid.

"Nate and I are trying to work through some things."

I saw the urgency on her face. "Mark, he doesn't talk, and I can see how that can be so frustrating for you."

It was such a relief that someone else in my life who loved me could see what I had been experiencing. Until Mom showed up, it was if I were living in a bubble with not enough oxygen. Hearing her words somehow gave me gave me permission to begin to breathe again.

"No, Mom, it's just that over time this is where we have come to as a couple, and it feels like shit. I have felt alone for so long." It was only in seeing her eyes tear up that I gave myself permission to cry.

Somehow using her interpersonal magic, Mom had Nate and I talking about our relationship to her while we all cooked dinner later that night. I watched Mom as she was careful to be extra gentle with Nate to get him to open up. I was shocked to hear Nate talk about how being close to his family wasn't a priority.

As I stood wiping down the counter after dinner, I said, "I didn't know any of this. I've loved spending time with your family and thought I was helping bridge a better relationship with y'all."

"Yeah, that's what *you* wanted," Nate said flatly. He could have been talking to a stranger about the weather. There was a slight edge to his voice and he seemed so cold. How is this the man I had fallen in love with?

"We've been together for six years—why didn't you tell me, especially when you saw me trying so hard with your family?"

"I don't know, Mark. I thought you'd just figure it out." As he said that I saw Mom's eyes widen with sadness. I knew she was thinking, "This is not good, Mark. This is not good." And she was right.

Although I was excited that he was actually talking to me, I could sense he felt ganged up against because my Mom and I were so verbal and could access our feelings in the moment. Nate often had to take time to figure out how he felt. His response to this conversation was to keep very good boundaries with both my mother and me, and to remain protected by an icy wall of stoicism. While the conversation was an opening, it didn't touch on our deep problems related to sex and intimacy.

Nate and I had not been back to San Francisco together since we had moved to New York five years before and had decided to make a trip there after the bris in Los Angeles. That night I had hope that the trip to San Francisco might be a chance of renewal for us.

We had to leave early the next day. My mother and I share an anxiety about traveling. Hers is more about the preparation of getting there and mine relates to a general fear of being thirty thousand feet off the ground. This general angst of traveling was in the air as the three of us scrambled to lock up the house and get out the door on time so we could make the flight. Nate is not a morning person and has to be shaken awake. He had done nothing to help with the packing or getting the house ready, which left me in the familiar place of being angry with him.

Although my mom is generally chatty, she was silent as the three of us piled into our car. There was a lot of traffic that I hadn't expected, which pushed us back about twenty-five minutes. In addition, I was unfamiliar with the setup of the complex roads going into Kennedy Airport because I often flew home to Virginia from LaGuardia. As I sped into the airport, I got confused going through the maze of overpasses and quick turnoffs. Whoever designed the airport must have been a huge Kafka fan because it seemed to have overlapping unmarked roads that were designed to make things unnecessarily complicated. In a shrill voice Mom said, "Mark, we have to make this flight!"

"Jesus, Mom, I'm doing the best I can!" I said as the pressure in my head pounded against my skull. I realized I had just missed the turn for Jet Blue and had to loop around twice to finally find the right place. Because my mother had bad knees, I planned on dropping her and Nate off and then parking the car.

"I'll meet you at the terminal. I'll park and will be right there," I said as I shoved mom's bag into Nate's arms.

"Hurry, Mark. Don't be late," Mom said as she scurried off with Nate.

"Yeah, yeah," I said but then moments later missed the turn for the parking garage and was led back out to the airport entrance. Once I reached the parking lot again, there were no spaces available. With a pit in my stomach, I realized I was going to miss the flight.

"Fuck! Fuck! Fuck!" I screamed and hit the dashboard as I sped around frantically looking for a place to park. The beating in my head seemed overwhelming. One of the many warm and fuzzy sayings my Mom used to say to my brothers and me was "Pretend you're an orphan and do it yourself." I thought about that saying as I said out loud, "I've been an orphan too long! Someone help me make my life easier!" Finally I gave up and phoned Nate to tell him that I wouldn't be able to make the flight. I called Jet Blue and immediately changed my flight to the first flight the next day and called Nate back to let him know I'd be a day behind him.

"Great, Mark," he said in his robotic voice with a hint of annoyance but then added, "It's okay, you'll still make the bris."

I got on the plane the next morning and spent most it thinking about how easily I had shut down and not told anyone about our problems. I had unfortunately become like my mother in my relationship with Nate. During my adolescence, Mom had caught Dad cheating twice with the same woman, whom he later married. Each time, Mom threw Dad out for six months. After we had all moved out of the house, she caught him again but told no one and instead seemed to implode. It was around the time she turned fifty and was going through menopause. She became clinically depressed and put on a huge amount of weight. To my brothers and me, she seemed to become a bit crazy, but years later when my parents divorced and we heard their whole history, I understood better what had happened. Mom had fallen into what my family calls a shame spiral; she was simply filled with a humiliation that kept her isolated.

I can only guess that my dad's guilt motivated him to repeatedly beg to stay when he was in love with another woman. The bottom line was that Mom hadn't reached out for support or help during that time, and I had done the same thing. In my silence, I had lost myself somehow. The daily rejection in Nate's aloofness had whittled away at my self-esteem. By not telling others about what was going on, I could deny the seriousness of what was happening in my life.

I sat in a stupor as the airplane buzzed with activity and noise. Somehow I had easily copied the behavior of my mother in the worst period of her life. As the plane landed, I turned on my phone and saw several texts from Laurie: "Spent all evening kissing last night!" She acted like a teenager with crush. It seemed so ridiculous and unfair. I simply texted back, "Sounds fun. Take it SLOW. You're married and he has kids!!"

I made it to my brother Paul's house just in time for the ceremony, and the first thing my Mom loudly whispered when she gave me a hug hello was, "Nate didn't say *a word* during the whole five-hour flight. I don't know how you can stand it."

I tried to focus on the joy of the occasion and was so happy to see my baby brother's first child, who was a beautiful boy named Peter. Paul and Hannah had a home that was built in the 1970s and was decked out like a Brady Bunch episode, which was how our house was decorated when we were kids. The room was filled with family and friends, and it felt good to be there. I gave my dad a big hug and as we pulled away thought of all the history between him and Mom, and how I had somehow fallen into the same pattern with Nate.

Dad looked a bit uncomfortable. He had decided not to invite his wife, and my other brother David had refused his request to stay with him, so he was the only family member in a hotel. Out of all of us, Dad could least afford to pay for his accommodations. I told him of the deals that Laurie was offering, and how Derek and other friends and I had already made good money. His eyes lit up with excitement—mostly that his son was doing well. I offered to talk to him more about it all when I got back to New York. After the ceremony was over, Paul and David took me aside and asked me what was going on with Nate and me.

"What do you mean?" I said.

"It's obvious you're full of rage at him and he's not talking to anyone. Look over there now: he's just sitting in the corner playing with a Gameboy."

"Yeah, we're having issues," I said, amazed that my family could sense all that was happening in such a short amount of time.

"We love you, Marky. Don't let him disrespect you." David and Paul's words echoed in my head that night when I caught Nate texting someone about a sex date he was planning while we were in Los Angeles.

"*What* are you doing?" I said angrily. "We're here to see my family and are staying at my brother's home. When did you think you are gonna to go fuck around with this guy?"

"I don't know, Mark. I was just chatting with him," Nate said in a chilly precise way. My heart was racing and the level of rage and sadness I felt seemed immeasurable. I went to bed that night with a deep sadness.

Nate didn't have time to have sex with anyone in Los Angeles that I know of, and we headed up to San Francisco for a long weekend. I had rented a cute apartment in the Castro, the gayest neighborhood in the United States, so we could have total privacy and cook our meals if we wanted to save some money. My hope of rekindling an intimate connection between us seemed remote, but I remained open to some type of healing away from our day-to-day life.

Throughout my time away, Laurie was furiously texting me updates about her fun with Stuart. "He's texting me that he can't stop thinking about my lips"; "I touched his penis through his pants last night"; "Laurie Silverman sounds good. I could be such a good mother to those kids. . . . Did I tell you how many millions he has!??!" It seemed extremely ironic and sad that my married boss was having more passion and fun cheating with her recently dead best friend's husband than I was with the man I had chosen to marry.

As we climbed into bed in the San Francisco apartment, the air felt heavy and thick. As we began calmly talking about our relationship, it hit me that Nate was no longer attracted to me, and nothing was going to change that fact. I saw it in his eyes. He didn't want to say it because he was afraid of hurting me, but prolonging the fantasy that we could have a life together had been much more painful for me.

In the dark of that night, we began talking about breaking up. There was relief in Nate's voice and an incredible pain in my heart as we both cried. Nate thought that we should both stay in the house and become roommates. I had been down this road before with Ira, who lived with me three months after we broke up, and knew the pain and loneliness of living with someone whom I used to love.

During the next few days, we continued to stay in the apartment together but spent days on our own. I chose to tell a few very good old friends, including Ira, about what was happening between Nate and me. It seemed the floodgates of emotion had opened up and I could not stop tearfully telling the truth to those around me. My friends were shocked at both the situation and that I had been so uncharacteristically silent for so long. Each offered support and encouraged us to try counseling before we made a final decision to split. When the time came for us to leave, Nate told me that he was going to stay an extra day; he had met someone online and wanted to spend the night with him. I was surprised that my heart could sink to a lower place, but upon hearing his newest travel plans, I felt like shit.

On the plane home, I sat alone and decided not to tell Laurie about the breakup. I didn't have any emotional reserves to deal with more drama at work, so I kept up the lie that I was happily married and kept feigning excitement over her new love while my life fell apart.

China Deals and Nate, Oh My

About a week after I got back from San Francisco, Laurie texted me late one night to tell me that I should come to work early the next morning. She had exciting news.

"Dick Goldstein's finally letting us in on his China Deals. Of course, I want to help you and your family, so you have first dibs on this one," Laurie said before quickly answering a text while two phones rang in the background.

Excitement about the new opportunity shook me from my stupor. "Thanks, sweetie! Fill me in on the details."

She reminded me that the $200,000 my friends recently invested was in one of Dick's deals. He worked directly with factories in China to have excavators made. These huge industrial machines were used to clear trees and brush from large parcels of land so they can be developed. Dick eliminated all middlemen and took orders directly from large building companies. The result was that he made a ton of money. Laurie handed me a brochure showing the equipment, which looked exactly as she had described.

As I looked at the brochures, I said, "In an economy with so much new development, this equipment makes total sense."

Betty walked in mid-conversation and chimed in, "Yeah, when I was with Dick and Laurie, he told us that is the best investment he has evah done."

"So what are the terms?" I asked Laurie again. It was as if she had ADD and got distracted easily.

"Dick puts up the money to have the equipment made and then the end buyer pays him over a period of a year to eighteen months. The profit margins are around 70 percent. I take 10 percent, and the rest goes to your investors."

"Sixty percent for us! That's crazy!" I jumped up.

"Calm down, my gay friend," Laurie said laughing. "Dick makes a helluva lot more than that. Because I did so well with the $200,000, he is upping my amount to $500,000 on this next one, but the payout will be over eighteen months. The first three months there is no payment and then after that, there are fifteen monthly payments that will pay 60 percent profit to investors"

"That's A-MAZING." I sang out. "How much are you looking for?"

"The full five hundred thousand, lovey. How much should I expect from your friends, and will you and Nate invest?"

"I'll take care of *all* five hundred thousand. When do you need it by?"

Laurie's eyes lit up and she paused for a second before she said, "I still don't believe you are gay. You're too sexy and amazing."

"Don't let my overwhelming sexiness distract you. You're already being an adulterous whore with Stuart!" I yelled out. Then we both started giggling.

I called my friends again but also included some family members. To my surprise, all of them were interested. Everyone was impressed that some of my friends had already made money in Laurie's deals. They were also happy to hear that I worked in Laurie's office. I realized how readily people trusted me in such a deep way. It was not a feeling I took for granted.

Laurie was shocked when I reported back in a few days that I had everyone lined up. She was extra happy that Nate and I put twenty thousand in as well.

"Whip up one of your magic spreadsheets so I can stay organized and on time with the payments."

"Sure, that's easy. Give me an hour and I'll have it for you." As she was texting someone, she called out, "Make sure that you put in the hundred thousand I'm giving you for putting this together. You get it paid out over the fifteen months."

I stopped what I was doing and turned around to look at her so that I could make sure I had heard what she had just said correctly.

"*What* are you talking about? Won't that cut into your profit?"

"Don't worry about me, love. For the first time in your life, you're going to be paid what you're worth. Keep helping me with these deals and there's lots more where that came from."

My face almost hurt from smiling as I typed up the spreadsheet that included the separate commission for me.

Meanwhile Laurie continued oversharing her personal adventures with me. "Stuart and I are going to have sex for the first time at my apartment at Avalon."

I stopped typing and turned around to face her. "Hold it, did you leave Vince?"

"Don't be ridiculous! My husband knows nothing about what is happening. I am keeping him happy and content." She told me that she kept the apartment in Long Beach, a few miles from Freeport where she lived. Steven Berber, the man who taught her everything about the entertainment business, shared the secret hide-a-way. "He brings women over to fuck them with his pencil dick on the weekends. I have the apartment during the week when I want it. I keep it in case I leave Vince."

My face must have shown how bizarre the whole situation sounded to me.

"I will *nevah* be dependent on my asshole of a husband," she said. "He may be brilliant and has a big penis, but he's horrible to me most of the time." The expression on her face changed instantly as she smiled. "I've never met anyone like Stuart, and tonight I am going to let him inside of me."

I tried to stay nonchalant even though everything she was saying sounded so crazy. "I thought after all these dates, y'all would have done it by now."

"I've sucked his penis and made him cum, but I've never let it get that far," Laurie said with a sense of vulnerability I hadn't witnessed in her before. Usually when we talked about sex, she sounded like a horny sailor, but as she spoke about sex with Stuart, the words sounded like they came from a high school virgin deciding to give it up for the first time.

"Don't you consider blow jobs sex? " I asked.

"No, to let a man inside of me is serious. I make men orgasm to control them, but sex is different," she said with a faraway look in her eyes.

I changed my tone to be more soothing. "Well, do you feel you're ready for this, sweetie? I mean, you are married, and this is all so soon after his wife died."

"I can't wait. He is a brilliant and successful businessman, and he is so passionate for me."

"Will you spend the night together?" I asked.

"No, I'll probably go home and let Vince fuck me in the hot tub." She laughed and then stared at me waiting for a reaction.

"That sounds like a porn movie, not a good way to help your marriage or your budding new relationship." I always tried to maintain a balance of giving her ethical guidance but not being too pushy.

She left the office for a Party Hearty meeting but texted me throughout the day with missives of what Stuart had said and the plans they had for the evening. Each romantic thing I read reminded me that I had a total absence of that in my own life.

Once Laurie had given me the details about the new China Deal, I had emailed contracts and wiring instructions to my family and friends. Because my dad was almost completely computer illiterate, I called him to explain the deal.

"Son, are you sure this is all legitimate, and that this Laurie is someone we can trust?" His voice had a stern timbre. My dad most often used a jovial tone of camaraderie when we talked, and this fatherly voice of concern had a hint of fear in it.

"Yeah, Dad, she's amazing." I explained that I had seen the invoices and products in the closeouts and that these deals would be very similar except bigger and longer. "Everything she touches seems to turn to gold for everyone around her. She's truly gifted at making money."

At the time, I felt that one of the few qualities that I shared with my father was that we were both risk takers. Dad took risks as part of a way to run away from responsibility. As far back as I could remember, I hadn't liked or trusted my father. Where my older brother Zack had a natural connection with him through the love of sports, I felt there was something in Dad that repelled me. When I was fourteen and my parents sat my brothers and me down for our first family meeting, I was not shocked to hear that my dad had been having an affair and was moving out. I was angry when he came home six months later because I felt he'd not changed. Within a year, I was again not surprised when Mom discovered that he had continued the affair and kicked him out again.

As a young adult, I made peace with my father enough to have a relationship with him, but there was always a wall between us. I simply didn't trust him enough to open up my heart. That all changed when I embarked on making a documentary about my family when I was thirty-one, a few years before meeting Laurie. The purpose of the project was to explore how both sides of my extended families dealt with a range of issues from intermarriage, religion, body image, depression, anxiety, and shame. During the project I asked Dad if we could have a few therapy sessions together, and within two sessions under the protective guidance of his counselor I was able to share all the anger and distrust I had held on to for so long. He and his wife, Sharon, heard the impact of their affair and asked for forgiveness. Since that time, there had been nothing but love flowing between us, and I had been happy to share the opportunity for Dad to make some money along with us.

Dad had not noticed trouble between Nate and me when he saw us in Los Angeles. After getting the business part of the conversation out of the way, I updated him so he would be in the loop. Although I had shared the news with my friends in San Francisco, there seemed something much heavier in telling my father that Nate and I were in serious trouble.

"I'm sad hearing that it's been so hard for you. You know I'm here for you anytime, Marky."

"Thanks, Dad. I love you, and I'll keep you updated on what's going on."

After only two counseling sessions, Nate and I decided to end the relationship. As I had sensed in San Francisco, his romantic and sexual attraction to me was gone. The months of silence I endured had been his way of feeling remorse and guilt for the pain he knew he would cause me if we broke up. He was right. My heart was shattered. I moved into the guest room and did my best to function in my daily life. Hearing him come in or leave literally pained my heart.

Prior to breaking up, we'd planned on hosting his family for the Jewish Day of Atonement meal. Twenty-five members of Nate's family were coming to our house. We had decided together not to tell his family about the breakup because it was too new and raw to invite the slew of familial interactions about our relationship. The isolation I was feeling and the finality of the situation pushed me to tell Laurie about the breakup. Her love and support were immediate. When we weren't together in person, she'd send texts or emails reminding me that I was in her thoughts: "Darling, I am so sad for you right now, and know how your heart must be broken. I know I am a happy whore right now with Stuart on the side and a husband to go home to, and can imagine how lonely you must feel. I am here for you night and day whenever you need me."

It felt so good to have her know the truth because she was the person I had the most contact with each day. "Thank you, sweetie. Just reading your words makes me feel not so alone. You know I don't have many friends out here."

"We will find you a handsome man to put your penis in soon!" She shot back in a matter of seconds.

"Lol, Jesus how are you making me laugh when I am so sad? For the record, I am nowhere near ready to meet anyone new. But it's good to know you have my back. XOOX"

"Love you more today than yesterday! XOXOX."

Laurie and Stuart mostly met at her apartment but also went out to local restaurants where people who knew her might have easily seen them. She also spent more time over his house with the kids, bringing them presents and taking them out on adventures. In between her many texts to me each day about Stuart, she always asked how I was feeling and whether I wanted to join her for dinner and even offered to go to the gym with me because she knew that was how I relieved my daily stress. Her love and support were consistent and palpable during an incredibly painful time for me. As I pulled away from Nate, I found safe harbor with Laurie.

She offered to help in any way she could with the holiday meal, but I decided to fly my Mom up to assist me. In previous discussions with Laurie about Nate and his family, I had told her that Nate's father had a friend who was very successful on Wall Street. When we first considered investing with her, Nate had approached his father, Louis, about taking out money from the account this family friend managed for him. Louis, an incredibly wise and successful corporate attorney, had advised Nate not to withdraw money from such a longstanding solid investment for something new that he didn't know well. Showing her intense competitive streak, Laurie had been furious that Louis had suggested her investments were not as stable as his friend's fund. I had placated her at the time saying that Louis was Nate's father and just trying to look out for him.

I hadn't invited Laurie to the dinner because there were already a huge number of people coming and it was a very emotional time. Her support of me came with the understanding that she would always be center of attention. For this night, I didn't want to deal with her. It would be the last time that Nate and I would be publicly perceived as a couple. He had told his parents the morning of the dinner, and they came a bit early so that we could all talk.

We all sat together for about thirty minutes before the other guests arrived. Ann, Nate's wonderful and loving mom, said, "I was shocked when Nate told us. The two of you keep a good secret. I am just so sad about this for all of us."

Louis added, "You've been a wonderful part of our family, and we don't want to lose touch with you. We want you to know that we care about you."

We were all sniffling back the tears and I told them I wanted to remain in contact because they had become family to me. The arrival of other guests silenced our conversation about the breakup. We made a pact not to ruin anyone else's day with the news. Nate stayed with his family as my mom and I shifted into catering mode and checked on the food in the kitchen. I decided to have the dinner in our largest room because it would accommodate everyone so easily. It was an old parlor that had been renovated in the sixties by enclosing the large wraparound porch, which left the room about five hundred square feet. Large windows ran around the whole room so we were bathed in light. Nate and I had recently paid for the floors to be redone and new windows put in. We had moved our furniture to the side and put the rented white tables and chairs in the center of the room to create some elegance. Prior to our breakup, it seemed so important to us that we share our home with everyone. Now it seemed like dining with a dead corpse. As more guests arrived, I dutifully gave tours of the house and Mom continued to replenish the food. At the appropriate time, we all sat down and everyone showered us with praise on the remodel. Midway through the meal, the doorbell rang, and before I could get up to answer it, Laurie and Betty walked in.

"Hello, Nate's family and Mark's mothah. I'm Laurie," she declared as she stood proudly at the door. I stood in horror as I saw that she assumed everyone in the room would know who she was and waited for recognition. She was dressed in a tight short-sleeve shirt showing at least six inches of cleavage and a weird floppy fedora that looked like it came from Sly and the Family Stone circa 1971. Only Nate's parents seemed to recognize who she was, so I quickly jumped in. "This is my boss, Laurie, and her assistant, Betty."

Everyone looked up for a few seconds and then slowly found their way back to whatever conversations they had been engaged in before she barged in. I walked over and gave Laurie a hug.

"How are you, sweetheart? I know this is such a difficult day for you." She whispered in my ear as she gave me a bear hug.

My jaw felt tense with stress. "I wasn't expecting you. There aren't any chairs for you two." I appreciated her gesture, but she was way out of line showing up uninvited on this very stressful day. She was used to being the center of my attention, but I had a room full of guests and was barely holding it altogether for the day.

"It's okay, love. I just wanted to bring over some presents for your mother and check on you." She motioned for Betty to bring over the boxes she had in her hand.

I gave Mom a look and she walked over to us.

Mom shifted into what I call cruise-line director mode. "So nice to meet you, Laurie. Mark has told me so much about you and how wonderful it is to work for you. I appreciate the way you've been taking care of him."

Laurie turned to me. "What an amazing and beautiful mother you have. I can see where you get your inviting personality from!" In an attempt to get Laurie away from the others, I herded the small group of women into the kitchen where we could have some privacy. Laurie motioned to Betty to hand Mom two boxes that contained several pairs of shoes. Weeks before I had mentioned to Laurie that Mom had an especially wide foot, and she arranged for a man who sold her shoes "that fell off a truck" to find some in her size.

"Don't be ridiculous," Laurie said when I offered to repay her. After a few minutes of small talk, I got hungry and went back to grab a quick bite and got engaged in conversation with one of Nate's aunts. About ten minutes later, I was horrified to see Laurie flirting with the Wall Street tycoon. She was explaining her closeouts and the new China Deal. He looked completely uninterested and unimpressed. It was like watching a street hooker approach the president of Wall Street to give him some stock tips. Laurie was licking her lips, playing with her hair, rocking back and forth, and of course her cleavage was doing a dance of its own whenever she moved or breathed. Thankfully, the mogul was skilled enough to get another plate of food and return to the main room without saying much.

"Oh well, I had to try," Laurie said with a laugh. "He thinks he is too smart to invest his millions with me, but he's only making 14 percent a year on his money, and you'll be making way more than that!" At the end of that sentence, she began walking toward the door. She had lost interest and was ready to move on in her day. As I gave her a kiss good-bye, I realized her whole purpose in coming over had been to meet the wealthy family friend.

I turned and looked at Mom, who whispered, "She looked like a total whore, Mark! It was embarrassing how she was trying to talk that wealthy man into investing with her."

I shrugged. "I know, Mom, I gotta take the bad with the good. She's amazing in so many ways but is not at all polished. She meant well in bringing you the shoes and checking up on me, but it didn't fit in with everything else tonight." I took a deep breath and let it out with a deflated sigh. "Let's just get through the rest of the night, okay?"

Mom looked at me for a second longer than she needed to. She was worried about me, but there was nothing to do in that moment but go back and enjoy the food we had spent the day preparing. The next day I received several emails from Nate's extended family thanking us for the lovely meal and expressing their sadness over our breakup. His parents had let everyone know the news after they left our house. Each email both touched and broke my heart. Almost overnight Nate and I had become a thing of the past.

A few days after barging in on our family event, Laurie invited me out to dinner with her and Stuart. As I walked into Waterzooe, a Belgian restaurant near Laurie's hometown, I felt awkward seeing the two of them holding hands and kissing at the table. I introduced myself to Stuart and sat across from them. For the duration of the dinner, Stuart either held her hand or stroked Laurie's thigh. We talked about his kids and what a special person Laurie was to all of us. But typical Laurie also steered the conversation toward business.

"Stuart owns hundreds of apartment buildings in the metro New York area. We talked about my company supplying his buildings with products, but he buys in such large bulk that I couldn't meet his needs."

"What about the closeouts, though? Stuart couldn't you use a shipload of cleaning products at well below wholesale every once in a while?" I eagerly offered.

He put his arm around Laurie and began caressing her neck. "It's a good thought, but I've been advising Laurie to go to hard lenders like a bank so she can keep more profit."

With a big smile on her face, Laurie put her head on his shoulder. "But I have all these people like Mark in my life who depend on me. I can't be selfish at this point."

"On behalf of all those little people, I say, 'Let's drink to that!'" and offered up my glass.

I left that night feeling happy for Laurie that she'd found someone and sad as I drove home to a house I shared with the man who used to love me. I had wanted either Nate or I to move out right away but he felt the opposite, so at the time we were living as stoic roommates. The silence between us felt deafening to me.

After a few weeks of living this way, I wrote him an email: "Walking in the door to see you is surreal to me now. It's just a parallel universe— you look the same but you're not my husband . . . he is somewhere in my head and slowing leaving on a pathway that will take him from my heart one day (not too soon). I thought my life was going to be one way and now it is simply a mystery as to what it will be, where I'll be, who I'll be, how I will get to be that person, and when I'll become each of the next chapters of my book of life."

Within a few weeks, Laurie unceremoniously dropped Stuart without telling him a thing.

"I don't understand why he keeps texting me all the time. I'm too busy and have all this work to do." She'd whine as she looked at the umpteenth text he'd sent her. A few days before, these texts would have sent her into a frenzy, but whatever spark she had felt about him was gone. When I questioned her about what happened, she didn't really have an answer.

"Look, I'm married and he has the children. It was just something we did for fun and it's ovah," she said with an annoyed shrug.

A bit horrified by the cavalier attitude she had toward this man with whom she had begun planning a future, I also recognized that he had recently lost his wife and had kids who had an established relationship with Laurie. I did my best to counsel her without sounding too preachy. "I get that it's over for you, Laurie, but please be gentle with him and the kids. You have spent a lot more time with them since the two of you were dating. They only lost their mom a few months ago."

Her eyes widened as she declared with righteousness, "I'm not going to change a thing with the kids. I'll always be there for them." And she kept her promise. Laurie remained an amazing auntie to all four of Stuart's kids. Although heartbroken at first, he eventually found another more appropriate woman whom he married a few years later.

In early December, I organized a big birthday party for Laurie, who was turning thirty-three, at 44½, a restaurant on the west side of Manhattan in Hell's Kitchen. I kept waiting for her husband or family to make a toast, but as the night wore on I realized no one was going to say anything. In the world of Long Island that Laurie inhabited, everyone seemed to be using each other to get ahead. There were few actual intimate friendships. Respect was won not by the integrity of character but, rather, how much money someone could make. I looked around the room and saw that every single person present was earning good money through Laurie's businesses or investments. Yet no one raised a glass in her honor. I leaned over to the table behind me where the birthday girl and her husband were sitting and whispered in Vince's ear, "Do you think anyone's going to make a toast?" He shrugged his shoulders and without making any effort to turn his head to make eye contact said, "Go for it." I took my fork and tapped it on my glass as I stood up.

"Everyone, can I have your attention, please? I'd like to make a toast to Laurie, who through her generosity and successful business ventures has helped so many of us transform our lives. I know she has been a true friend and angel in my life, and I feel grateful for our friendship. Happy Birthday, and a wonderful year ahead to you!" I looked over to Laurie, whose face was beaming with an ear-to-ear grin, and blew her a kiss. Troy, who was very competitive, immediately stood up and gave a toast, and then Vince, who was drunk, awkwardly stumbled to his feet to raise a glass to his wife.

In the previous month, I emailed all my friends and family who had made money with Laurie during the past year to let them know about her birthday and asked them to contribute to a gift. We pulled together enough money to buy her a Coach handbag, the only thing she said she wanted. Later in the month, around Christmas, she handed me a small wrapped box.

"You were the only one at my birthday party who really cares about me. I loved what you said in your toast, and I love you too, my friend." For what seemed like the first time, she had no phone in her hand and was giving me her undivided attention.

As I unwrapped the gift I saw a blue box with a crown symbol on it. She saw that I didn't recognize the brand. "Oh my Gawd, you still don't know what the gift is? You're so precious and nothing like the spoiled ass-holes from here. Go ahead—see what it is." As I opened the hinged box, I saw it was a Rolex watch. "You know what this is, right?"

"Oh, Laurie, this is so generous. I feel like it's too much, I mean, thank you, sweetheart, but it's too expensive."

She put her hands on my shoulders and looked me in the eyes. "Too expensive for you who gave me a platinum coin for the one-year anniversary of starting to work with me last May? Like you said when you gave me that coin, our friendship and working relationship are made of the same precious metal and will last forevah." I gave her a hug and accepted the gift.

Although I was very uncomfortable with owning something that was such an obvious symbol of wealth, my family was very impressed. "Mark, do you know how much that must've cost! This shows that you're a success now," my mom gushed as I showed it to her when I flew home for the holiday. She urged me to wear it to all the family dinners and get-togethers so that I could show it off. The watch felt heavy and awkward on my wrist, and as person after person asked me to see it, I felt no less a fraud than had I brought a woman as my date and pretended to be straight.

On my flight back to New York, I had a pit in my stomach thinking of having to see Nate when I got back home. He finally moved out the weekend of New Year's Eve 2007. We had both agreed not to make any legal decisions about the house or other investments for a year, until our emotions cooled. The plan was for me to eventually buy him out of his share of the house and continue living there. He moved to Manhattan with a new friend whom he'd he met at the gym.

I didn't want to watch him move his things out and so accepted an invitation from Joe, the friend Nate and I owned the house with, to come to the Pennsylvania countryside. He had told me of the wild parties that his friend Chip threw at their house. Joe thought it might be just the thing to cheer me up.

When we arrived at Chip's eighteenth-century mill house, it turned out that the only guests for the weekend were Joe, his partner, and me. While I had hoped to ring in the New Year meeting new people in a festive setting, I sat around all weekend watching two couples play footsy and whisper sweet nothings when they weren't lovingly staring into each others' eyes. It was pretty much emotional torture for a guy who was trying to distract himself from his breakup.

I went to bed at 11 p.m. on New Year's Eve. As I lay in a fetal position trying to keep warm in the drafty room, I prayed that the year ahead would be better than the one I was leaving behind.

Bitch Mom, Poor Mom

Laurie leaned across the round table toward my mom. Soft music from the 1980s was playing and the smell of high-quality beef filled the air.

"So, Judy, Mark has told me such lovely things about growing up in Newport News, such a funny name for a town. I understand you had to move from your lovely home after the divorce. How do you like where you are living now?"

I had flown my mother up to Brooklyn for the weekend. She and I had driven to Long Island to meet Laurie at George Martin's, one of her favorite lunch spots. This was the first time that the two of them really had a chance to talk. Based on my pleading, Laurie had agreed not to look at her cell phone the entire lunch and was doing a wonderful job of focusing on getting to know my mother.

Mom's hazel eyes got surprisingly watery in response to Laurie's question. She looked down at her food for a moment and swallowed to prevent herself from a full-out cry. "I loved the house that Mark grew up in. It was very difficult for me to leave. The townhouse I rent now is very small, and I'm sad that I can't have all my boys there together when they visit." The tears were streaming down her face. "I love art and contemporary furniture, so my place is vibrant in the way I like, but small. The neighborhood isn't the kind I had pictured I'd be in at this point in my life. I do the best I can on the salary I make, and help from my boys." At the time, Mom was making $11 an hour.

I picked up my burger and paused before I took a bite. "I've been trying to save to buy Mom a place of her own with the money I've been making on your investments." I was used to my mother's dramatic emotions so didn't make a big deal about her crying.

Without hesitating, Laurie put her fork down and turned to me. "We've got to get your mother out of that horrible neighborhood. Look at what a warm and loving person she is, so beautiful, too." Laurie transformed into a politician up on a platform making a speech to the masses. "I'll figure out a way for you to have your own closeout where you make my share of the profit. It will happen this year, Judy. Don't you worry!"

Later as Mom and I got into my car after we hugged Laurie good-bye, I turned to her almost laughing. "You couldn't have planned that any better. Jesus, where did that Jerry Springer moment come from?"

"I honestly don't know, and didn't plan it." Mom put her hand onto her chest, a little taken aback. "I just got so emotional when she asked me the question."

Laughing, I said, "Well, you just made sure that we'll have enough money this year to buy you a new house! This is how life works in Laurieland, Mom. We didn't plan it that way, but Laurie will sprinkle her magic dust, and everything will be all right."

Mom turned to me with parental concern. "Mark, she seems a little bit out there. Are you sure this is all going to be okay?"

"Yes, Mom, and I'm hoping to find a way to let you retire soon, too."

At the time, my mother was working as the in-house caterer for the Jewish Community Center in my hometown. The position was a sad denouement to a twenty-year career of operating her successful catering business. The job provided a very modest income and enabled Mom to remain involved in the Jewish community. It also gave her precious insurance, which was vital because her health had been failing for the past ten years. She was only in her early sixties, but her body was like that of someone twenty years older. A combination of serious hard work, horrible eating habits, lifelong stress, and genetics had resulted in her having a myriad of chronic conditions that made work painful and very difficult. She was a one-woman catering show: all the food prep, lay-out, and serving were her duties. She also had to scrub down and mop the kitchen. When she and my dad divorced ten years earlier, Mom was forced to move from our large four-bedroom home into a tiny rented townhouse. Neither of my parents had done much financial preparation, so my younger brothers and I helped my mom with her rent and luxuries like airline tickets or new outfits for special events.

A few weeks later, Laurie told me she had arranged for the closeout to help buy a new home for my mom. I would net exactly what I needed to combine with my savings to make the down payment. We went out to eat to celebrate the mitzvah we were giving my mother.

As we finished the chocolate pie, carrot cake, and ice cream sundae, Laurie said, "I wish my mother was more like yours and not such a mean asshole."

Trying to get the last of the melting ice cream into my spoon, I looked up and said, "You never told me why you two aren't close."

Laurie stopped eating and yelled out, "*Not close*? She doesn't speak to me!"

"But you introduced us at her store the other day when we dropped off a check."

"Yeah, she'll act polite around others, but ever since I hired Betty, she cut me out of her life."

Laurie explained that a few years before I had met her, her sister Jill and Betty were best friends. The two sisters didn't get along. Laurie needed an assistant to help her with personal and business errands and offered Betty a job. When Betty accepted, Jill freaked out and acted as though Laurie was stealing away a precious lover. Seeing Jill so hurt, Laurie's mom, Nancy, demanded that she fire Betty.

"My sister must be gay or something. She acted like she was in love with Betty. She kept calling her crying and saying she felt so betrayed. I think she may have even slashed Betty's tires."

I stopped eating and just focused on what she was saying. "God, that sounds crazy, Laurie!"

"I was just trying to give Betty a break because she was divorced and barely making a living as a waitress at Denny's. She needs the money she makes from me to support her two kids."

As always, Laurie insisted on paying the bill, and as we walked back to her huge black SUV, I said, "It sounds like you really miss your mom. If that's true, maybe it's best to reach out to her since she's not going to budge on her position. Couldn't you just talk to her?"

With her eyes on the road, Laurie said, "Nice suggestion, but she'll never talk to me about it unless I fire Betty first."

"Well, I can help you write a letter or email if you want. You're doing so much for me and my family. I'd love to give something meaningful back to your life."

With a big smile on her face, Laurie turned to me and said, "That would be nifty. You are so good expressing your emotions in that gay way."

I scowled. "I hate when you say things like that."

"You *are* very talented in communicating . . . that's all I'm saying," Laurie said with just a tinge of apology.

The next day, I helped her craft a letter to her mother that explained the situation with Betty and expressed how much she wanted to have her mom back in her life.

Later that week, a car pulled up in front of the office and Laurie stoically got up and went outside. A woman who looked like a blonder and slimmer version of Laurie got out and handed her an envelope. From what I could see, there seemed to be a bit of a heated exchange before Laurie came back in.

Like a child overwhelmed with too much homework to do, Laurie said in a voice full of defeat, "That's my mom. Let's see what the bitch wrote." I walked over and read over Laurie's shoulder. The letter slammed her for not taking full responsibility for upsetting her sister. Her mom made it clear that Laurie would continue to be punished until she corrected the mistake of hiring "that woman." She also sprinkled in a few biting jabs reminding Laurie that since she already had had a handful of abortions, she most likely would never be a mom and wouldn't understand the pain of seeing her own child hurt.

"Oh well, I guess I don't have a mom anymore," Laurie said softly. I felt terrible because my suggestion had only made things more clear. As long as Laurie kept Betty on the payroll, her mother would have nothing to do with her.

My own mother was thrilled when I told her on the phone that I was ready to buy her a house.

"But Mark, can you really afford this?" she asked with hope in her voice.

"Yes, Mom. With the amount of money I'm bringing in, I can afford to pay a mortgage as long as David and Paul help out, too."

"And you want me to retire," she almost sobbed.

"You've been working a long time and have had a really rough time these past few years. I can afford to give you more than you have been making each month."

"But what about my insurance, Mark? I need the health insurance with all my problems," she groaned.

"We already talked about this. I got that covered, too. Our lives don't have to be such a struggle anymore. Take some time to think about this and let's keep checking in the next few weeks."

The extra two or three thousand dollars a month I was now regularly making from investments had already given me a sense of freedom, but my daily life remained isolated and lonely. I was at work or with Laurie all day long Monday through Friday. On the nights I didn't eat dinner with her, I went to the gym, ate at a diner, and drove home to an empty house. I began frequently signing on to gay dating and hook-up sites. The attention I was getting from guys online stroked my ego and helped me heal from the breakup. But I was mostly meeting random guys for bootie-call sex. Even though it was exciting, it felt like subsisting on a diet of chocolate cake instead of eating nutritious, balanced meals. While I love sex and dessert, my body and heart needed genuine nourishment, and that was still in short supply.

Of the nights that I ate with Laurie each week, at least one of them was with her husband, Vince. The dinners were usually at one of a handful of fine-dining restaurants very close to her house, which was only a mile from work. Dinners with the two of them meant that I had to be the sole witness to him criticizing and humiliating her.

"If my wife was a normal person, she'd have a mother to talk to instead of all this fucking drama!" he'd bellow. He was handsome with steel-blue eyes. Like his business partner Troy, he seemed to only be able to yell in his raspy Long Island accent; there were no soft tones or whispers. He was full of machismo, and as he consumed more alcohol, he became meaner to Laurie.

"It amazes me what she orders when she has thighs like that. Wives should want to look good for their husbands, but mine just shovels in the food," he would declare for the whole restaurant to hear.

During these diatribes, Laurie would shut down and silently eat and text throughout the meal, which added to Vince's fury and my annoyance. The woman who ate powerful men for breakfast and had continued having sexual trysts with a myriad of other men after she broke it off with Stuart was a timid beaten-down child at dinner with her husband. Worse was that because she was so checked out, I became Vince's default dinner partner, which meant hearing him pontificate on whatever topic he felt like discussing. His mother had been a school principal and somehow that translated in his warped mind into the right and authority to lecture others on any topic.

One night when Vince was exceptionally drunk, his comments about her weight seemed especially cruel to me. I was furious that he would attack my friend and someone I saw as a loving person in the world.

"Fuck off and stop acting like an orangutan marking his territory." I had stepped out of the polite gay man role people in Laurieland put me in, and it freaked both Vince and Laurie out. The next day she urged me to apologize to Vince or otherwise he would demand that I be fired and that she cut me out of her life. I acquiesced. When I apologized to Vince, I blamed the whole thing on too much wine. Because of his familiarity with being drunk, he understood and quickly accepted my apology. Life with Laurie was full of drama, and every so often I was glad to be the cause of it instead of the person who was always helping her clean it all up.

Within a few weeks of my initial conversation with my mother, she agreed to retire and let me financially support her until her Social Security kicked in. When Laurie heard that Mom had agreed, she suggested we go out to Italian for dinner.

As I ate chicken parmesan and spaghetti, I thanked her profusely for all she had done. "Laurie, without you none of this would have happened. I'm so grateful for your friendship and the opportunities you've given me. You've totally changed my mom's life!"

"Your mommy deserves it, my love. You inspire me with your good deeds, and I wanna help you achieve your dreams." She took a few bites of her pasta and paused a moment before speaking. "There's one thing I'd like to ask you to do for me."

I stopped eating and put down my fork. "Of course, whatever I can do, just let me know."

"Please talk to my mothah for me. You're so good with your sensitive words. You can make it better. I know you can." Her eyes were pleading with me.

"Do you think she'll listen to me?" I asked.

"Yes, she'll respond to your handsome looks and hear that you're being sincere. Tomorrow you could convince her to take me back."

Laurie had helped my mother so effortlessly. Of course I wanted to return the favor and assist her in rebuilding a relationship with her mom. The next afternoon, I left work early and drove ten minutes over to her mother's party supply store. As I parked my car, I took a deep breath to center myself. I looked around and saw Nancy walking toward the store. I jumped out and quickly jogged over, calling out, "Excuse me, Nancy. Can I have a word, please?"

Although similar to Laurie in physical appearance, Nancy had none of the warmth that gave Laurie her strength. As she turned her head around, I could immediately see that she was an ice queen.

"I'm sorry to bother you, but it's important. I'm a friend of Laurie's, and I think you'll want to hear what I have to say."

She turned her whole body to face me. In her white pantsuit, she was an older, slimmer, perfectly coiffed version of Laurie. "I'm listening," she muttered.

"I've known Laurie for almost two years, and I've never seen her as upset as she has been lately over her relationship with you. She's distraught about what to do and really misses you."

Nancy blinked hard a few times. As she spoke, I could almost hear the emotion she was straining to hold back. "I appreciate that you care enough about Laurie to come talk to me, but my daughter knows what she has to do to make things right."

"Look, I am putting myself in a weird situation here and don't wanna overstep my bounds, but isn't there a way you can be mad at her and still have her in your life?"

"Laurie knew what she was doing when she hired that woman. She's not stupid." Her eyes hardened.

"My mother and grandmother didn't talk for over ten years, and when my nana was on her deathbed, they both realized there was so much that they had missed out on. You and Laurie live ten minutes away and work in the same industry. You refer clients to each other and see each other on-site as you set up for events. It seems like such a waste that this incident is getting in the way."

Nancy looked at me silently. I was getting through. I took a breath and tried to be as empathetic as possible. "Laurie told me that you two used to be so close, 'Like two peas in a pod,' she said. Don't you miss that, too?" I observed more silence from Nancy. I could see that my words were melting her.

By the end of our thirty-minute conversation, she was willing to talk to her daughter. Once again, Laurie had been right, Nancy had responded to me. The next day Laurie gave me a big hug and joyfully reported that they had made up. "We made up! Thank you, darling, for speaking with her. I knew you could do it."

I stepped back from her and said, "She was pretty icy at first, but in the end she seemed pretty lovely."

She looked down at her phone to check emails. "Well, lovely or not, I still had to tell her that I'd fire Betty because my family is more important."

"What? Oh shit. What are you gonna do?"

Without looking up, she said, "Don't worry. I'll just make sure Betty is nevah here when my mother shows up. Laurie knows how to handle these situations." She gave me a big kiss on the cheek leaving a mark of her cherry-scented lipgloss. "Thanks for getting my mommy back!"

While Laurie adjusted to having a mom again, my mother had found a place that seemed perfect for her. I had wanted her to live in a one-story house near our old neighborhood. She preferred a townhouse in a neighborhood with other seniors. I flew down to take a look before we made an offer.

Her side of the duplex had an open floor plan, which gave an air of spaciousness. There were two bedrooms on the second floor that Mom planned on using for me and my brothers when we came to visit. The master bedroom was on the first floor and overlooked a beautiful backyard shaded by huge pine trees.

After giving me a tour, Mom teared up as she looked up at me.

"Mark, can you really afford this? I don't want to be dependent on you at such a young age."

I turned and kept walking around the unit. "Mom, this place looks great, and I love the master bedroom being on the first floor. You won't have any more pain going up and down the stairs."

Mom didn't budge from the spot she was standing in. "I'm serious. I want to make sure this is the right thing to do."

My mom had struggled financially since the divorce from my father. Arthritis in her knees meant she could barely make it up the stairs of her current apartment. This often left her trapped upstairs at 6:30 p.m. It was a no-brainer for me to use my first windfall to help her settle into a better living situation.

I walked closer to her. "You need a new place and I can afford it. What else is there to say?"

Mom looked at the ceiling and yelled out, "Thank you, angel Laurie Schneider!" In her small town, there was no bidding war and the inspections showed no problems. She moved in April 2007.

On every long drive to work or crazy dinner with Laurie and her husband, I silently reminded myself that helping mom find her way back to being proud of her home and having enough space to host family parties again was one of the highlights of my life. All the ridiculousness of Laurieland was worth it, if just for this one thing.

Taking the Bad with the Good in Laurieland

When word got out that I had bought my mother a house, relatives and family friends came out of the woodwork making inquiries about how they too could get a piece of the action. It was like a billboard advertising that I had become a success and that there were riches to be shared. The force of people's interest often took me by surprise.

Patty, a distant cousin of my father, was in her late seventies and known to be one of the wealthiest women in my hometown. I never would have approached her about Laurie's investments simply because I assumed she was too fiscally conservative, but I was wrong. At an informal brunch at my mom's new home, she approached me. "So, I hear you're doing pretty well for yourself." The gentle sounds of Southern accents were music to my ears after being immersed in Long Island. Patty stepped closer and with a sly smile asked, "Is there room for me to get in on the action?"

Without any prompting, she launched into a lengthy explanation about exactly how much money her parents left her and how she turned it into her current fortune. By the end of her monologue, she had told me the amount of her bank accounts in addition to her children's substantial trust funds.

"I'm a little surprised that you're interested in these investments, Patty, but I'm happy to explain how Laurie's deals work."

"Just tell me the percentage of profit and I'll write you a check today for $50,000." I tried not to show how shocked I was that she didn't want to hear the details first. I received a check a few days later.

Within a few months, the list of potential investors went from a handful of my inner circle to twenty-five family members and a larger group of friends. Of course, Laurie was very happy with the new influx of Morewitz family investors.

"Who knew that a nice social workah would turn out to be Mr. Moneybags!" Laurie joked to Betty after I told her another relative wanted to invest.

"Hey, you know better than anybody that I'm not the one with the money. I'm just trying to help out people I care about." I did not place much emphasis on making lots of money when I first moved to New York. Since working for her, I had learned the many benefits money brought.

She put her hand on my shoulder and looked me in the eye. "Of course, sweetheart. I was just joshin' you. Keep it rolling in and all of us will get rich very soon!" With these last words she dropped her head back and laughed as she clapped her hands like an excited little girl.

People in my life started treating me differently. Being associated with the woman who was making everyone money made me a sought-after commodity. I could see a wild hunger in people's eyes when we met. They were extra gregarious and overly fascinated with anything having to do with Laurie. It made me extremely uncomfortable.

"So, what's it like to work with Laurie every day? I mean, it sounds so exciting and glamorous," said my aunt when she called to tell me she had more money to invest.

"How's Laurie doing? Please send her our best and give her a big hug!" said a jolly family friend sounding like she had taken a tab of ecstasy.

Sue and Bennett, my father's cousins from Rhode Island, were a good example of the ridiculousness of people's projections on Laurie. They too were fascinated with Laurie and wanted to meet the person whom they were trusting with a chunk of their retirement funds.

"Look, Mark, we trust you, but we heard Laurie is so fabulous that we just have to meet her," said Bennett on the phone one day when we were discussing his next investment. "We're coming to New York next month and will do whatever we need to so we can finally see this famous Laurie face to face."

They didn't realize that making plans with Laurie was not easy. Unless she initiated a social engagement, chances were that she'd not make it a priority. An annoying part of my job with her was to placate her friends and business associates who called in frustration because Laurie had missed an appointment. I was constantly making excuses for her. When Sue and Bennett wanted to meet Laurie, I pushed her hard to commit to seeing them.

"Hey Laurie, my cousins want to meet you. They've invested $75,000 in the closeouts. Can we make a date for next week when they'll be in town?

"How cute! The little country mice want to come meet Laurie in the big city." She laughed.

"They'll only be in town for one night so I need to make a concrete plan. *For real.* No fucking around on this," I said in a serious tone.

"Yessir!" She put up a hand in a mock salute. "Have them meet me for a drink around eight at the KitKat bar on Saturday night. I have a few musicians playing in the band across the street and will be bringing potential wedding clients to see them perform."

I was glad to have a plan but knew that it wouldn't work out the way my cousins expected. Laurie was never predictable.

When Saturday night came, I met my cousins for a drink. They were both retired and in their mid-sixties. Bennett is five-five in tall shoes and Sue close to five-three. When I greeted them each with a hug, their heads barely cleared my chest. I answered every possible question about Laurie and texted her as a reminder that we were meeting in a half-hour. As I feared, she ignored my texts repeatedly. I continued to make small talk as my feet and hands became increasingly sweaty with nervousness. Although I was used to covering for Laurie's lack of consideration with her people, I resented her being disrespectful to my family.

Finally a text came: "Can't make drinks. Meet me at the club in ten minutes."

I rushed to pay the bill and get my cousins into a cab. I didn't want to miss the window of opportunity for them to meet Laurie.

The band was playing in the basement of a bar where Laurie frequently met potential bridge-and-tunnel clients who were impressed with going to a "real New York night club." The upstairs club was hip with ambient music piped in through an excellent sound system. The basement was a dive with a stage just big enough for eight band members and a 10 x 10 dance floor. The rest of the room was filled with cocktail tables huddled close around the structural beams and a long bar in the back. The room had a dank, sour smell of a college frat house that had too many years of beer spilled on its floors night after night.

After walking down the long stairway, I led my cousins to Laurie's table. "This is Sue and Bennett," I shouted so she could hear me over the loud music.

Already a little tipsy, Laurie got up and gave them each a big hug. "You're both so adorable! Look at these two tiny tushies!"

Both Sue and Bennett turned beet red and had huge smiles on their faces. The powerful Laurie thought they were cute! My cousins thanked her for the opportunity to invest and make money. Laurie was very demure and gave me credit. "Mark is such a wonderful human being. I want to help all of his family and friends!" And with that she excused herself to go back to her clients. "Have fun and enjoy my band!" The meeting had lasted all of three minutes.

I was worried that Sue and Bennett would be upset at the brevity of the interaction with Laurie but they were thrilled to have met her in person. Both seemed to be on cloud nine. Wanting to impress Laurie, they bopped around to the music for another twenty minutes before I took them back to their hotel.

"She's a dynamo for sure!" squealed Sue as we left. Even though Laurie had barely acknowledged their presence, my cousins were overcome with excitement.

Once again I was reminded of the strange power Laurie had over others. I was thankful that my dynamic with her was different. I didn't so easily fall under her spell. In fact, I was the one who most often was able to call her out on bad behavior. When she was rude to Betty or other employees, I made her aware and suggested that she apologize. Even when she went off about Vince, I was the one to ask her what she may have done to worsen the situation with him. During these times, I didn't dare bring up all the guys she continued to date in the hopes of finding her "next husband," or the sex she had with various playmates on the side.

The most disturbing behavior I experienced in Laurieland was overt racism and homophobia. After having lived and worked in very progressive environments, I felt it was like a surreal nightmare for people to openly use words like *faggot* or *Chink* in jokes and during business meetings. From day one of working for Laurie, I always stopped the person who used the offensive language. My method was far too abrupt for the schmoozy culture of Laurieland: "Please don't use that term in my presence; it's very offensive." My outspokenness was considered disruptive to the natural friendly flow of Laurie's world. It was the one area we openly disagreed. "You're just too nice to see that some people are bettah than others," she'd chastise as though I needed guidance.

Ironically, Laurie is actually part-Latina because her maternal grandmother was originally from Argentina. "I was a simple Catholic farm girl before meeting my husband," the older woman told me in a thick accent as she cooked us dinner at her house and told stories of her homeland. Laurie loved to have me join her when she was with her family because she could escape to her phone texting and emailing while I engaged in polite conversation with those left behind. In these situations, I was a dutiful surrogate husband. Once I found out about where her grandmother was from, I confronted Laurie.

"How can you let people around you say such terrible things about people of color when your grandmother is Latina!"

She responded as though I was a child asking a silly question: "Oh, what are you talking about? She's white, just from a stupid country that speaks Spanish. Once she came here with my grandfathah, she became Jewish, and so my mothah's Jewish, and *I'm* Jewish."

I was astounded by her lack of understanding of her heritage and of a similar ignorance of most people in her life. At a dinner one night at which several of Laurie's business associates and their wives joined Laurie, Vince, and me at a local Mediterranean restaurant, there was a lull in the conversation. These dinners were usually very boring because all that Laurie had in common with most of the people in her life was making money, and after that conversation was over there was little else to talk about. One of the business associates brought up the fact that he had a fourteen-year-old daughter who wanted to date a "little nigger" from her school.

With my mouth full of food, I put out my hand. "Stop it, right there. Don't use that word around me, or *ever*." I swallowed. "What, are you crazy? It's 2007!"

"Okay, buddy, calm down," said one of the other men.

I looked around the table. "Seriously, stop it with the racism and homophobic comments. Almost all of you are Jews or Italians. You seem to understand when people call you a filthy name. Why can't you see it's the same thing?" I could feel my heart racing. It was as if I had gone back in time thirty or forty years.

"Okay okay, so this filthy black kid wants to screw my daughter, and I told her, 'Fuck no. I'd rather you be a dyke than bring home a pickaninny baby one day.'"

Another woman at the table said, "Do you really feel that way? I mean, is it better to have a fagala kid than let them screw around with a nig—I mean black kid?"

"I definitely would rather have black grandkids than know my kid was a lezo or fag. No offense to you, Mark. You're a nice guy and all, but you know what I'm saying."

My head was throbbing in anger. I looked at Laurie, who was focused on her phone not saying a word. I knew she was avoiding the conversation.

Several others made similar comments, all weighing the evils of either having a gay child or allowing their kids to date someone from another race.

I stared at the floral tablecloth for a few seconds before pushing my chair back and standing. "You're all completely disgusting and should know better," I said. "May all your kids grow up gay and only date African Americans!" I walked out to my car in a whirlwind of anger.

I got a text from Laurie as I approached my car: "I apologize at the stupid conversation but you know how ignorant we all are. I'm sorry you're so upset. I love that you never stop saying the right things. I love you."

I ignored the text and on my drive home reminded myself that I didn't belong in this world. Most of the people at that table had grown up in Long Island where they were surrounded by people just like themselves. Their world so totally insulated. They had no idea what it was like to be a Jew from the South told by schoolmates that I was going to hell for not believing in Christ. Newport News, Virginia, in the 1970s and 1980s was full of business signs that said "Jesus Is Lord." Being a Jew was an abomination. The people in Laurie's world would never understand such feelings: they had never ventured out of their little kingdom to experience anything else. It didn't make what they said right, but it made me understand even more that I needed to get the hell out of there sooner than later.

The next day, Laurie sent me a text at 5 a.m.: "Down at the docks with Betty looking for deals to make us all lots of moohah! I am so sorry for last night and promise not to use naughty words anymore. Can't wait for you to come to work. Have a big surprise for you."

In addition to late-night texts telling me "I love you. Can't wait to see you tomorrow" or details about her most recent sexual encounters, Laurie often texted me at dawn when she was down at the docks scoping out potential closeouts. I learned quickly to turn my phone off when I went to sleep so these texts wouldn't wake me. Even though she had become goddess of my universe, my sleep was still more important.

When I texted her that I was on my way to work, she told me to meet her at another location. I knew she was looking at big office space for all of her businesses and assumed we were meeting at a potential new site. As I pulled up to the large one-story brick building in the industrial area of Oceanside, a mile from her house, she was getting out of her big black car, phone pressed to her ear. She motioned for me to follow her.

"Look, Larry. I gotta get off. My favorite man in the world just arrived." She gave me a kiss on my cheek. "I'm so sorry about last night, love. You're a very sensitive boy."

I gave Laurie a hard stare. Early in our friendship, she had stopped using overtly racist and homophobic terms when I told her they were offensive. However, she never stopped others from making their ignorant remarks. I knew better than to engage her in a discussion on the topic because it would go nowhere. "I'm really disturbed by the whole thing. Let's just focus on whatever you want to show me."

Smiling ear to ear, Laurie motioned like a pretty model on *The Price Is Right*: "How amazing is our new office!" She proudly reported that the landlord reduced the rent on the 10,000-square-foot space because she agreed to sign a ten-year lease.

As we toured the office area, she filled me in on her plans to buy her own party event planning equipment to rent out to other companies. She called out a list of things she was considering, including photo booths, lounge furniture, and dance floors. The other half of the warehouse would store all the janitorial supplies and paper products that she couldn't sell immediately from the closeouts.

"This place will help me make my million this year!" she said with excitement.

With the business expansion came a new cast of characters to Laurieland.

Over the next few months, Joey, her friend, business associate, and former sexual playmate, renovated the building to her specifications. He was from a very nice solid Italian family. His two brothers were Laurie's attorneys and his mother, Mary, was a partner in Laurie's entertainment and janitorial supply businesses and continued to serve as substitute mom when Nancy and Laurie fought.

Built like a Mack truck, Joey often had a cigarette in his hand, increasing the baritone of his thick accent. On first glance, he looked intimidating but was actually a sweetie pie whose bark was worse than his bite. The black sheep of the upstanding family, he had worked for organized crime but now owned a porn shop and oversaw landscape construction projects. I found out through him that the Mafia had control over all the highway and street maintenance in New Jersey and New York.

Joey and Laurie met through her friend Keith, a younger-looking Don Rickles with the voice of Danny DiVito. Joey and Keith had met in prison. Keith had been doing time for drug sales. He had a habit of keeping his sunglasses on when he was high on speed and always had a funny story to tell. The man was definitely a character.

Keith's and Laurie's paths crossed literally on the street ten years before when Laurie was trying to develop her closeout business. The way he told the story, their eyes met while each was driving. Keith motioned for Laurie to pull over. They struck up a fast friendship. After Laurie explained her ideas for closeouts, Keith showed up at her door the next day with $5,000 cash to invest. Along with the bundle of cash, he had brought framed pictures of his family that he had ripped off the wall of his house. "So she'd understand that I have a family to support. I didn't want her to screw me over." Laurie told me that somewhere along the way, she and Keith had had sex, but that their connection never turned into anything more than a solid friendship.

Keith was disgusted at the disrespectful way Vince treated Laurie. One night, he stormed into a bar where Vince was playing saxophone on stage. He pulled out a wad of cash and shouted from the peanut gallery, "Here's ten grand. Start treating Laurie right or stay the hell away, *asshole*." Laurie told me that when she and Vince got married, he forbade her from seeing Keith again.

"So always refer to Keith as 'Kenny' when my husband is around. I think he found a way to check my voicemail and emails. Vince would kill me if he knew I still saw Keith."

There was also Ivan Rosen, a successful businessman who had retired early from running the women's division of a successful international clothing company when the business had been bought out a few years before. Ivan had money to last the rest of his life and spent his days playing basketball at the gym. He also brought in his friend and business associate Mike, who had helped him run the women's clothing line. Mike was an adorably cute Italian guy who spent as much time as Ivan at the gym and had the bulked-up body to prove it. These two had a lot of liquid cash and helped Laurie with some of her bigger real estate and business strategies. Ivan was also a partner in her janitorial supply company and was sent monthly profit checks.

After the renovation of the new building was complete, it was more common to see Keith, Joey, Mike, Mary, or Ivan stopping by the office to talk to Laurie or to pick up or drop off a check. Part of my job was to remind Laurie when the payments were due for each of her investors and partners. I set up a simple Excel spreadsheet, and for the first time Laurie had someone tracking her investments and payment schedules. "Thank God you're so organized. Sometimes I don't remember the percentage of profit, and between you and me, I think people take advantage of my generosity."

Ever since Laurie had opened up FlippingMax Realty earlier in the year, her business ventures had grown exponentially. She had decided to take advantage of the amazing market for flipping houses and, of course, had found great success using her existing investor network. Because he had bad credit, Keith let her take out loans against his two houses to use for flipping foreclosed houses. As part of the deal, Laurie agreed to pay Keith's mortgages for the rest of the terms of the loans.

"Isn't it risky to keep Keith in your life?" I innocently asked one day when we had been concerned that Vince could drop by the office when Laurie was meeting with Keith.

Laurie looked incredulous. "*No one* tells me what to do. Fuck Vince. Fuck my mothah. I tell them what they want to hear, and I do whatever the hell I want."

I laughed out loud. "I'm actually living in a real-life soap opera. This is *crazytown*."

The Birth of Collective Good LLC

On one morning toward the summer of 2007, Laurie took me aside at the office.

"See this?" she pointed to a sore on her lip. "And this?" She opened her mouth and pulled her lip inside out to show more sores. "You won't believe how I got these last night."

"Are those cold sores?" I asked.

"Ewww! Are you fucking crazy! Steven and I finally did it."

Steven Berber was Laurie's mentor in the entertainment business. He was a good-looking Jewish guy in his late forties trying to hang on to his looks and his cool. He and Laurie had always had a flirtatious relationship. They bragged to each about sexual conquests and there was a certain tension in the air when the two of them were together. Ever since Laurie dumped Stuart, she seemed antsy to find something else to distract her.

"Laurie, I've had a lot sex in my lifetime, but I've never woken up with sores on my lips," I said drolly. "What the fuck happened?"

She brought her index finger and thumb about three inches apart. "I sucked his pencil-dick for hours." Her eyes widened. "I swear it was *hours*. We were totally drunk and I went down on him after we started making out." She paused, thinking through the events of the night. "He musta taken a Viagra or something because he stayed hard *forevah*, but wouldn't cum. It turned into a contest."

"What were you competing for?" I asked stupefied.

"I wanted to make him finish first, and he wanted to keep proving his manliness by staying hard and not letting me win." The smile on her face didn't budge.

"And the result is that you look like you've got leprosy of the inner mouth." I paused briefly. "So I guess you won?"

"Of course, darling, Mother Laurie always wins!!" She clapped her hands together and then pulled out lipgloss to coat her lips. "Now, I have a new play-toy. We'll see where this goes . . . isn't my life glamorous!"

"It's another *crazy* situation, Laurie. I mean Steven and Vince work together and are friends. You're one risk-taking crazy mo-fo!"

"Okay, lovely, now I'm switching topics." She was now at the mirror staring at her face and hair. She spent a lot of time each day looking at herself regardless of what she was doing and who else was in the room. "So, Larry my accountant had two things to tell me today. Numbah one, he referred a bookkeeper to help with my ongoing accounting. Second, he doesn't like all these small investors you've brought in. He would rather I keep the $50,000 minimum I used to have before I fell in love with you and changed the rules."

I gave her a harsh look. "Laurie, you know we're not in love."

"Only kidding, cutie pie, but I was thinking that it would be so much easier if you had a company that could put all your people together to make one large investment. That way you could manage it all, and I'd only have to write one check. Right now, I have to keep track of all these transactions and deal with giving everyone a 1099 at the end of the year."

I shrugged. "Oh, I'm sorry, I've never thought about it from your perspective."

"Well, that's what Laurie is for, to do all the thinking for everyone." She gave my cheek a big kiss. "We have some big China Deals happening later this year. Try to get a company up and running before then. You can speak to my CPA, Larry, and my attorneys to set up an LLC. It should only cost $760."

Laurie's suggestion of starting my own business didn't excite or stress me. It seemed like just adding a layer to what currently existed. I contacted

Larry and asked him about the idea. He was very open to working with me but seemed to have strangely limited knowledge of what Laurie was doing with the investments. He was a Jewish guy in his mid-fifties but looked seventy with his white hair and weathered red face. Like most people in Laurieland, he was unpolished and spoke as though he was chewing on marbles. He always had a ball of spit at the corner of mouth that I kept expecting to fly across the room at me.

"So you're telling me that these buyouts she does make 25 percent profit in three to six months?" he asked, as though hearing it for the first time.

"Well, they're called closeouts, not buyouts, and yeah, Laurie buys the goods below wholesale because they're irregular or slightly damaged. Then she sells the stuff to wholesalers and retailers." I paused. "How are you her accountant and not know all of this?"

He looked at me in disgust. "She's crazy to work with. You gotta know by now how scattered she is."

I felt protective whenever anyone spoke harshly against her. "What do you mean? I think she's brilliant—maybe a little ADD—but definitely brilliant."

"One day she runs an entertainment company, another day it's a janitorial Supply business." Larry said like it was an insult.

"Isn't that what entrepreneurs do? I mean, she's kind of building a tiny empire for herself," I responded. "Didn't you tell her that the small investors are complicating her books and that I should have a company to bundle them all together?"

"She told you I said that, huh?" His poker face didn't betray what he was thinking. "I could have said something like that." He gave me a constipated look and after silently watching the spit bubble on the corner of his mouth grow for thirty seconds, I left without hiring him.

The meeting had not given me with a confident feeling about working with Larry. I searched around for other accountants but found that they had no way to comprehend the business structure I was proposing because of the unusual model of Laurie's closeouts. I finally approached

Louis, Nate's father, who was a brilliant corporate attorney. My former father-in-law quickly understood the concept and had a few ideas of how to structure the business.

"What name are you thinking of using?"

"Collective Good, because its purpose is to be for the common good of all my family and friends. Together we'll share in the amazing opportunities that Laurie's offering."

When talking about business, Louis had a flat affect; he stayed completely focused as his mind filtered through the many possibilities to find the best option. "I'll give it some thought and will give you a call when I've got some ideas."

The next day, I received a call from his secretary. "Hello, Mr. Morewitz. Please hold for Louis." A second later I heard him pick up and he immediately launched into his explanation. "Okay, the business will be the managing partner of temporary partnerships. Each partnership will invest in another one of Laurie's deals and may have different investors. You'll be managing member of Collective Good. My firm will take care of filing for the LLC and will develop the investor agreements to use for your family and friends, and another set to use for the partnerships to contract with Laurie. I'll assign all of this to someone lower in the ranks but will look everything over myself."

"Wow, that's amazing!" I said, getting excited. "Thank you so much, Louis."

"It's important that you keep very good records, so you should have a bookkeeper and an accountant set up everything."

Louis advised that I go back to Larry because, even if I didn't have initial confidence in him, he had an established relationship with Laurie, and it might be the best place to start the business. I called Larry and told him what Louis had proposed.

"Oh, why didn't you say that before? I can make that work," he said smugly. He explained that we could set up the company books so each partnership had distinct records but everything would be run out of one business account. "Use Chase Bank because it'll make the transfers to

Laurie's account easiest." Even though I didn't like or trust Larry, I took Louis's advice and hired him.

After a month or so of working out all the details with the lawyer at Louis's firm and Larry, Collective Good LLC was incorporated in early October 2007.

Serendipitously, there was a new China Deal happening right around the time that Collective Good became a reality. As I was finalizing the details of the company, I put out a call to all of my family and friends who had shown interest in previous deals and explained the new company structure. Within a short amount of time, I raised the $500,000 she needed for the deal.

"So far I like this Collective Goods *a lot!*" She beamed.

"It's Collective Good without an *s* on the end, sweetie. It means the company is for the good of everyone involved."

"You social workers come up with the strangest concepts for a business."

At the time I started Collective Good, I was becoming weary of all the drama in Laurieland. I also realized that between the commissions and investment profits, I no longer needed the salary Laurie was paying me. Remembering that she had originally told me I'd only have to work three days a week, I offered her a deal during breakfast one day. Laurie knew this incredible hole in the wall with the best bagels and homemade cottage cheese.

"I've been thinking that you should stop paying me a salary. I'm making enough to live comfortably from the investments, and you already have so many people to support. You've hired a bookkeeper and new office people. You don't really need me to come in every day anymore." With a mouth full of cottage cheese, she said, "But I want to see you every day, and even on the weekends. I miss you on days I don't get to be with you!"

I had anticipated that she would put up a fight so I had prepared. "Let's compromise. I'll come in a few days a week to help out but will still have dinner with you whenever you want . . . even weekends."

Without irony, she said, "I think my intelligence is rubbing off on you. I am very sad, but it's a brilliant idea."

And with that, I bought my partial freedom from Laurieland.

Cancer Cancer Everywhere

At the beginning of 2008, Laurie texted me early in the morning.

"I want you to come to a meeting today with Ivan and Mike and me. We're trying to cut out the Hasids as middlemen, and go right to the source in China."

"Not sure what you're talking about," I texted back, confused.

"Go get me some bagels and cottage cheese at the deli across the street. We'll talk when everyone gets here. I've got to make a hundred calls before the meeting starts."

When I arrived with bagels in hand, Laurie was on the phone with another breakfast already in front of her, so I put the food down on another desk and went online to check her emails. A few minutes later, Ivan and Mike walked in together.

"So I contacted my associate in Xi'an, and she's willing to scout out some factories for us," Mike said as he and Ivan sat down. The conference area consisted of six plush leather chairs surrounding a glass coffee table. It gave meetings a kind of intimacy.

"Can these factories handle exact specifications that I give them for paper towels and toilet paper?" Laurie asked as she applied another coat of gloss back and forth across her lips.

I felt like they were speaking code. "Sorry, I'm behind on what's going on. Could someone catch me up?"

Mike explained. "I've been telling Laurie that although we really appreciate the money we are making in her deals, it doesn't make sense as a long-term business model for her to keep paying out such high profit rates."

Ivan jumped in. "When Mike and I used to run our corporate division, he worked directly with factories in China."

"I spent a lot of time going back and forth to Xi'an, where most of the factories are located," Mike elaborated. "I still have contacts there who are scouting out factories for us."

I was shocked to see Laurie actually sitting and paying attention. "These ambitious guys think I can cut out the Jews and just work directly with the Chinese to make paper supplies."

"Sounds amazing," I said considering the plan in my head.

"The best part is that I want you to go to China with Mike to work with the factories," Laurie said, beaming as though she was presenting me with an award.

"Me? *Really*? That would be so exciting, but shouldn't Mike just take care of it all? I mean, he has all the expertise." I felt flustered that another layer of the business was being offered to me.

"I'm gonna make you an international businessman," Laurie declared. "Your mothah is going to be so proud of you!"

In the weeks that followed, Mike ordered samples of goods from several factories to gauge their quality. When the boxes arrived, we'd gather around as Laurie held up the paper towels or the party streamers and announced whether she approved.

The plan was that once we received consistent shipments of quality goods, Mike and I would fly out to the factory to negotiate a deal—actually, Mike's contact would negotiate the deal. Mike and I would visit the factory to give a presence of the American investors. We planned to increase Laurie's market to other states. Mike was a bona fide corporate manager with excellent business skills. The strategy he had mapped out made sense and seemed like a win-win for everyone involved.

When I told my mother I'd be going to China on business, she was elated. A week after telling her the news, I received a box delivered by UPS. In it was a briefcase on wheels, perfect for a long flight, and a money clip. The note inside the box read, "To be a successful businessman, you have to look like one. I'm so proud of you! Love, Mom."

Like all things in Laurieland, the plan of my going to China depended on Laurie maintaining interest. After a few shipments of samples arrived from China, Laurie was distracted by another new man.

Jason Steele was a gorgeous Jamaican with a tight surfer's body and a great voice for singing reggae. She took him on as her new project. "I'm going to make him a star and get in his pants!" she said to me like a schoolgirl. Her focus on Party Hearty didn't completely wipe out the China factory project but temporarily put it on the back burner.

Fate brought another huge distraction in my life. During a routine visit in March, a dermatologist found a suspicious mole directly above my right ear.

"This doesn't look good to me. No, I don't like this one bit." She handed me a small mirror to look for myself. "I want to get a biopsy of this before we do anything else. See how dark and misshapen it is?"

"I just had this checked a few months ago by another dermatologist because my brother said it looked weird. The doctor said it was nothing to worry about." I took a look at the dark spot. "I think it's doubled in size since them."

The intended purpose of my appointment with Dr. Eastman that day was to have a few age spots removed. Now she wanted to do a full body scan, concerned about the amount of moles I had, and the history of skin cancer from my dad's side of the family.

She injected the area with an anesthetic and began slicing off a thin layer of the dark pigment. "Look, I tend to be conservative on collecting biopsies. I'd rather be safe than sorry." I sat silently because she had told me not to move my jaw. She finished and put on a Band-Aid. "I'm sure you'll be fine. Don't give it another thought until my office calls you with the results."

A few days later on a Friday afternoon at 3:45 p.m., I received a call. "Please hold for Dr. Eastman," said the receptionist. I tried to ignore my annoyance. How much time did it take for her to dial my number herself? A moment later I heard the doctor's voice. She was obviously in mid-chew of a sandwich when she picked up the phone.

"Listen, it's melanoma, Stage three. It's nothing to get scared about. My receptionist will give you the name of a surgeon who will scoop it out."

My mind went blank. I usually had a thousand questions, but I was unprepared for the results to be so serious. "It's late in the afternoon on a Friday. Can this really wait until next week?"

"Mark, don't worry. It will be fine." And with that she transferred me back to the receptionist who gave me several numbers to call. I was stunned by the news and by the lack of compassion in her delivery.

My first call was to my friend Joe whose opinion as a doctor I very much respected. He didn't like the news. "Stage three of four means you gotta get that out soon, Kitten." "Melanoma is an aggressive cancer that can spread quickly."

My next call was to Laurie. "Oh My Gawd! How horrible! You'll use Howard Silverman, the best plastic surgeon. He did my breasts and one of my lipos."

Although Laurie was still what my mother called "a big girl," she had undergone four liposuction procedures during the years before we met and another one the previous summer. Her somewhat tight midsection and arms showed the pinch marks of the surgeries, but her zaftig proportions revealed gluttony for frequent and large portions of food.

I bristled at her suggestion. "Thanks, but I'm gonna just go to the specialist my doctor recommended."

"Whatever you decide, sweetheart, I am here for you and will be praying night and day for this to be ovah soon." I knew Laurie didn't pray at night or during the day, but I knew she was genuine in her concern and appreciated her offer to help.

I was not really worried about the situation until I visited the surgeon the following Tuesday. He suggested that the only way to do the procedure would be to cut a fifty-cent-piece–sized flap of skin above my ear "to make sure we get all the margins of the cancerous cells." That part sounded fine. But when I asked how that hole would heal, he told me he would have to cut the right side of my face from eye to ear and pull that flap from the right side of my face to cover the hole.

"So I'd have a face lift on one side of my face?" I asked in horror.

"Well, the right side *would* be pulled differently than the left. And the incision would leave a raised red scar from your eye to your ear." He seemed surprised when I left without booking an appointment. Over the course of the next five days, I got referrals from Nate's family and other people I trusted. Surgeon after surgeon said the same thing without showing any regard to the fact that they were talking about completely transforming the way my face looked.

On my fourth doctor in a week, I'd finally had enough. After receiving the same spiel, I stood up in frustration. "Doctor, pretend that I am someone you care about. Let's say your son or the President."

He let out a nervous laugh.

"Imagine that the way I look mattered to you as much as it matters to me." He seemed to puff up his chest as I continued. "I am only thirty-eight. I'm single and I'm gay. My appearance matters to me, and I like the way I look now."

He looked down and nervously shuffled some papers on his desk. "I don't know any other way to approach the surgery."

I let out a sigh. "Well, at least that's an honest answer. I need to find someone who can be a little more creative. Thanks."

While I continued my attempt to find a surgeon who would keep my face intact, I received a call from my dad. Seeing his number as I picked up the phone, I assumed he was checking in to see if I'd found someone to operate on me.

"Hi, Marky." Dad was silent for a second. "I got some bad news today."

I felt a pit in my stomach. "What's going on, Dad?"

"The doctor found something. He says it's my lungs and that it's gone to my liver and brain."

"Oh God. Did he use the word *cancer*?"

After a pregnant pause, Dad softly said, "Yes, that's what the doctor said it was."

My temples pulsated with pressure, and I did my best to shower Dad with love and support. At the same time, I wanted to know everything the doctor had told him because my father was a simple man and I didn't trust that he had asked the questions to get the fullest picture of his prognosis. After a few minutes of talking, he mentioned that the doctor had emailed Sharon, his wife, the MRI report with the results.

"Would you please have her email me that document? I wanna talk to Joe and Ira about what it says. Both are very competent doctors whom I trust to help us figure out how to best help you."

Within the hour, I received the email from Sharon. While I was waiting for callbacks from Ira and Joe, I opened up the document to see what I could understand on my own. Through my previous work as a medical worker, I had gained a good amount of general medical knowledge. I knew that the analysis of tests were often at the bottom of a report, so I skipped to the end. My eyes scanned the page: "Multiple enhancing lesions of the right cerebellum and right frontal areas," which was what Dad had told me. "These findings are strongly suggestive of metastatic disease to the brain." I dropped my head and averted my eyes from reading any more. The word *metastatic* jumped off the page. I knew this meant that Dad either had a hard battle ahead of him or no chance at all.

Both Joe and Ira soon called and confirmed that the kind of cancer Dad had was untreatable. It was only a matter of weeks or maybe months until he died.

Still feeling numb, I shared Joe and Ira's interpretation with Sharon and my brothers. First I emailed them all and then called everyone including my mother. Although divorced for fifteen years, Mom and Dad had formed an amicable friendship during the past five years. I knew that

Mom still thought of Dad as an extended family member and was as concerned about him as the rest of us.

"Oh Mark, we knew that something wasn't right with your dad at Nana's birthday last month, and now it's too late."

"I know, this is so sad," I said whimpering a bit. "There's so little time left with him."

Dad had seemed vaguely withdrawn at his mother's ninety-seventh birthday brunch in late February and very different from the outgoing person I saw in December when I came home at Christmastime. In the six weeks in between, he had experienced a persistent flu. At the February birthday party, I took him aside to urge him to see a doctor.

"I'm worried about you. I can tell that something's not right. I see it in your eyes."

Dad shyly looked down at his hand as he rubbed his fingers and thumb together. It was something I knew he did when he was uncomfortable. "The doctor said I have the flu."

"A flu doesn't last this long. How about requesting to go to a neurologist? I'm thinking maybe you might have had a TIA—you know, one of those mini strokes."

His eyes widened as he turned to look at me. "Why do you say that?"

"You seem slower than your usual slowpoke self, Dad. Slow to process, and slow to respond. And it looks like you're not so stable on your feet."

He had a pained look on his face and looked away again. "Funny you mention that. I had some trouble walking when I went away to St. Martin last month. Sharon had me in a wheelchair for a while."

I didn't filter my exasperation. "Dad, the flu doesn't put you in a wheelchair. Sharon's a nurse, she should know that." He blinked and looked down again.

I put my hand on his shoulder. "Please go see a neurologist. I'm gonna keep bugging you until you do."

Surprisingly, Dad listened to me. In the two weeks since I'd seen him, he had gone back to the doctor to request more tests. After hearing the sad news, my first instinct was to drive down that night to be with him but Joe nixed that plan.

"You've got to get your melanoma taken care of immediately. Then go help your Dad. Remember to put the oxygen mask on yourself first, like the airline attendants say, *right?*"

Later, as I got off the phone with my brothers on the West Coast I glanced at the clock and saw it was approaching midnight. "My daddy's gonna die," I meekly said to no one. I was still shell-shocked, and Joe's reminder that I had to pay attention to my own health issue felt like it put me over the edge.

I texted Laurie: "Can we talk tomorrow morning? My dad's really sick and I'm sad." The phone rang a few minutes later.

"I'm so sorry I couldn't call you sooner. I'm working a pawty and had to walk outside. What's wrong with your fathah?" As I filled her in on the details, I felt myself nestled in her loving embrace.

"I'm so sad for you and your lovely and sexy Dad. I'll help you til the day we both die holding hands." This was not the first time she shared that fantasy with me. "I told you that the man for your surgery is Dr. Howard Silverman. He studied dermatology before specializing in plastic surgery and even did some special study of melanoma in medical school."

"Why didn't you tell me that before? I thought he was just another plastic surgeon."

"You didn't ask, sweetheart. I know you have so much on your mind right now, so I'm going to text you the address: plan on going in first thing tomorrow morning. I'll call ahead and make sure he will see you."

One of the many huge payoffs of living in Laurieland was that I was part of the entourage of the queen bee. This meant that I had access to all of her kingdom because everyone bowed down to her. Of course it turned out that Dr. Silverman was an investor and business partner in yet another of her ventures—to develop the first sing-out-loud hip-hop greeting cards.

The next morning I was sitting in his office while he pulled out an old textbook to show me a particular type of stitch that he planned to use. "To cover the site of the biopsy, I'll move the scalp from the back of your head. Your face and your good looks will be intact. Your hair will cover up the scar." I booked the first available surgery appointment he had, which was a few days later.

Laurie took me to dinner after my consultation with Dr. Silverman. "Listen, darling, I'll take you to the surgery, pick you up, and take you home. Then I'll cook you a nice meal and will stay with you until you feel better."

I took her hands in mine and gave her a big kiss on the cheek. "First, I love you. You are the absolute best and sweetest for helping me. Second, I'll take a car service because it's a very long drive from your house to mine and then Jersey where Dr. Silverman's office is. Third, you don't even know how to boil water, but I so appreciate you wanting to help."

She beamed a big smile. "Then I'll get you all your favorite things: cupcakes, feta cheese, pizza, and I'll have my grandma make her famous chicken soup."

"Sweetie, I love that you know me so well, but just a ride home would be enough. He said I would be fine after a few hours of sleep and may just have a headache."

"I don't want anything to happen to my favorite man in the whole world."

A few days later the surgery went off without a hitch. When I woke with my head bandaged, Laurie was there to walk me gently to my car. She gave me the gift of quiet on the hour-long drive home and helped me get into bed. And when I awoke several hours later, I was happy to find she had honored my wishes to leave the house after I fell asleep. I was genuinely grateful that she was so supportive, but her love felt smothering in a way that I didn't want to deal with while I was healing.

After a day of rest, I flew home to Virginia to be with my dad for his next doctor's appointment. The physician was around my age and had the formality of a true Southerner. Out of ridiculous politeness, he hadn't told Dad the severity of the disease. In fact, the doctor offered chemotherapy, an option that Sharon and Dad's very protective younger sister

Faye wanted him to do. With Dad, Sharon, and my older brother Zack in the room, I felt we needed to hear the full truth of the prognosis so we could deal with the reality of the situation.

"Doctor, what kind of impact would the chemo have?" I asked.

The doctor put his hands in his pockets and looked down at the floor before speaking. "Well, Mr. Morewitz, the treatment may slow the progress of your father's cancer a bit."

"My understanding is that the type of cancer my father has doesn't really respond to chemo." I looked over at Dad, who was looking at his feet as he tapped them lightly with his cane.

The doctor took a moment before speaking. "Well, that is correct."

My older brother Zack then spoke. "Then why prescribe chemo, which would make him nauseous and tired? I don't get it."

The doctor cleared his throat. "The treatment has been known to extend life of the patient for two weeks to two months."

The room was silent for a beat. We all looked at Dad whose face was blankly staring at the floor. Huge teardrops fell from Sharon's eyes as she pulled out a Kleenex.

I asked, "Doctor, in your experience how long have other patients with similar cancer diagnoses lived? I know it is uncomfortable, but I feel we need to say this out loud."

The doctor spoke slowly and with incredible empathy as he proceeded to tell us that Dad had a very short time to live and recommended radiation to shrink the tumor in his brain to help with balance. Dad had been using a cane for about a month but had fallen a few times.

A few days later, David and Paul, my younger brothers, flew in from Los Angeles. Along with Zack, we all took Dad out to breakfast. Somehow through his illness, he had gotten a voracious appetite in the morning. Tommy's Restaurant, a delicious southern diner, was a perfect solution because we could get huge portions of food for less than $10.

After Dad ordered a ham and cheese omelet, potatoes, coffee, and waffles, he took a breath and a sip of water. "Sharon and your Aunt Faye want me to take the chemo treatment. I don't want you boys to think I'm a coward, but I'm not gonna do it." He looked around at each of us with an eagerness in his eyes for validation.

Paul spoke first. "That's what I would do, too, Dad. The treatments sound like they'd make you really uncomfortable."

"And all we want for you is to feel good," David chimed in.

"Sharon and Aunt Faye just love you so much," Zach said sweetly.

I added, "There is nothing *not brave* about choosing to avoid medicine that's gonna cause you suffering, Dad."

Dad's face beamed with love. "Thank you, boys. It means the world to me to have your support." Like a perfectly choreographed play, the waitress appeared with two arms filled with plates of yummy food. Dad said, "Dig in!" with a big smile on his face as he picked up a fork and started tearing into his waffle.

The next day I flew back to New York City to take care of business.

Saying Goodbye to Pop

When I returned, I drove to Long Island to have dinner with Laurie. She wanted me to fill her in on the details and was upset to hear that we had dealt so openly with my father.

"You made your daddy listen to the doctor telling him he's going to die! How horrible and nasty. And I thought you were such a sweet boy!"

I took a bite of my chicken Parmesan ravioli and a sip of pinot gris. "Okay, Oprah, what would you have done?"

"I would have treated him like I do a kid who's crying. I'd just distract him and make him happy. What's wrong with that?" she said incredulously.

"Nothing, sweetie. I'm not wired to avoid, and I didn't want Dad taking medicine that would have made him sick in his last few months."

"Oh yeah, I guess that's true, but I still think it stinks."

"By the way, my priority right now is Dad. I'll be spending as much time with him as possible."

"Of course, dawling. I wouldn't have it any other way." She dipped her fork into my ravioli. "I'll keep you in the loop on deals, and you just let me know if any of your peeps are interested." At the time, there were about forty of my people investing with Laurie through Collective Good.

"It's such a relief knowing I'll have money coming in while I focus on Dad. But how can I transfer money while I'm out of town?"

"Just call or email Matt Baker at Chase in Rockville Centre. He will take care of everything you need." As she lunged for the last piece of bread she asked, "Can I have that?"

Laurie was in and out of her local Chase Bank so much that she was on a first-name basis with most of the staff. Matt had opened her accounts. I had heard her call him to transfer funds to cover checks and knew she had helped him and his wife find an apartment. A common unspoken motto of relationships in Laurieland was "You scratch my back, I'll scratch yours."

I was relieved to learn that I could do all of my business from Virginia because I really wanted to spend every minute with Dad. However, prior to learning about my father's diagnosis, I had hired a contractor to completely renovate the first floor and basement of Hazel. The plan was for him to gut my kitchen and build it back from the studs. He would also finish the basement that currently looked and smelled like an ancient dungeon. Work was scheduled to begin in late April. When I met with him to go over my plans, I explained that my father was dying and that I would be down in Virginia for much of the project.

He shifted weight from his right to left foot and leaned against my kitchen wall. Tom was a white guy in his fifties who was trying too hard to look like a guy in his late thirties. He had a whiny voice and wore clothes that harked back to the grunge scene from the late 1990s. There was something about him that made me think of Weird Al Yankovich. "We're gonna need your ongoing input to help with the *many* design decisions."

"Can't we just go over what I want now?"

He laughed at my naïveté. "There're a lot of surprises in these old house that we can't predict. So we'll have to take it step by step. For example, only after we demolish the kitchen will we see if the floor needs a complete replacement or just strengthening a few sags in the middle."

Tom and I agreed that it made the most sense to start in the basement so that my life would be the least interrupted during this stressful time. He advised that I come back to New York at least every seven to ten days to check on progress and give input so the job could be done to my satisfaction.

"Do you have to start this project now? Isn't it enough that your father's dying?" Mom asked when we were talking on the phone about plans for me to return to Virginia.

"I know it's crazy, Mom, but the construction world is really busy and competitive. I got referred to this contractor by an architect who highly recommended him. And I gave him a deposit before we found out about Dad."

"For most people the stress of either would be too much."

"The thing is that I am not gonna be making money with Laurie forever, and I want to do this renovation when I know things are solid. The house is a big part of my future. It's where I hope to raise a family one day. And right now it's really difficult to book a contractor because so many houses are being renovated."

"I was strong like you when I was young, Mark. You get that from me," Mom said with confidence.

She was right. When she was young, my mother did more in a day than most people did in a week. That is one of the qualities that I found attractive and familiar in Laurie. In one twenty-four-hour period, she did a myriad of huge business deals, managed personal issues, and always had time for a celebratory dinner. Her business day often began around 5 a.m. when she went down to the docks to arrange for a closeout. Of all her investors, she usually texted me so my family and friends would have first dibs on the moneymaking venture. I'd often wake up to her messages: "Hi Love. There is a shipment of toilet paper that I can get tomorrow for 120k. Can pay 150k in three months. Let me know if your friends are interested ASAP."

If I came into the office at ten, I'd see Laurie eating while on the phone with a Party Hearty client planning an event while emailing someone else about flipping a property. Late mornings, she'd either be looking at property to flip or going to various wholesale paper companies to sell what she bought through closeouts. By noon, she would have a huge lunch delivered to the office for the staff and eat with us even if she had another business lunch scheduled right afterward. Her stomach seemed to be bottomless, but her back widened and her huge legs got even thicker.

"I only had a few bites for breakfast so I'm okay to eat the pastrami and roast beef sandwich. It's not going to make a difference to my disgusting fat thighs. Ugh, I don't know how Vince can stand fucking me!" she'd say as she popped a French fry into her mouth.

Her afternoons were often spent driving with Betty to nicer areas of Long Island or western New York to woo new clients to book her band, DJ, and dancers for their event.

"They were typical rich assholes with ugly, *retawded* children, but I have a deposit for ten thousand dollahs stuffed in between my breasts as I'm calling you from my car."

Dinners were either spent with Vince or potential clients for Party Hearty. I always got a play-by-play report via texts or emails: "My husband's a handsome man with a big penis but he's being an asshole tonite ☹."

After dinner, she would usually head from Long Island to the KitKat Bar in Manhattan to show potential entertainment clients her hot lead singers who performed several nights a week as the house band. On her drive back to Long Island, I usually received several texts or calls filling me in on her day and the amazing business possibilities she had come across. Everyone Laurie met seemed to have the potential to connect her with the next "big deal."

About ten days after my surgery, I was happy to receive an email from Dr. Silverman telling me that the original biopsy had gotten all the cancer out of my head so the surgery had not really been necessary. I would be fine. Not having to stay in New York for more procedures meant I could fly back to Virginia to be with Dad, which felt like the thing I most wanted to do.

During that first week, it really sank in that we didn't have much time to deal with some important logistical issues. I began gently talking to him about whether he wanted to be part of making his own funeral preparations.

"Dad, it's time for me to start thinking about making arrangements for you—can we talk about this together?" I gently asked one afternoon as I sat next to him. He shifted his position on his cream-colored leather sofa and slowly nodded while his mouth made the movement of a cow chewing its cud. He had always had a habit of randomly making chewing motions with his mouth, but as he had gotten sicker it happened more frequently. The oxygen machine made a loud hissing noise in the background as it pushed air into Dad's nostrils. The room smelled musty and full of sickness.

I pulled my chair closer to him and held his hand. "Do you have a cemetery plot?"

"No, never got one," he said meekly as if I were scolding him.

"Do you wanna be buried with Sharon? I checked and the cemetery on Warwick Boulevard would work, but the Jewish cemetery won't allow someone of another religion to be buried there." My mother had been correct in her concern that Dad's interfaith marriage might be a problem for the rules of the Jewish cemetery.

"I'll be buried alone," he said softly. The anxiety medication was working but flattened out his tone and left him sounding hollow. I contained my surprise that Dad wouldn't be interred with the love of his life and simply asked, "Have you talked about this with her?"

His lips dry, he spoke slowly as he nodded. "We talked about it a few nights ago. Would you find a place for me where my family is buried? Sharon can tell you how to pay for it."

I patted his hand. "Dad, I'm paying for it and it's no big deal."

With his eyes closed, he took a sip from the straw I held to his lips and paused a moment before exclaiming, "*You're* the one!" in the tone and cadence of an evangelical preacher calling out to his congregation. He had begun using this phrase with me, and each time he gathered the strength to open his eyes wide and bunch his lips together with intensity. When he had first used it, he gave no explanation and so I made up my own, which I felt was a catch-all for, "I love you," "Thank you," and "I turn to you as a son does to his father."

Although we never had had a traditional relationship, our roles had completely transformed in the days since we found out his diagnosis. I had always been the grounded and strong one but had never chosen to use that strength to take care of him before. In the past two years, Laurie's investments had also enabled me to become the family breadwinner, a role that he had never felt he could adequately fulfill. Dad had spent his entire life struggling financially and feeling bad about not being a better father or husband.

It was a surreal experience to make the call to Abe Firestone, the man who has handled our synagogue's cemetery plots for the past forty-five years. I remembered him seeming ancient when I was a young boy. How was it that at sixty-eight, Dad was dying and Mr. Firestone was still here to help me with the details? After acknowledging the sadness of the situation and asking about my family, he delicately launched into the locations available within the cemetery that was arranged with lettered rows and numbered plots. He let me know that there were few single plots available including one close to the fence where people who had killed themselves were buried. I shuddered at the thought and instead chose a place toward the front of the cemetery where everyone could see and greet Dad's headstone. It was also only a row away from his father's grave and where his elderly mother would soon be buried. Throughout his life, my father had experienced so much internal and publicly aired shame about cheating on my mom and his business failures that I didn't want the community to perceive that our choice of his final resting place was anything but full of love. Some part of me also didn't want my dad, who had struggled with self-esteem for so much in his lifetime, to be alone and isolated after his death.

"In the front near my father?" Dad repeated back to me when I told him. He nodded his head in thanks and closed his eyes as his face went placid. He was exhausted and didn't have the energy to keep his eyes open much anymore.

"I gotta go now, Dad. Remember, I'm flying back to New York tonight and will see you in a few days."

With his eyes still closed, Dad whispered, "Love you, Marky."

"I just can't believe what you talk to your dying father about," Laurie said the next time we met. "You amaze me with your strength. You're such a good man . . . sometimes I wanna be more like you."

Laurie was a constant presence as my father faded. Her texts, emails, and calls helped me stay strong and present for my family. Of course, the money I was making, that we all were making, helped tremendously. For the first time in my life, I didn't have to consider cost before need. For that I am thankful—that in my father's final days, he was proud of me for the man I had become and relieved that he didn't have to worry about our family for whom he had nothing to leave.

Odd Behavior at a Funeral

Dad died at home a few weeks later, three months after his diagnosis.

I ended up making most of the funeral arrangements. Through the incredible sadness and stress, Laurie checked in with me frequently to let me know I was not alone and that she would do anything I needed or wanted. When she told me she would be attending the funeral, my heart felt a little lighter simply because there was someone I could lean on.

The day of the funeral was overwhelming. As I watched the casket being lowered into its final resting place, I wept alongside my family. Since I was in the front row, I was only a foot or two away from the grave. As we had gone through the litany of traditional prayers, my mouth was able to recite the proper sounds but my eyes had blurred into intense focus on the wooden box that contained my father's body.

I stared at the casket, my heart aching and my face wet with tears. Since the breakup of my marriage, I had cried more easily, and today the sadness was a waterfall of grief. It washed over me again and again that these were the last moments that I would be in the presence of my father's physical form.

The rabbis explained the Jewish tradition for the family and community of the deceased to shovel three distinct portions of dirt onto the casket until it is covered. Everyone under the canopy except my frail ninety-seven-year-old Nana stood up to perform our last act of love for Dad. The cemetery workers had unfolded pieces of material that looked like artificial grass to uncover a large pile of dirt. A brass shovel was on either end of the mound. The rabbis took their turn and then the family moved forward.

I felt the heat of the June sun as I picked up the small shovel. The sun's glare was a spotlight on my face, but I was aware of the people around me, watching every move that I made. It was strange but I had never felt more grounded and present except at my wedding four years earlier. This was my father's funeral. The people all around us were there out of love and support. My heart was achingly open out of love for Dad, with whom I had made a complex journey in my lifetime.

I collected the dirt in the shovel and burst into tears as I watched the brown bits scatter the coffin below me. I repeated the action twice more and through my tears said out loud, "Bye, Daddy, I love you."

I walked back to my seat and sat crying. Somehow the act of getting up to shovel the dirt had dispersed my family. Aunt Faye, my father's sister, had shifted closer to my nana, who sat stoically, her shoulders down in defeat and her gaze to the ground in front of her. In an effort to console my mother, my brother David sat next to her, and my two married brothers were huddled with their spouses and children. Dad's wife, Sharon, had her son and sister's arms around her. I sat alone in the second row as I watched at least thirty people from our extended family and community stand up to take their turn at the shovel. With compassionate determination, each person awkwardly picked up the tool and found a way to the dirt in front of them. I felt my body heavy with emotion and heat from standing in the direct sun. I had a random thought that it would have been a perfect beach day had we not been burying my father.

I felt a hand on my left shoulder from behind me. From the whiff of coconut, pineapple, and cocoa butter, I knew it was Laurie. I didn't look up or put my hand on hers. I honestly didn't have the strength at that moment to do anything but receive, and so I let her give me comfort in the most compassionate and appropriate way I needed. Just having the acknowledgment that she was there for me felt right.

A few hours before the funeral, Laurie had arrived at my mother's town-house after completing the eight-hour drive she'd made from Long Island. She'd chosen to make the car trip instead of flying because she wanted to surprise me with a carload of sweets from the Little Pie Company, my favorite bakery, and bagels from H&H, the best in the world.

"Hi, my sad friend," she said getting out of her car with a tray of chocolate-iced cupcakes with creamy white fluff in the middle that had been baked in New York City that morning. Through our many texts and emails during the past week, she understood the enormous emotional toll and the amount of stress I was experiencing with the coordination of all the logistics of the day.

Laurie had a way of knowing just what someone required in the moment to feel good, and as I sat at my father's funeral, the warmth of her hand on my shoulder was just what I needed to be connected to something more than the well of sadness I was experiencing.

After our part of the burial was complete, we headed back to my dad's best friend Charlie's house, which was a huge 1930s mansion on Chesapeake Bay. My father was loved by many different communities. Three hundred and fifty people attended the funeral and about two hundred came to the lunch. The house was so crowded that I could barely make my way through to the room with the food. I had arranged for a smorgasbord of Southern cuisine from the Grey Goose, a local restaurant that was a favorite of mine. The table was laden with deviled eggs, turkey, ham, tuna biscuits, assorted cheeses, fruit, and lemon meringue, coconut cream, and chocolate pies. There was plenty of beer and wine outside on the porch. I hadn't eaten all day and my sugar-o-holic senses could only make out the smell of the chocolate pie, but I didn't have the stomach to eat anything. I had just buried my father. Instead I headed out the back screen door onto the huge southern plantation–style porch where the other hundred or so people were milling around. With only a few trees in the backyard, I was glad we had ordered tables with umbrellas to provide some shade.

I saw Laurie sitting at a table off to the side and made my way toward her. I smiled as I thought of a scene from Dad's favorite movie *The In-Laws*, in which Alan Arkin dodges enemy bullets and Peter Falk is screaming "Serpentine! Serpentine!" I followed that internal cue and weaved in and out of the crowd to avoid any more conversation as I made my way to Laurie, my comfort zone.

Walking toward her table, I noticed the outfit. She was dressed like a common whore in skin-tight black stirrup pants and a scoop-neck tank top. Seeing the inappropriateness of her clothes when she dropped off my baked goodies earlier in the day, my mother quickly grabbed a black shawl and suggested that it would go perfectly. So Laurie's gallon-sized breasts were each covered appropriately for the solemn occasion.

Laurie seemed very uncomfortable sitting at the table. My cousins, Bennett and Sue, who had met Laurie at the nightclub several months before, were standing on either side of her chair. Across the round table was Annie, one of my dearest friends from college, and Franny, her mother. Everyone at the table had invested with Laurie, either directly or through Collective Good LLC. In typical southern fashion, Franny, through a slow, heavy drawl, was attempting to graciously thank Laurie for the opportunity to invest.

"I just want you to know how much it means for me and my family to be making this extra money." She sighed heavily and continued. "I'm divorced and in poor health. Life has not been easy these past few years, but your investments have changed my outlook on life."

I could see Laurie was avoiding her gaze.

After a long awkward pause with no response from Laurie, Bennett jumped in. "We're also so appreciative. Nothing like this has ever come our way before. Mark tells us how wonderful you've been to him during his father's illness."

Laurie had been looking down at her phone. She wasn't texting or emailing anyone but was doing her best to avoid the increasingly awkward one-way conversation. At the mention of my dad and me, she simply said, "Mark is a true mensch," without raising her head.

"Did someone say my name?" I said with a tired smile as I walked over to give her a kiss on the cheek. She seemed relieved to see me and got up from the table without saying anything more to the people around her. I greeted everyone before she took my arm and pulled me aside.

"I can't believe you had to put dirt on his casket and watch him be buried right in front of you. Is that even normal?" she asked doubtfully. Part of our dynamic was having me translate regular life experiences or pop-culture references so that she could understand a conversation at a group dinner or business meeting. Today's event seemed to be no different.

"Yes, sweetie, it's done at every Jewish funeral, and although I was really sad, it was a beautiful thing to do for Dad." I turned to face her. "So you've never actually been to a cemetery before?"

"Don't be ridiculous, of course not! I only came today because you're so important to me."

Laurie was like my father in wanting to only live in the happy and joyous part of life. Of course she had avoided anything as sad as today's burial. My ability to experience deep emotions and to deal with complex issues was one of the gifts I brought to our friendship. I imagined she had never come close to a coffin before, let alone watch it being lowered into the ground. We sat watching the beauty of Chesapeake Bay awhile before she let me know it was time for her to leave.

"I'm sorry, sweetheart, but I've got to get back on the road so I can make it to a meeting with a potential client tonight. It's a long drive back!" It was typical of Laurie to not be away from home for more than twenty-four hours and to have left no down time for herself. When travel was necessary, she seemed nervous and introverted, qualities that seemed out of place with the outgoing, brilliant businesswoman that I had come to love.

"I understand. We all know that your superpowers don't last if you stay away too long."

"I'm glad you can still be silly on a sad day like today. It shows your spirit is still shining through," she said through a smile as she hugged me.

I smelled her coconut scent as I kissed the top of her head. "Thank you so much for coming down. You know I would never have been able to spend so much time with Dad if I hadn't been making money with you. I am so grateful to you in every way."

Looking me right in the eye, she said, "I'll take care of you forever, my lovely friend. I promised your father that I would always be here for you, and I shall do just that." She had stumbled into her fake British accent.

I believed what she said was true because Dad had asked me to arrange a call with her a few weeks before he died. When I handed the phone to him, he had asked for privacy. After he hung up, he looked like a cat that had just swallowed a canary.

Dad and Laurie had met the November before his diagnosis when I flew him to New York City for what turned out to be his last birthday. In addition to seeing some shows and enjoying the big city, he of course had wanted to meet Laurie.

I arranged for lunch at the same restaurant where I'd taken Mom to meet Laurie. The moment Dad's eyes locked with hers, I could unfortunately feel a spark between them. It made sense because both were natural flirts. When Dad went to the bathroom after lunch, Laurie gave me a full report of what she thought of my father.

"I have to be honest, I didn't expect for him to be so cute, and those sweater vests make him look so sexy!" she said with a big smile. "Boy, is he a charmer!"

"Yeah, my Dad is definitely a nice guy."

"You're wonderful in your ways, but I bet he would never be as direct as you are."

"My harshness definitely comes from my mom. Dad is pretty much all sweetness."

Looking over at the bathroom door, she said, "If circumstances were different and we were both single, I think I would go for your fathah." She was grinning ear to ear.

My stomach turned at the thought of the two of them, but I didn't want to share my full disgust. "Too bad my dad doesn't have any money . . . not really your type."

Licking her lips as she put on a fresh coat of lip gloss, she patted my arm and said, "You know me so well my friend and yet you still love me for the greedy whore that I am."

I hadn't thought about that lunch with Dad and Laurie until she began to say good-bye to my mother and a few of my brothers. I was reminded of Shirley MacLaine in *Sweet Charity,* the hooker with a heart of gold. That was Laurie, the eccentric businesswoman-whore with a heart as big as the universe.

Watching her sulk off to her Escalade, which seemed especially gauche in its extravagance on that day, I noted the strangeness of her behavior with my family at the lunch but assumed the intensity of the day had been unsettling for someone who liked to stay in a happy fantasy world. After all, she did drive all the way down to bring cupcakes and to support me on this most difficult day. As I went to bed that night, I counted her as one of the blessings of my life. Her friendship helped me be the person I needed to be during such a sad time for my family. If there was any inkling of a tiny intuitive voice warning me of what was to come, I was too emotionally raw and physically exhausted to hear it.

Signs of Trouble

While the summer of 2008 brought dramatic changes to my life, Laurie's world also began to shift in big ways. She became increasingly practical in her business decisions and began talking about wanting to sell off her small empire. She also became obsessed with a less traditional and more disturbing business plan that involved Dick.

Party Hearty core services always included a band or DJ. This meant that Laurie had to rent sound equipment for every gig. Although she always negotiated the lowest price possible, it still cost her several thousand dollars each weekend just for the cost of doing business. Her solution was to steal the best sound guy she could away from her competition and open Ocean Sounds LLC, a sound equipment company. This enabled her to get equity in equipment that she could use repeatedly and rent out for profit to other companies.

"I'm *so* proud that you chose such a practical route for this business. Have I finally been rubbing off on you?" I asked tongue in cheek when she told me of the new venture. We were walking through the warehouse to see all the new equipment.

"Very funny, Mr. Smarty Pants. it may not seem like a sexy idea, but the business will make hundreds of thousands off the initial investment. You know, I guess I'm paying more attention to expenses because I'm close to seeing my bank account with a million dollahs in it," Laurie said as we returned to her office.

As I held the door for her, I said, "How much do you have right now, if you don't mind me asking?" I never could figure out her personal finances because she was always putting money back into investments or new businesses.

She flung herself down on the leather chair and began typing furiously on the computer. "Hold on a sec." She opened up her bank website and logged in and pointed to the screen. "I have a lot of my money tied up in two big real estate deals with Floyd, so I only have about eight hundred and eighty thousand right now."

I took a brief look and saw that she had that amount in the account.

She logged off and turned back to me. "You aren't in the office enough to know everything about what's going on, but I'm negotiating a deal to buy a party planning business in Westchester. I'm thinking with an office there and Long Island and all the business I already do in New York City, I'll be the biggest in no time."

I looked down at her breasts. "Uh, sweetie, you're already the biggest." We both laughed. "Seriously, that's incredible. How do you figure out the worth of an entertainment company?"

Touching my chest lightly with her carefully manicured hand, she said, "Oy, you with all the questions. I love that you care so much about what is happening but don't want to take anything away from me."

She went on to tell me that William and Shirley Kaplan had owned their business for twenty-five years and were looking to finally relax and retire. The plan was for Laurie to buy them out over a period of a few years. During that time William would still appear at parties and help sell jobs. This way his reputation would help Laurie maintain old clients and build business in an area that was somewhat new to her. She had been working on the deal for a month and wanted to keep meeting with the Kaplans to see how well they worked together.

"But listen, my brilliance doesn't end there. As you know, my FlippingMax Realty has been making a bundle all year long buying and selling properties close to foreclosure. At each of the closings, I pay someone between $400 to $600 to certify all the documents. It's so retawded that I'm paying some idiot that money when I could be paying you instead."

I was totally surprised by her statement. "But I don't know anything about real estate."

Her tone changed to one I recognized from when she was trying to sell a party to a potential client. She reached over to put her hand on my shoulder. "Take that stressed look off your handsome face."

"I'm just not sure what you're proposing."

"I want you to go to school to become a real estate closer. I'll pay for your training, and in the end you'll save me money, because we can work out a rate so you make something and I don't pay as much. It'll also help you learn more about real estate, because I want you to be more involved in that side of the business. I've noticed that you have a good eye for property."

Laurie and I had done drive-bys to view several properties for sale, most of them in foreclosure, and I had been the one to point out issues with the roof, heating, or drainage systems.

A bit flattered, I shrugged. "Okay, I mean, I guess I can look into it and see what it all entails."

"It's just one certification course, Marky," she said in between putting on layers of gloss. "I asked one of the closers when I signed the papers for my last property."

Satisfied that she would get her way, Laurie moved on to another topic. "In the meantime, let me tell you about giving Freddy D a very skillful blowjob under my desk."

I said playfully, "Wow, if there was a contest, you would definitely win biggest whore in the room."

Laurie was looking through her purse. "Silly gay man, don't you want to hear how big his penis was? It was huge and thick." She said raising her eyebrows.

"Hmm, okay, that does pique my interest, but you're seriously delusional if you think this won't bite you in the ass one day. Freddy D and Vince work the same parties together, right? How can you prevent your husband from finding out?"

"Don't you worry your pretty bald head. Freddy D and Vince never work in the same room at a pawty. Freddy's DJ booth is always in the kid's room, and Vince always heads up the band. And regardless, Freddy won't say a word 'cause he wants more of my special oral attention."

Exacerbated, I yelled out, "I see danger, Laurie, lots of danger!"

She understood I was chastising her in a loving way. "Listen, I am the smarty pants around here, and I do what I want. For example, I set up that beautiful Jamaican musician in an apartment only a half-hour from here and leased him a car so one day I can finally get his big black penis inside me. When he records in our studio with Vince every day this month to work on his new CD, I'll visit the studio and will look them both in the eye." Her chest was puffed up and it was almost like she was beating her breast to show she was the alpha of the universe.

"Be careful, sweetie—careful with your heart, careful with your body. And careful with who you trust with all this playing around."

She put her arm around me and her head on my shoulder. "I trust no one as much I as do you, love. I am going to share my millions with my favorite gay man and we're going to be best friends forever." Then she pulled away and looked at me more sternly. "I don't know why you're choosing to stay in your house while it's being renovated when you could be living in my apartment on the beach out here."

Laurie could see I was exhausted and emotionally spent. Although the stress of watching my father die and planning the funeral was done, my house was still under complete renovation, which meant there was a construction crew on-site six days a week. While Dad was dying, the stress around the house dimmed in volume and I was able to pop in and out of it to deal with specific issues. Now that I was living back in Brooklyn full-time again, the stress was draining at best and sometimes overwhelming.

I had made sure that construction crews entered the house no earlier than 7 a.m., but they often woke me up earlier talking loudly as they waited on my front steps to be let in. Tom the contractor had been correct about the project having frequent unexpected issues that needed my ongoing attention. The floor in the kitchen was completely unlevel. It had to be stripped down to the studs and completely rebuilt before installing the new wood. The plan for putting in air conditioning for the unit I was living in hit a snag when the subcontractor couldn't find routes for all the ductwork. I helped him measure closets and the space between the basement ceiling and the ground unit subflooring to come up with a suitable plan. Similarly, there were problems with plans for making the basement apartment ceiling high enough so it didn't feel like a cave because of the steam pipes leading to the boiler. I had never designed anything before, but as anyone who has lived in their house during a renovation is sure to tell you, I became an expert at seeing what needed to be done.

Laurie and I were in touch each day via email, text, or calls, so she was up to date on all that was going on at the house.

"My apartment's on the beach and so peaceful. You can find hot men to bring back every night. I promise to stay away while you're living there."

Even in the stress of living in my house, I didn't want to get overtaken by the chaos of her life; nor did I want to only be a mile from her. She would want me with her every minute of every day, and my life would be taken over by her melodrama. So I declined as politely as possible.

"That's such a sweet offer, but I need to be at my place every day to check the work of the contractors, and the hour drive just feels like stress in itself. But maybe I'll stay there sometime if I ever have too much to drink at dinner with you."

I'm not a big drinker and never did stay at the apartment, but I still appreciated the offer. She was the only one in the vicinity really checking in on me after Dad died. Her love and support felt palpable and comforting in a way that I needed at the time. My phone buzzed constantly with texts and emails from her: "Morning my favorite man on this planet. At the docks with Betty checking out closeouts and thinking of you. Shall we bring bagels to you for breakfast?" She invited me to meals, meetings, and parties. "With asshole cheapskate client trying to plan bat mitzvah party. Join me for lunch?" Even while eating with her husband, she was thinking of me. "Hate my husband, but love you. Shall I bring over dessert after I ditch scumbag Vince?"

Laurie had an old-school formality in her language. Dotting her conversations with words like "mimeograph" instead of "copy" and every so often using "shall" in a British accent. I chalked this up to the fact that her father, Donny, was in his seventies and that instead of watching *Mr. Rogers* or *Sesame Street* as a kid, she had hung out with him and his alterkochers discussing various business schemes. When she was ten, he began taking her to Atlantic City as a cover for various liaisons with women. He offered her money to keep his extramarital fun away from her mom and let her go shopping while "Daddy has some fun." Her parents had both been married to other people when they first met and started sleeping together.

This screwed-up childhood left her with no interest in anything but money, power, and sex. She literally had no idea about songs, TV shows, movies, or other pop-culture references that the average thirty-three-year-old American would know.

One day over lunch she filled me in on her latest attempts to seduce the Jamaican musician. A bit bored hearing about all the ways he didn't sound interested, I started talking about a fun movie I'd been to recently and asked if she'd seen it.

"You know I don't do anything like that," she said with a mouthful of fries.

"Is that a decision you made, or what? I don't get why you wouldn't wanna see them. If nothing else, it's something to talk about with clients."

With a dramatic shrug of her shoulders, she said, "When do I have time to see a movie? I'm up at dawn to go to the docks, and then work all day and take clients to see our band at night." The last bite of pastrami sandwich disappeared in her mouth. "But I'd see one with you if you wanna go. I'll do anything to spend more time with you."

"I'm going to take you up on that offer, Ms. Laurie Schneider. When do you have a free evening?"

She clapped her hands in glee. "A date with my gay husband! Let's do Thursday. I wanna go to whatever is playing at the theater a few blocks from my house. You know I don't like going far from home." She took a bite of fruit and swallowed. "We can eat at that yummy Italian restaurant where they make the salad at the table just special for me."

The only movie playing that Thursday night was *Happy Feet*, a computer-generated movie about penguins that sang and danced. I had to tell Laurie to put her phone away several times because she was texting and the light and noise were disruptive to me and other movie watchers. As we left the movie, she declared in hysterical laughter, "I haven't seen a movie in two years, and you take me to *that*?"

"Hey, give me a break. It's the only thing that was playing at the theater you wanted to go to!" I gave her a hug and we kept on laughing. "By the way, I signed up for that real estate closer class. I'll start going one night a week for four weeks."

She jumped up and down with her giant purse secured in the nook of her elbow. "That makes me so happy to know I'll be seeing you more." Then she turned to face me. "Make sure that you get a check from the office to reimburse yourself for whatever it cost."

"No worries, sweetie, I'll cover the cost."

A few days later, she invited me to Long Island for dinner. First we visited Donny, who had been very ill with a mysterious case of internal bleeding. He'd lost a lot of weight and was generally fatigued. I had been to her parents' home a few times before, but the visits had been very quick. They lived in a nice two-story house about five miles from where Laurie and Vince lived. As we entered, Kiki, their white poodle, began barking until Laurie gave it some of her special love. Soon it was purring like a little kitten in her lap as we sat on the couch. Looking around, I noticed that the living room was decorated like most of middle America with nondescript furniture, a large television, and a shelf full of family mementos and pictures. Although we were there to see her father, once inside she seemed totally disinterested in going upstairs to see him.

"Come ovah here and look at my pictures." Laurie let the dog off her lap. We walked a few feet over to the glass shelves.

"This is me at my prom. Aren't I hideous?" She pointed at the picture but her eyes were already looking for others. "Hey, wait a minute—let me get the album. As I sat back on the couch, Kiki jumped up on my lap and I felt obligated to pet it even though I didn't particularly like dogs. She came back and we went through pictures of her family through the years.

She put her arm around me to give a sideways hug. "I'm so glad you like going through these with me!" Laurie said like a little kid. I always enjoy looking through friends' and boyfriends' pictures because it gives a history of the person I care about. Laurie turned the page and a big smile crept onto her face.

"This is me and my first boyfriend. He lived down the street and was a few years older. I had to convince him into going out, but he ended up staying with me because I gave him head."

I laughed. "Wow, that's not the average first love story."

Without looking at me, she said very matter-a-factly, "Who said anything about love? I wanted him, and I got what I wanted."

I had been looking at Laurie as she talked. When I glanced down at the picture, the image brought bile to the back of my throat.

The person in the picture was hideous—a monster. The picture showed her in a ridiculously confident pose typical for a teenager. She was dressed in Day-Glo yellow tights and a mismatched tight purple sweater showing two tiny chocolate chip–sized breasts. Her permed hair was shaped like a triangle and her nose seemed too large for her face. It wasn't just that she was physically unattractive: there was something deeply vulgar in her. For a brief second, I had a chance to look behind the cloak of smoke and mirrors that Laurie spun for the world, and it disgusted me at a very deep level.

I closed the album and said, "Cute guy, but I need a bathroom break. I'll be right back." I leaped up and walked through the kitchen to the back bathroom and looked at myself in the mirror.

"Holy shit, what the fuck was that?" I thought.

It wasn't as if she resembled the Elephant Man. There was just something shocking in what I saw, and I didn't yet understand what that raw ugliness was. After taking a minute to get my bearings, I went out and was happy to see she was on the phone and motioning that we had to go back to the office. Thankfully, I would not have to look at that picture again. The visit with her Dad would have to wait until another day.

That night I lay awake. Anger was pulsing through my body and I felt it throb in my temples. For a reason I could not put my finger on, I was furious with Laurie.

For the first ten years of my life, I lived with almost unbearable insomnia. I knew too well the helpless feeling of lying in bed exhausted but unable to sleep. I had learned various kinds of relaxation techniques that had enabled me to have peaceful sleep for the past twenty-five years. However, this night was the first of many in which I could not get this seething rage at Laurie out of my thoughts. There was nothing specific I could point to, so I attributed my nocturnal anger to the fact that Laurie was smothering me.

I didn't have much time to consider what was going on: the next day a new drama had unfolded that took my attention.

"PLEASE CALL ME AS SOON AS YOU WAKE UP! HORRIBLE NEWS L"

I had learned to check my phone as soon as I woke up to see if there was anything new from Laurie. I immediately called her.

"Oh, I'm so upset. Reverend Stevens, his wife, and their grandchildren were in a horrible accident last night. Everyone's dead except the reverend, who is intensive care." In a shrill voice, Laurie filled me in. "They were driving back from a concert and a drunk truck driver sideswiped them.

"Oh, sweetie, I'm so sorry, but I don't know who these people are."

"You know Carson, the drummer I fly in from Vegas all the time for our Party Hearty Jobs. It's his parents and niece and nephew."

I had called her while still lying down as I awoke.

"Since Joy died, whenever I hear of someone dying in a car accident, it just kills me. I'm driving over to the hospital today to see if there is anything I can do."

"You're such a lovely person to help the family," I said on my way to the kitchen to get some water.

During the course of the next weeks, Laurie became obsessed with helping Reverend Stevens, who it turned out, was well know in many African American Baptist church communities throughout the country.

Over a lunch of bagel sandwiches, Laurie said, "You know these shvartza families never have insurance or plan for emergencies. None of the reverend's kids know what to do. You're a social worker. Can you help me help them?"

I was taken aback at Laurie's generosity. I gave her some suggestions, and she dove in and devoted herself to being a liaison between the family and the hospital. When she found out that the reverend needed comprehensive rehabilitation, she researched and found out that the best hospital in the area was in New Jersey and began attempts to get him moved. She quickly found out that his insurance would soon run out and wouldn't pay for the hospital stay.

"I hope this makes you proud of me. I want to be more like you and your big-hearted self."

Laurie emailed me a link to a website soon after. When I clicked on it, I was surprised to find an open letter from Laurie to the African American Churches across the country:

Hello, my name is Laurie Schneider, and I would like to inform everyone that Rev. Joseph Stevens has a C4 Spinal Cord injury, which has left him unable to breath without a respirator.

The cost for his care is exactly $4,033.00 per day. We are praying to raise $70,000.00 during the concert at the end of August. I have a credit card with a high limit that I am going to use so that he can be admitted tomorrow. My credit card will get him through the first week, and the ambulance which I am giving $31,956.00. I have paid for the hotel rooms for his sons to stay *with him, and food for his grandchildren. I took care of the limos and food during and after the funeral. I am willing to put all of his sons to work, so they can continue to pay their bills. I can only afford to keep him hospitalized for ONE WEEK. I am going to host a fundraiser within the next 4-6 weeks, and pray to raise another $100,000.00. I need help from everyone who can and is willing.*

Please call me with any questions or concerns you may have.

Before I had time to react, she texted me: "You won't believe what's happening. Hundreds or maybe thousands of black churches across the United States are already coming together to collect money to help pay for the reverend's medical care and transfer to the new hospital!"

I picked up the phone and gave her a call. "You're so wonderful to be doing all of this! And how great his community is pitching in to help him."

"Well, I mean they are all poor, illiterate black people giving their life to Jesus, so I'm not sure how special it all is, but I'm making sure there will be money to pay for him to get treatment."

A week later I received a summons from Laurie to come meet her at the office. "I have big plans for you, Mr. Social Workah. Get your ass down here for a late breakfast."

When I walked in the door a few hours later I was shocked to find a pile of money on Laurie's desk.

She held up a clear plastic bag filled with money for me to see. "The churches are collecting cash and putting it into a vacuum-packed bag with a sheet showing the total so no one can take any of the money. Can you believe how stupid they are?"

I paused for a moment before speaking. I thought it was amazing what the churches were doing, and I still didn't understand why Laurie had gotten so involved. "I think it shows ingenuity and dedication to the reverend."

"I don't know what that first word means, but I'm not here to argue. I am starting a new charity called BADD: Brothers Against Drunk Driving." She paused for a second. "Do you get it? Brothahs, like black men call each other *brothah*?"

I pulled up a chair and sat across from her at her desk as she sat down and put the bag of money on the table behind her. "I know you want to help but starting a nonprofit is a complex thing. Did you check to see if that name already exists?"

"No, that's *exactly* why I brought you in today. You're brilliant, and I know you're bored and think we're all disgusting with our money obsession out here. I want you to be the executive director of BADD. It will be great for your career and will help prevent this tragedy from happening again."

"That's such a sweet gesture in so many ways."

"I already put some of the money sent from the churches into an account I opened for the charity. Tell me what you want, and I'll make sure to give you all the money you need."

A panic washed over me and I shook my head. "No, Laurie, the money being sent to you is for the reverend's medical care. To start a nonprofit, you have to apply to the federal government to get what is called a 501(c)3 status to operate as a charity. If you divert funds this way, it may be a federal crime." I knew all of this from my experience working in nonprofits and city government.

In a flat tone she asked, "What are you saying?"

"I know your heart is in the right place, but for right now all this money has to go directly to the reverend's medical care. If one day you want to start a nonprofit, I'll totally help you, but this is not the right time to do this. You have to focus on the reverend and running your businesses."

Several of the workers in the office had called me to ask her to focus on Party Hearty and Scrub-A-Dub-Dub because she had been ignoring her responsibilities as owner of both companies.

"There're so many worthy charities that you can get involved in," I offered.

"You know me, I don't want to get involved with anything. You're the person who likes that. I just want to make people feel good."

I walked over to her and gave her a hug. "Sweetie, everything you're doing is already enough. Let's just leave the new charity as an idea to talk about in the future when Reverend Stevens gets better."

After more protesting, Laurie finally got the message that every cent being sent to her had to be accounted for in the account for the reverend. By the time I left, she had called the bank and had all the funds she had inappropriately transferred put back in the correct account. I drove home thinking that I had just stopped a catastrophe from happening.

It didn't take long for Laurie to find another project. Within a few days, I was summoned again to Laurie's throne. "I have such exciting news. I am going to be rich forever. Come find out the deets so you can share in the wealth with me!"

Luckily, there were no piles of cash on Laurie's desk this time when I arrived at the office. She grabbed my hand and led me deeper into her private office as she shut the door and then dramatically turned around.

"I found a way to make our dreams come true!"

I sat down on one of the leather conference chairs. "Oh shit, that scares me. Which particular dreams are you referring to?"

In a playful tone, she whined, "Since you won't have a baby with me, which by the way I think is ridiculous since I would be putting your sperm with my egg in a poor woman's uterus in India—"

My whine was not playful. "Laurie, come on, we've talked about this. The answer is NO."

She crossed her arms over her huge breast and gave me a pouty look for a few seconds, then reached over and gave me a kiss on the cheek laughing, "I'm only kidding you, Mr. Serious Man. I know you want to have a baby with a husband one day. But I have figured out a way to make me rich while fulfilling a dream of an old man."

"Oh shit, what are you talking about? Please don't tell me what I think you're going to say."

"I'm going to have Dick's baby!" she said clapping and jumping up and down. "Dick's children are total asshole losers who have no interest in his business. With the China Deals, he has been mentoring me while paying a lot of attention to my beautiful breasts." Laurie opened her blouse to reveal the depth of her cleavage.

Putting my hand up to block the site of her gigantic breasts, I called out, "Jesus, Laurie, put those away. Get to the point. What the hell are you planning this time?"

Bragging, she said, "Dick shoved his tongue down my throat the other day and told me that he would like to put his sperm in me to make a beautiful bab—"

I interrupted her. "Hold it, have you been having sex with him this whole time?" I felt angry and nauseous at the same time.

"Calm your pretty little head down. I let him hold my hand and touch my breast when we meet about the China Deals. I do it so you and your family and the other investors have a chance at making such good money."

I felt a rush of pity and disgust. "Do you think he is attractive? I mean, do you want him to touch you that way?"

She reached for her purse and began looking for something. "Look, he's seventy-nine years old. I have no desire for him, but as you know the thought of being rich makes me cum and he has a lot of money." She pulled out a deodorant stick and lifted up her arm to apply it.

"He told me that his girlfriend, Robin, no longer has sex with him because she's in her seventies. The whore he pays to sleep with him weekly is in her fifties and can't give him a baby."

She lifted her other arm.

"He hates his asshole kids and wants to leave behind an heir to his fortune." She dropped the deodorant in the purse.

"I can't believe how crazy this is," I said. "You're married. What about that?"

"Dick and Vince both have blue eyes. The baby will look like Vince, and he nevah has to know."

"I thought neither you nor Vince ever wanted to have kids. I mean, haven't you had three or four abortions since you got married? What's he gonna say if you get pregnant?"

Grabbing the desk as though holding herself back, she spat out, "Vince is a vile, obnoxious man who will make a terrible father. My body is already hideous. I've had *seven* abortions so that I won't get any more fat."

Her lack of poise usually released the same in me. "And how the fuck is all of this making any sense? By the way, I can see the white stuff from the deodorant showing under your arm. You should switch to a clear stick."

"Gotta love being besties with a gay man!" She turned and smiled at me. "Dick will leave the baby a huge portion of his fortune if I am the one to give it to him. Before he dies, he will teach me everything about his business. My husband will never know a thing, and we'll all live happily ever after."

"And how about all the men you're messing around with? What about them?"

"I'll tell them my husband forced himself on me. Don't worry, Laurie gives the best head and the men will always want that."

I sat in silence for a few seconds stewing. "Laurie, every word out of your mouth is so fucking offensive, I don't know what to say. I'll have nothing to do with any of this. Nada. Do you understand? I mean it."

"Oh, you're so funny. Of course you'll change your mind . . . and don't forget, you are the guy I'll be relying on to help me run the businesses."

I put my face in my hands. "No, Laurie, no way. To bring a baby into the world for greed is the worst thing I can think of. It would be a sin."

"You, who puts his penis in another man's tushy, saying something is a sin? Ha ha." Laurie approached my chair and nuzzled my head in her breasts.

"I didn't mean to upset you. You're such a good man. But just know that I'm gonna have to eat less to get in shape so my body is ready to accept his old-man sperm to make a *brilliant baby*." Her last words were said in a happy singsong voice.

Over the course of the next months, my conversations with Laurie were peppered with updates on the reverend and whatever the latest thing Dick said about her breasts or having a baby. Although I had known Laurieland was light on ethics when I signed on, the current situation seemed a grotesque caricature of the world I had first entered two and a half years before.

The pinnacle of absurdity and obscenity was a voicemail message from Dick that Laurie played on her speakerphone to the whole office as she held her hand over her mouth giggling in a very creepy way. In the message, he told her how much he wanted to lick her "down there" before "entering you to make a baby together." His voice sounded very old, and unfortunately for all the people in the room who heard it, it was clear that he was masturbating while speaking.

My mother used to say, "I wanted to run screaming down the street naked" when she felt caught in an uncomfortable situation. That saying seemed to fit me perfectly as I sat listening to the pornographic message of a septuagenarian, who was planning an adulterous affair to create a human life that I was sure would be ruined the day it was born.

As strange as it sounds, I felt relieved that I had an excuse to spend time in Virginia when my mother had a serious colon surgery the next month. During that time, as much as I could, I limited my communication with Laurie to texts and emails so I didn't have to hear details of what she was planning with Dick. I was really disgusted with how far she had gone into a personal Sodom and Gomorrah.

While in Virginia, I bought shades for Hazel's kitchen from Robert Bloch, an old friend who ran his family's custom blind and drapery business. Robert had been my camp counselor when I was eight, and we had remained friendly ever since. As he showed me samples, he asked how I was doing and about my work. I explained my relationship with Laurie and gave a summary of the kinds of deals that she offered.

"That sounds amazing. Is there room for me if my wife and I were interested in joining? I've got two kids in college and earning some extra money would be great."

This type of interaction was commonplace for me. Wherever I went, people wanted to join in and make some money. I was happy to include him. "Sure, I can email you when the next round of opportunities come up."

I didn't give any more thought to my conversation with him until a few weeks later when I was back in Brooklyn and I received a call from my mom, who seemed upset.

"Robert Bloch called today. He's very worried that you are involved in a pyramid scheme."

I was infuriated. "What? I don't get where he would get that from, and why the hell he didn't say anything to me directly?"

"He said a good friend of his was involved in a Ponzi scheme and that he sees signs that Laurie could be doing the same thing." There was a pause. "Mark, could he be right?"

"Mom, there's no way Laurie is running any type of scheme. I work in her office and see all the receipts and hear the phone calls when she makes her deals. Tell me exactly what he said." She explained that one of Robert's best friends worked for a financial investment company for several years, and it turned out that the fund he worked for was a total scam. The man running the scheme had already been arrested and Robert's friend had been emotionally devastated and financially ruined. Robert was concerned that Laurie's investments were too lucrative to be legitimate.

Even though I made it clear I didn't think Robert's accusations had any merit, I promised my mom that I'd check with Laurie, whom I called right away and explained the situation.

"What should I tell someone who is concerned that the investments aren't real? I mean, it *is* unusual what you are doing."

Laurie sounded annoyed. "Ovah the past four years, my investors have made hundreds of thousands of dollahs. You know I always pay on time." She paused. "There will always be assholes who take advantage of other people, but you know how much I love and appreciate you."

"Of course, sweetie. I'm not accusing you. I'm just trying to have a response for this guy and others who may be hesitant."

"Look. The stock market is a gamble. Buying gold is a gamble. And even buying property can be a gamble. But I guarantee everything I do because it's such a small operation and I have it all down to a science." She popped her gum a few times. "You see the invoices and checks from buyahs of the closeouts . . . I text every morning from the docks when I'm checking out possible new shipments . . . nobody's evah lost a dime in any investment I put together."

After my conversation with Laurie, I sent Robert a terse email, telling him that I appreciated his concern but to communicate directly with me if he had any questions or concerns about Laurie's investments. I ended the email by saying, "I trust Laurie implicitly and don't appreciate that you didn't have the courtesy to approach me directly. Please don't upset my mother anymore."

I didn't speak to Robert again until I called him to apologize years later.

The Crystal Ball Does Not Lie

In early December 2008, Laurie made the trip to Brooklyn to finally see all the work I had done on Hazel. Almost all the renovations were complete. The house was transformed and looked amazing. The bubble wrap for the custom sofa and chairs that I designed was still sitting in the back corner of the room from when it had been delivered the day before.

Laurie walked around the house like a child in a museum. "This place is unbelievable!"

"Thanks, sweetie, you know how awful the remodeling process has been during the past six months. At least now the end is near and I can finally enjoy living here."

With her purse handle still cradled in the crook of her arm, she turned toward me. "How much did all this cost?"

I didn't want to reveal how much I had spent because Laurie might have questioned why I hadn't invested every dollar with her. I had learned how to appease her simply to get her off my back.

"Every cent that I have not reinvested with you I put in the house."

As Laurie sat on the new white sofa, she curled up like a cat. I went to get her a drink. When I returned, she was gazing at a framed picture of my family that sat atop the coffee table in front of her.

"You and your family are all so real," she said with a dazed look on her face.

Sitting across from her on a wingback chair I bought at a thrift store and had recently had reupholstered, I responded, "That's why I have such a hard time when Vince or other people in your life are so mean to you."

My statement seemed to lure Laurie out of her trance, and she sat upright drinking the Diet Pepsi I had brought her.

"Where are you spending Christmas this year? Come and spend it with me and my asshole husband. Our families are coming to our place on Christmas Eve, and having you there would make me so happy. At least I'd have someone to talk to who actually wants to be with me."

"Sure, I don't have any plans that night. Is your grandmother gonna cook?"

"NO! I want her to have the night off! We'll order in from somewhere nice."

"You've been so down lately—how about if I cook dinner for everyone? You do so much for me during the year, please let me do this for you."

There was an awkward pause and she looked down at the floor. "You're really such a good person."

"We've already been through that. I know I'm a handsome, loving, adorable, and very sexy guy," I said with a laugh. "Lemme bring you some happiness with my food!"

In the weeks after that conversation, I had consulted with my mom to come up with a menu of beef tenderloin, fusilli with feta cheese and garlic, salad, rolls, broccoli, and my special chocolate cheesecake for dessert. On the day of the dinner, I spent all day cooking, happy to cheer up Laurie.

That night I worked in Laurie's small kitchen while her family and in-laws relaxed and talked in the den area. Nancy, Laurie's mother, had recently had surgery to remove a large fibroid, and so I made sure to mention how happy I was that the surgery was a success. Although I never could predict what mood Vince was going to be in, he was jolly that night, and his parents and sister were all lovely. Everyone was drunk and very appreciative of the food. Laurie seemed distracted and depressed, sitting alone at times staring at the table. Not surprisingly, no one was paying any attention to her dramatic mood, so I walked over and quietly checked in with her.

"Sweetie, this is such a lovely night with your family, but you seem so down. What's going on?"

Still staring at the table, she said in a monotone voice, "Mike analyzed my books and said both Party Hearty and Scrub-A-Dub-Dub are losing money. He says I have to completely change the way I do business to stay afloat."

"I know about all that. Mike told me a few weeks ago that he had told you that you had to stop giving entertainment items away for free and cut back on office staff. You need to stick to the prices you've written down for customers. Your clients are going to understand that you're just doing what you have to . . . everybody is tightening their belts since the Madoff thing."

She continued staring off in a trance.

"I still don't get why you don't just focus on the China Deals and closeouts," I said. "Both are such easy moneymakers for you and all your investors."

She turned toward me and said in a childlike voice, "But the two companies are how I meet everyone I do business with."

Her statement didn't make sense to me, and I assumed she'd had too much to drink, which may have also accounted for her demeanor, so I just put my arm around her shoulder and gave her a little sideways hug.

"And Bobby stole my share of the condo we bought together in DR."

I had no idea who Bobby was or what she was talking about. I did my best to get the basic information so I could be supportive. "Who's Bobby? And what's DR?"

Without looking at me she told me in a flat voice that Bobby was the attorney who had defended her in 2001 when she was arrested and convicted for drug smuggling in the Dominican Republic.

"Before you get upset—I had only taken down some prescription pills for a very sick friend who lives there. I wasn't selling them or doing anything wrong. Bobby is a brilliant lawyer and got me house detention. After that, we began to hang out and party together."

I was shocked at what she was telling me but didn't let my face register any emotion. "That's why it is hard for me to get credit for big things like mortgages or cars because I have a felony on my record."

"So tell me what happened with Bobby, sweetie."

"A few months ago, he put together a deal to flip a condo in the DR and then the asshole took my share of the money. He won't return my calls or emails." She looked forlorn. "We used to work so well together and all our deals made lots of money, but he said I owe him this one. I was counting on the forty thousand. I really need it right now."

I was still processing that she had been arrested for a felony and at the same time trying to be supportive. I put my arm around her and gave her a squeeze. "Isn't there anything legal you can do? I mean, if you bought property together, isn't there a contract or at the very least wire transfers showing you invested?"

She put the side of her face on the table and looked down at the floor. In that position, she resembled a Bassett hound with her sad puppy eyes.

Behind us, members of her family continued having an increasingly raucous time and the room was filled with laughter. It seemed surreal that no one noticed she was in a really bad place. Or maybe no one cared but me. After a few minutes of just being by her side, I gave her head a kiss and stood up and went back to finish up my duties in the kitchen.

As I drove home that night, I felt good doing something to make her family event warm and loving, especially when she seemed to be in such a funk. But I woke later seething with anger. Each night for the next few days, I spent hours tossing and turning. I could not seem to put aside a rage I felt for Laurie, even though I had no idea why I felt that way.

A week later, my mother flew up to see the new renovations and to help me prepare for a New Year's Day brunch that I hosted. The year 2008 had been such a shitty one that I wanted to open my house up as a symbol of wanting the New Year to be one of love and friendship. I encouraged the tenants on both the second and third floors to invite people, and we ended up having around forty guests. Everyone was in awe of how wonderful Hazel looked. Most had seen her "before" state and so truly appreciated her facelift.

The day turned out to be a sweet one for me. Everyone congregated in my unit. As I walked from the kitchen to the living room, I was smiling ear to ear. My house was beautiful and filled with people who were having fun.

Later as we were cleaning up after the lovely day, Mom asked, "Where was Laurie today?"

"I didn't invite her." I explained that whenever she's around, I'm expected to attend to her as if I were part of an entourage. I didn't want my party to be another stage for her to play out some drama.

"Remember what she did at the dinner when Nate and I were breaking up?"

Mom nodded. "I know she can be a bit much, Mark, but she's done so much for you."

"I'm just realizing I need to figure out my next step after Laurie. You know I need more of a sense of purpose than making money—even if it does help everyone I care about."

Mom's eyes suddenly grew large with a look of fear. "That scares me, Mark. What will happen if you don't work for Laurie anymore? How will you be able to keep helping me?"

I told my mom that I hoped to make enough money through Laurie's investments to buy another apartment building, which would give me permanent financial security. "Then I have to figure out what I'm actually going to do in the world, because I can't just hang around and watch TV."

In a maternal tone, Mom responded, "Of all my boys, you always wanted to help people. Do you think you'll move back to San Francisco? You always seemed so happy there."

A big smile crept across my face. "That's so funny you asked, because I'm going in two weeks to check it out!" I wasn't ready to move yet but knew that going for a visit could help me figure out a plan.

Of course I didn't tell Laurie my real motivation for visiting San Francisco. But her superpower intuition rarely let me keep a secret from her. Two days after the conversation with my mom, I visited her office.

"I don't want you moving to San Francisco, but maybe we should scout out a West Coast office to double our closeout capacity," she said.

"Wow, where did that come from?"

"I know you're lonely and miserable except when we're having fun together. If you could fly out there once a month for business, I know it would make you happy, but then you could come home to me so I could be happy, too."

As I boarded the plane to California, I thought that like many things with Laurie, she hadn't thought out any details of a plan. Her relationship to the local dock owners in Brooklyn enabled her to do closeouts and her ever-increasingly intimate connection to Dick let us all partake in the China Deals. She had no connections outside of Long Island that would enable us to expand the business. As I closed my eyes to doze during takeoff, I had a smile on my face thinking how happy I was to be leaving New York. Yes, I had a newly renovated house and would be making a lot of money on the new China Deal for which I had just transferred almost a million dollars, on behalf of my family and friends, from Collective Good to Laurie. However, I had never been someone who lived to make money. In my gut, I knew that the isolation and loneliness I was experiencing were a sign that it was time to make a change.

San Francisco quenched a thirst in me. I rented an apartment for a week in the Castro so that I could feel like I was actually living there during my visit.

Walking through the city felt like being in a charming village. The streets were not crowded, most of the buildings were no more than four or five stories tall, and the air felt fresh and clean. My phone kept ringing with invitations from old friends who wanted to see me and catch up. I was in such demand that I had breakfast, lunch, and dinner dates each day. In each conversation, I saw my life reflected in the compassion in my friends' eyes. They knew I was in the wrong place.

"Marky, why don't you move back? You seem so lonely in New York," I heard them say over and over.

I felt an inner calm I had never experienced in New York. On a walk around Lands End, the most northwestern point in San Francisco, the beauty of the Marin Headlands against the colors of the Bay and the Golden Gate Bridge stopped me in my tracks.

"You *are* coming back here," I felt my inner voice say, as clearly as if there were actually a person speaking to me.

I soon found myself telling friends that I was definitely moving back to San Francisco within a few years. By then, I hoped to have made enough money to buy a building in San Francisco. With rental income from two buildings, I could live comfortably and likely go back to school to finally become a therapist.

One of my birthday rituals when I lived in San Francisco was to visit an astrologer named JoAnn, who often provided some sage wisdom and random things to watch out for or look forward to in the upcoming year. Even though it wasn't my birthday, I thought it would be fun to have a visit with her since so many things had shifted in my life since I had last seen her five years before. When I emailed her to get an appointment, she told me I was lucky that someone had just canceled a session for the following day.

"How cool," I thought to myself. "Things are finally clicking into place for me again."

That night I went to bed exhausted from a long day of hiking and socializing. As I turned out the light, I snuggled in the cold sheets and closed my eyes looking forward to a long night's sleep.

Two hours later, I jolted upright to a sitting position and called out, "Write it all down—the story has to be told."

I looked out the bedroom windows to the neighbor's backyard. My breathing was heavy as I tried to make sense of what just happened. Even though I've always had vivid dreams, there has never been another time in my life in which I woke myself this way. I decided to write down the words of my exclamation and try to get back to sleep.

When I awoke the next morning, I studied the words I had written down during the night and thought it must have meant that I should write a book about all the things that happened in 2008: my recovery from my breakup with Nate, my Dad's death, my cancer scare, Mom's surgeries, and Hazel's renovation. I had always been someone who kept a journal. Maybe this was an inner sign of what to do as part of my plan to move to San Francisco. Writing about the many difficult events of the past year might help me fully understand and digest them so I could be ready to move on to a new chapter.

As I walked out of the apartment on my way to my astrology appointment, I was satisfied with the explanation I had come up with to make sense of the strange event of the night before. I still intended on bringing up the incident with JoAnn to see if she had any other information.

Climbing the stairs to her office, I was excited to see if JoAnn had any groovy advice to offer. As she opened the door, I laughed with glee at the site of her outfit, which was a mishmash of retro sixties clothes, Doc Martens boots, and a multicolored poncho. She was substantially shorter than I, so when she said, "Hi Bubbie" and reached out to give me a hug, I had to bend down to meet her open arms. She pointed to a chair and said, "Have a seat and lemme pull up your chart."

I smiled at the throwback feel of the space, which was painted a mellow orange that resembled the dreamsicles I used to devour on a hot day as a boy. I watched as she put on her oversized red glasses and brushed back her large brown curls with each hand. Her many bracelets and baubles clanked softly as she typed on a computer and turned the pages of a book.

Then she seemed to internally switch gears and said in deep serious voice, "Okay, I have your chart open. Please tell me why you're here today."

I gave a very brief synopsis of my current situation and asked whether I should sell my house in Brooklyn when I move back to San Francisco.

She closed her eyes and was silent for a moment, then turned toward me.

"Before I get to your question, I need to tell you that there is something very wrong in the astrological house that holds your financial picture. Tell me more about this business that you're involved in."

Surprised at her statement, I went into a brief explanation of my business investments with Laurie.

JoAnn turned the pages of her book and stared at her screen. "I don't know how else to say this. You'll have three years of horrible ruin, and there will be enormous trouble due to your finances. I see a lot of drama around money for you."

"Oh, that can't be right," I said without thinking. "In the next two years I'll be making enough money to invest in real estate so I'll never have to worry about money again."

JoAnn closed her eyes and asked, "Are you sure this person you're dealing with is trustworthy? Is she someone who really loves you?"

She kept her eyes closed.

"Yes, she drove eight hours down to my father's funeral with a load of cupcakes and bagels to cheer me up. She helped me buy a condo for my mom and has been the only support I have in New York."

Satisfied at my own response regarding my finances, I repeated my original question. She told me it was my choice to sell or not depending on whether I wanted to manage a house from three thousand miles away. I thought it was input that anyone could have given me and went on to issues of romance.

"So, I've been single since 2006 and haven't really had a date since then."

With a sly smile on her face, she asked, "But I see in your chart that you have had a lot of fun with the boys, haven't you?"

Laughing, I responded, "Yeah, I've had my share of fun, but no real intimacy at all. Do you see anything for me in that area?"

"Let's take a look," she said adjusting her glasses. As she checked her sources again, her face soured. "The same issue is coming up again. Your financial issues will impact your ability to find intimacy." She closed her eyes and sat silently for a moment.

"You're not in physical danger, but your life is not stable. I'm very concerned about this picture I see and want you to reconsider looking into your financial world. There's something you're not seeing that's going to hurt you . . . devastate your life."

I left the session a bit perplexed but chalked it up to hippy-dippy astrology and went on with my day. Later that afternoon I received an email from an old friend, asking if it was too late to transfer money to the latest China Deal. The deadline had already passed several weeks ago, but I went ahead and emailed Matt at Chase Bank to transfer money to Laurie's China Deal account. I then emailed Laurie telling her that I just moved over another $45,000 into her account and that it was the last of the money for this investment. I received a quick response from her: "Thanks for the surprise money! It made my day ☺."

I made sure to email my friend that her money had been included in the deal. When I got back to the apartment, I edited an investor agreement for her, included my electronic signature, and sent it off. It felt good to be able to do business while I was in San Francisco. It confirmed that I could make my business relationship with Laurie work long distance if I chose to go that route.

As I got on the plane to go back to New York, I felt elated that there would be an end to my sad times in Brooklyn. I closed my eyes to take a nap as the plane took off and made a mental note to visit San Francisco as often as possible in the next two years, as I planned my return to the place that held my heart.

The Telling

On the evening of January 23, 2009, I left the house feeling agitated, although I couldn't put my finger on why I felt so out of sorts. On the drive to Long Island to meet Laurie for dinner, I didn't dwell on my uneasiness. After all the lonely years in New York and then the chaos of being in Laurie's entourage, I'd gotten used to living a life that didn't feel right. As I sped down Belt Parkway, I reminded myself to be grateful for all the gifts Laurie was sharing with me and my loved ones. I just needed to bide my time before I could start living again in San Francisco. Of the eight million faces in New York City, it seemed that only Laurie truly saw me. Yet, I'd started feeling like her prisoner. Being part of Laurieland meant being at her disposal and socializing with people whose values I abhorred. However, I knew that sticking around for another few years would enable everyone in my life to fill our coffers with the manna she miraculously continued to provide.

I cranked up Madonna's "Confessions on a Dance Floor" CD and emptied my mind on the long drive.

When I arrived at the office, I followed the sound of Laurie's voice, taking the long way around to see what changes had been made in the month since I'd last been in. The new party planner had repainted the money-green walls a robin's egg blue, and Laurie had built herself a new private office in the warehouse. It was decorated with huge blown-up pictures of Vince, which looked better than the TJ Maxx tchotchkes that

Laurie had on the walls before. The only thing that remained constant in Laurieland was that nothing stayed the same.

Laurie gave me a tired smile when she saw me in the doorway. "Hi, love. Come give Laurie a kiss." I walked over and she offered me her cheek. "I'm just finishing up the prep work for this week's pawties. I've got a wedding and a bat mitzvah."

"Can I help in anyway?" I asked out of habit.

"No, dawling, got it covered." She continued discussing last-minute details with Goldie, a Party Hearty event planner, and I leaned against the doorframe to observe Laurie do her thing.

"And my ridiculous sister got her tits done, thinking it's gonna take attention away from that fucking *ugly* face," Laurie told Goldie. "She keeps pulling up her blouse for anyone to see her new perky little boobs. It's so pathetic."

"Sounds like she's taking after her big sister," I blurted out. "How many times have you offered a peek under your shirt, Laurie?" The biting words were not said in jest. I was angry, although I didn't know why.

The few seconds that Laurie paused before looking at me seemed to take forever. We'd never exchanged harsh words before.

"I guess you're right. We're both ridiculous," she said quietly. In that moment I realized I was ready for a fight and still had no idea why. I remained silent while Laurie finished up her work. As we walked across the parking lot to her car, Laurie handed me the key.

"You drive tonight, sweetheart, Laurie's tired." The significance of her giving up control felt right since I was bursting with resentment and aggression.

During the ten-minute drive to the restaurant, we gossiped about how annoying Goldie was, and then she gave me an update on her latest marital drama. With uncharacteristic luck, I found a parking spot a block from the popular restaurant. Inside, we were seated quickly at a small table toward the back, close to the long bar. Ambient music played and the air was filled with the smell of garlic, cheese, and meat. Laurie had suggested Italian since it was my favorite. When the waiter came, I ordered a glass of wine and Laurie a dirty martini. "Tonight I need this more than evah," she said, her voice quivering with stress.

She asked about my trip to San Francisco. As I was recounting some highlights, I could tell she wasn't listening and was lost in her own thoughts.

"Listen, I have to talk to you about something," Laurie said meekly in the middle of her second martini. Her eyes were watery. I looked at her plate and realized she'd barely touched her food. My heart sank. I knew something really bad was about to happen.

"I can't pay the closeouts next week."

I put my fork down.

"Whaddayamean?! What am I supposed to tell the investors?"

She locked her eyes with mine. "The closeouts are fake. I made them u—"

"WHAT are you talking about?" The anger was pouring out.

"I needed cash flow last fall and made up the closeouts so I could cover payments to other investors. I am *so* sorry."

"*Sorry*? You owe my family almost a million dollars this month! What about *them*?" I could feel my heart beating inside my chest.

"I'll pay every cent back to all of them. I just need time." She took several big gulps of her drink. Her eyes were pleading with me. "I didn't want to tell you, but Larry said I had too or he would call you."

I let her words sink in. "I don't understand how you could have lied about so much when you knew my family doesn't have *any* money to spare." I picked up my fork and started stuffing my face. It was the only thing I knew to do as I tried to stay in the moment. Food in my stomach helped me feel my body and kept me from floating away from this nightmare.

"When Larry was reviewing my books and saw that last wire transfer from you, he figured out that your money was not going to an investment and told me I had to tell y—"

"Jesus, Laurie, what about the China Deals? Are they fake, too?" I put my hand on my forehead. "Oh shit, my people have millions invested in those deals!"

"No, all the China Deals are real. I swear. But I want to be honest with you. I didn't transfer all the money you gave me for the last China Deal because I needed to pay back othah people."

My head was pulsing with anger. "How much *did* you put in, Laurie? *What the fuck?* That deal is almost $2 million!" Random bits of food were spraying out of my mouth. "You know my family put up their houses and retirement money."

Looking into my eyes, she said, "I'll pay it all back. I swear to God, I'll pay it all back. I am so sorry. I never wanted you to know all of this."

My eyes were laser beams cutting through her. "How would I not find out if you owed my family millions of dollars and didn't have any money to pay us b—"

"I have all my real estate and the other China Deals. I'll have the money. I just need more time."

I could see she was totally spent from the truthful discussion, and I resisted the urge to pound her with my fist. I stood up and then sat back down.

"Jesus, Laurie, I can't believe any of this!"

She kept her eyes on her plate. "And there's another thing, which doesn't have *anything* to do with me. Dick changed the payout timing of the last two China deals. He gave a ninety-day extension to the buyer, so those payments will be late, too."

"How late?" I was fuming. She could see I was angry and so she was trying to disclose everything now.

"Everything will be delayed three months. Because of the changes in financing, the buyer needed to refinance his loan."

Leering at her, I said, "But you always said Dick would cover the deals if there were any problems."

Her voice shifted into a more soothing tone. I could see that she wanted to reach out to touch me but knew I wasn't receptive. "I know this is upsetting, but it's just a delay. Everything will be okay with the China Deals—you'll just have to tell your investors that everything will be just a little late."

I continued digging to ascertain whether there were any more secrets lurking around the corner. After I was convinced that Laurie had told me all the information she was going to share, I paid the check because I had been the one to invite her to dinner. We drove back to the office in silence. As I opened the door to get out of the car, I turned to look at her. I knew in that moment that the only chance my family and friends had for being paid back was if Laurie continued to feel I was *on her side*. I took a deep breath.

"I know that this was very difficult for you to tell me, and I appreciate that. But you should've told me long ago, so I could have saved all the people I care about."

"I'll make all of this right," she said quietly. "I'll pay everyone back."

I did my best to stay calm. "I say this as a friend, Laurie. You're sick and need therapy. You've lied to me every day, and to every other person who trusted you. Please get help and see a therapist."

"But *you* are my therapist," she said with pleading eyes.

I got out and slammed the car door. My legs felt like rubber as I walked across the parking lot. I could feel her eyes on me. I knew she was afraid of losing whatever connection we had, and her fear was as visceral as my anger. As I sank into the driver's seat, my lungs struggled to pull in oxygen. I was filled with panic and dread. As soon as I drove away, her texts starting coming in. I took a quick glance at a stoplight.

"I'm so sorry. Please don't hate me."

"I'll make it up to you. Can you ever love me again?"

"If I put my face close to a bowl of bleach and breath, will the fumes kill me? I want to DIE."

"You crazy fucking bitch!" I yelled. I turned off the phone and drove home in silence, my tears and the occasional gurgle of a cry the only sound. My mind raced:

How much of what Laurie told me tonight was a lie?

What do I tell my family and friends?

What will happen to everyone who got second mortgages or used their retirement or kids' college funds to invest in the fake closeouts or the last China Deal?

What have I done by inviting Laurie into my life?

At home, I walked into the living room and began pacing the floors, the lovely new floors, thinking through every word Laurie had said that evening and trying to figure out what was real and what was a lie. I walked around my house like a mental patient on Thorazine. I didn't cry; I was too full of fear and shock. As the sun came up, I was still shuffling around, talking to myself. "I'll never give my life to anyone again. Never give my power away again!" The day passed without sleep or any word from Laurie.

On Sunday, I called my friends Tracey and Derek and told them everything I knew.

"You *have* to call the police," Tracey said. "You could be implicated in all of this."

Derek was angry. "I thought you were sure everything was solid!" He and several of his family members were heavily invested in Laurie's businesses. "Nate's dad's an attorney right? Call him *ASAP.*"

Louis had helped me set up Collective Good LLC and was the closest thing I had to a father figure. I sent him a vague email asking him to get in touch with me and got an automatic response stating he was out of town and would return the following day. That night, after eating a few bites of oatmeal for dinner, I sat down to write Laurie an email. I wanted to remind her of our close relationship so she wouldn't shut me out, jeopardizing my chance to possibly recover the $5 million my family and friends had invested in her businesses:

> I want to reiterate that I love you and appreciate you telling me what you did. The fact that you accepted $1.8 million for a new China Deal when you knew there was trouble is beyond my understanding of selfish. Even when I told you ALL my family and friends were freaked out about the market and Madoff, you said this process was untouchable and all was fine. That would have been a chance for me to protect my family and friends. I'm at a complete loss right now. I need a 100-percent true honest realistic plan with specific timelines for how and when you are going

to pay out the money listed below. I need that plan in two days so I know what I can do on my end to recover this money for my family and friends.

I ended by listing all the Collective Good investments. The total amount of principle that she owed was $5,212,200. After I pressed the send button, I lay my head on the desk and cried.

The next day, Laurie emailed back:

> All I ever did was to try to pass on what I thought was a great opportunity. I was told it was guaranteed. I've always paid all my investors since I started, sometimes late, sometimes on time. No one is happier than me when I help someone else make money.
>
> You are my only concern. I only want to keep your investors happy by making them an enormous amount of money. So don't think for a minute I have used your money for ANYONE or ANYTHING but to buy right and keep you current and on time. All I can do is promise you this: I'll pay you and your investors. We have the receivables to cover it. It will be late. It will be there. I love you and I'm sorry. I just want to kill myself then maybe you can have money from my life insurance policy and love me again.

When Louis called, I was too afraid to tell him the full truth. I only told him about the late China Deal payments, not the fake closeouts. I still hoped she'd somehow find a way to pay the money back at the end of the month. But that evening, I realized Louis needed to know the full truth and called him back.

"What else aren't you telling me?" he asked.

"Nothing, I've told you everything. I'm sorry and scared and embarrassed at having to come to you with something so horrible."

If Louis judged me, he kept it to himself. "Okay then, I'm here to help. Let's get started by discussing your options."

While I was married to Nate, I had always enjoyed being around Louis. He was fun, intellectual, and a very loving father. Occasionally when Nate's family and I were out to dinner or at a family gathering, someone would come up to thank Louis for his help or gush about what a skilled attorney he was. Now I was able to experience his brilliance firsthand. By the end of the phone conversation, I understood that I needed to find out exactly how much money Laurie had transferred in the last China Deal and to get a sense of when she could pay back the fraudulent closeouts. I immediately texted her and asked to meet as soon as possible.

While I was waiting for a response, I called Nate. I assumed Louis and I would be working together and I felt he should know what was going on, too.

"Laurie told me last Friday that she made up some of the recent closeouts," I told him. "I'm really afraid all that money is gone."

"Oh shit, Mark!"

"You warned me about her."

"No, Mark, we both knew Laurie was eccentric and at worst inconsistent, but Jesus, we had *no* idea she was a criminal. What did my dad say?"

"He wants me to wait to go to the authorities until I know exactly what happened with all of the money—God, everyone I know is involved." My voice broke.

"Sorry, Mark. I just got a text and need to go meet someone about possible work—it's something I've been waiting for all day. But I'm glad my dad is going to help. Talk to you later."

He hung up and I stood staring at my phone. Nate was supportive, but I simply wasn't on his radar anymore, and even the severity of this situation wouldn't change that.

I sat down in my favorite chair and gazed out the window, waiting for Laurie to contact me. Although she had often delayed returning a text or email, I knew that it was purposeful this time. When she did finally respond, she suggested we meet at Betty's house that evening.

On my way over, I realized that she didn't want to meet at the office because the other employees would hear our conversations. Many of them also had money tied up with her. As I walked into Betty's house, I was surprised to see Keith, one of Laurie's thuggish friends, wearing his sunglasses as he stood next to her like a guard dog. Laurie fiddled silently with her phone, and Keith pointed me to the chair farthest away from them. I ignored him and handed Laurie a sheet of paper with the total amount invested by Collective Good.

Without making eye contact, Laurie pointed to the paper. "Everything there except for the last China Deal is on the books with Dick and should be fine—just late, like I told you before." She started texting on her phone. "I still have to talk to Dick about how much I actually put in for the last deal."

Trying very hard not to sound aggressive, I knelt down to look directly into her eyes. "I don't understand why you can't just look at your bank account to find that amount." I could feel Keith glaring at me.

"I transferred some money to Dick, and then we went back and forth on a few deals," she said in a flat voice. "I need to ask him what his books show. You know I nevah keep good records."

I knew that was true. Her bookkeeper asked *me* questions about transfers between Laurie's company and Collective Good because Laurie never wrote anything down. I left the meeting with a promise from Laurie that she would get the information from Dick.

The next day, she texted me to confirm that she had checked my numbers and everything except the last China Deal had been transferred to Dick. I asked her to meet me at our bank to have some documents notarized—before I hadn't gotten her to sign the Collective Good investment agreements for the last China Deal before I left for San Francisco. I wanted proof that she owed Collective Good investors millions of dollars.

At the bank the following morning, I was surprised that she actually showed up. A stranger observing us would have never known that a week before we'd been such close friends. Laurie didn't make eye contact with me and turned her body away from me as much as possible while we waited for a notary.

"I need to meet Dick face to face to hear from him how much you transferred for the China Deal," I told her as we sat on a bench in the middle of the bank. "I need verified information for investors."

"Fine," she said, without looking away from her texting.

When the notary came in, Laurie signed the documents I'd brought without reading them. She continued to email and text as we walked out of the bank.

"I'm meeting an attorney who will figya out a payment plan," she said, still avoiding eye contact.

Later that day, she texted me saying she'd arranged a meeting at her attorney's office with Dick and me the following Monday. I felt a mix of relief and fear knowing the meeting would give me answers but dreading more devastating news.

Since I'd found out the news a week before, I hadn't eaten anything but oatmeal or slept more than a few hours at a time. When I looked in the mirror, I could see my ribs. One night when I couldn't sleep, I went to the gym, thinking that working out would exhaust me enough to collapse in sleep. Afterward I stepped on a scale. The day Laurie and I had gone out to dinner, I weighed 184 pounds. Now I was seventeen pounds lighter; my high metabolism had gone haywire with all the stress. I looked up at my unshaven face and saw a ghost.

By midmorning the day I was to meet her and Dick, Laurie had still not sent me the address. I texted her for the umpteenth time: "I have no idea where I'm going today. Send me your attorney's name and address."

She responded immediately. "It's Beatty in Garden City on Old Country Road. 600 block across from Citibank building."

Completely annoyed that she was being so cryptic, I shot back, "What's the street number and the attorney's first name? I need all the information."

She didn't respond. After ten minutes, I did an online search for "Beatty attorney in Garden City" and found Rick Beatty on 426 Old Country Road. "Never mind, I found his name and address," I texted her. "Looking forward to finally meeting Dick and hearing about the payment plan."

There was a brief pause before she responded.

"All your questions will be answered."

I knew she had chosen her words carefully. Later, as I drove to the meeting, I had a sick feeling in my gut. I had spoken to Louis for guidance on the exact information I was to gather. But I knew there was no way to prepare for what was about to come. Bile rose in my throat as I walked into the attorney's building.

Rick Beatty, Laurie's attorney, was an attractive guy about my age with a friendly smile and of course a Long Island accent. He greeted me in the reception area and walked me back to the conference room where I expected to see Laurie and to finally meet the infamous Dick. But when I turned into the room, Laurie and Dick were nowhere in sight. Instead, Laurie's mother, dressed in a white pantsuit, stared up at me from where she sat at the table.

"Where's Laurie?" I managed to say even though my chest felt like an elephant was sitting on it.

"Laurie didn't feel safe being in the same room with you, so she asked me to be here," Nancy said sternly.

"Unsafe with *me*? She's afraid of *me*?"

"Look, I don't know what transpired between you two, but I do know my daughter's a liar, so I want to hear from you what's going on."

I stared at this Laurie look-alike and I felt as if I were on Mars without air or gravity. Beatty motioned toward a chair.

"Please sit down."

I sat and explained why I was there. There was a long, awkward pause while the attorney looked down at the table and Nancy and I waited for him to speak.

"Dick Goldstein owes Laurie *no* money. Laurie never invested a dollar with Mr. Goldstein. In fact, she took out several large loans from him over the past three years."

I stood and walked to a bookcase across the room, which I held on to for support. I started sobbing as it hit home: my family and friends had been swindled out of $5,000,000—their life savings.

After I calmed down, I asked all the appropriate questions, trying to gather as much information as I could. There was not much to tell me. Both the attorney and Nancy were there to protect Laurie. But then Beatty opened up a bit.

"Listen, I know people on both sides of Ponzi schemes and understand how difficult it is. I also have a colleague who lost huge amounts with Madoff. However, I must advise my client not to admit anything else to you."

From the volumes of media coverage that the Madoff case had garnered, I'd learned that a Ponzi is a fraudulent scheme where returns are paid to investors from new investors' money instead of from legitimate business ventures. It was clear that the attorney was admitting Laurie's guilt. I only wished I had a tape recorder to capture it.

On the way out of the building, I saw Nancy in the parking lot. She approached me with a look of concern on her face. "I'm saying this as a mother. You have to take care of yourself. Get some sleep and eat something."

I blew up at her.

"I don't have money to pay the mortgage on my house or my mother's! Didn't you hear that Laurie owes my family $5 million? Laurie lied to all of us. She's a criminal and should go to jail."

The ice queen kept a total poker face, but with every word her head gave an aggressive nod toward me. "I understand that you're upset, but if you go to the police, you won't be giving Laurie a chance to pay you back."

"You should sell Laurie's house and pay my family back, Nancy. I know it's in *your* name."

"*I'm* not selling anything," she said defensively.

"You just made it clear that you don't care about what's right or fair— you're just protecting your sociopath daughter. Goodbye, Nancy," I said through my tears and walked away.

On the long drive back home, my thoughts were bleak: *How am I going to break the news to everyone? Will they believe me? Hate me?*

Living in Laurieland had turned into a total nightmare.

Defensive Strategy #1

Louis called me the next morning after he spoke to Laurie's attorney. He and Beatty agreed that Nancy and I would take over as conservators to Laurie's businesses. This meant that Laurie wouldn't have access to any of her business accounts. Louis advised me to contact Laurie and Nancy to arrange a meeting at the bank to sign over the accounts as soon as possible.

"I'm still not sure I shouldn't go to the authorities now," I said.

"It's always an option, but if you do, then you lose the possibility of getting any money back for your family and friends. Investigate the facts so that when you go to the authorities, you'll have information that'll be useful to them."

When I got off the phone, I knew the next step was calling my mom to tell her the news. I knew she'd need extra support when hearing the horrible news. I also was aware that I had no reserves at the moment, so I called my older brother Zack first. After telling him what was going on, I was grateful that he agreed to go over to Mom's place to be there when I called.

As I dialed her number, acid poured into my stomach. I knew how hard she had worked in her lifetime and how much she deserved what I had provided for her during the past few years. Now that I had no way of knowing what the future would hold for us, I felt totally overwhelmed and helpless. I took a deep breath and cleared my thoughts.

As I began to share the little bit of information I had, Mom shrieked, "Oh no, Mark, so many people depended on you!" Within a second, she added, "What does this mean for my house? You won't be able to afford this, will you? Oh God, this is terrible news. What are you going to do?"

There was nothing she was saying that I had not already thought or actually said to myself, but it was still deeply unsettling to hear her so upset. "I'm working with Louis to figure out the best way to move forward."

Mom continued in a shrill voice, "I just can't believe all those wonderful things she did for you, and all along she was lying and stealing *everything* we had. What a sick and miserable bitch! I wish you'd never met her!"

After letting her know that I'd be sending out an email to everyone in the next few days, I encouraged her to talk to Zack and not bottle up her feelings. I also reminded her that I was under incredible stress and needed her support in whatever way she could give it.

"Of course, Mark, you were only trying to do good. Your heart was always in the right place. Look, you named your company Collective Good and tried to help so many people. You even encouraged us to donate money from investment profits to charities. Who else would have done that with the opportunity Laurie made you think you had?"

"Thanks, Mom. I needed to hear that right now."

As I put down the phone, I walked into my den and let out an audible sigh. I'd emailed all of the Collective Good investors a few days before Laurie told me about the fake closeouts, asking everyone to confirm their Social Security numbers to assist Larry with tax document preparation. In the days that followed, while I had been having a nervous breakdown, my inbox had been full of cheerful emails from people expressing their gratitude for the financial opportunities. Each message was a painful reminder of the trust that each person had put in me and how I had failed them all horribly by introducing them to Laurie's world.

With Louis's guidance, I crafted an email that conveyed all the relevant information for the Collective Good investors:

Hello Everyone,

About a week ago, Laurie Schneider and I had a discussion about her companies. During this discussion, I found out that Laurie had mismanaged a large portion of a recent Collective Good LLC investment.   . . . This is what I know as of the writing of this email:

1. Some of the deals that Laurie raised money for didn't and/or do not exist.
2. Laurie Schneider apparently used some of the money that was raised by Collective Good LLC to pay other debts—including some payments to other Collective Good LLC investors.
3. Laurie does not currently own assets with value near the amount owed to Collective Good LLC investors.

I went on to explain the steps that I was taking to gather information and do all I could to reclaim the money that Laurie owed everyone:

1. Collective Good LLC has been granted authority to review all of Laurie Schneider's business and personal financial records with her accountant so that we can determine what assets and liabilities she really has.
2. Laurie has agreed to grant Collective Good LLC a security interest and lien on anything she owns (which mostly includes her businesses). If she attempts to liquidate or borrow further against these assets, Collective Good LLC would then be protected, and if she defaults on our agreements, Collective Good LLC could begin foreclosure proceedings.
3. Collective Good LLC will become de facto receiver over Laurie's businesses and affairs, which will include signing authority over her checkbook/accounts and continued access to her books and records.
4. I am actively working with her attorney, my attorney, and our accountant to develop a reliable and meaningful payment plan with

the goal being to get as much principal back to everyone as soon as possible.

5.   Upon the advice of my attorney and accountant, we will be treating any payment (whether called "profit" or "principal repayment") you received as repayment of principal. This will ensure that you pay taxes only on the money that actually is profit for you.

In the most difficult part of the email, I did my best to acknowledge the horror of the situation and apologize to everyone:

I know this is a huge shock and that each of you has invested precious money in part due to your trust in me. I also have invested all my assets in these deals and can relate to the huge disappointment and anger you may be feeling. Almost every one of you is a close relative or friend of mine or my family. I feel the responsibility of this situation heavily and am doing my best to act with integrity and honesty. I apologize from the deepest place within me that we are involved in this precarious situation.

I created Collective Good LLC to assist all of us and my intent during this difficult time is to work so each of you gets as much of your principal as soon as possible. I know each of you will want to speak to me with questions, concerns, and emotions. So that I can devote time and focus to each of you, please email me three time slots in the next day that I could call you.

Again, I am so very sorry to report this news, and I intend to continue doing everything I can that is possible and appropriate to best handle this situation.

On February 2, 2009, as I got ready to send the email after rereading and editing it several times, I was acutely aware that by pressing the enter button, I would be spreading havoc and fear among those closest to me.

But it was the only responsible thing to do. I also knew that many of these people would never feel the same about me again.

Up until that moment, I had been overwhelmed and ready to fall apart. In pressing that button, I called on something deep within to give me fortitude.

Within a matter of minutes, I started receiving responses. Almost everyone expressed devastation at their loss.

Sue and Bennett, the Rhode Island cousins who had seen Laurie at my dad's funeral only months before, were understandably outraged. As soon as he received the email, Bennett picked up the phone and called me.

"I simply don't understand how this happened. You worked with her in the office, and we assumed you were on top of everything."

"I know this is incredibly upsetting, Bennett. It turns out Laurie laid a brilliant web of deceit and used fake invoices and contracts to give all of us the idea that her deals were real. She lied to every person in her life. We still don't know if others were involved."

"Well, all that may be important, but honestly, I just want my money back," Bennett said in a flat tone that reminded me of Jack Benny. "We'll probably have to sell our house to survive."

"I am *so* sorry for all of this and know you two put your trust in me." I had my hand over my eyes as I sat in my office chair at Hazel and focused on being supportive in any way I could. "I'll continue to do all I can to investigate what happened, and find any money she has to pay everyone what they're owed."

Although many shared their anger with me for not doing a better job of knowing that Laurie was a fraud, another cohort responded with incredible grace in their concern for me, with full understanding that most of my family and friends were involved.

Franny, who was also at the table with Laurie at my father's funeral lunch, tried to be supportive in her voicemail message to me. "I love you, Mark, and know your heart was in the right place. I will pray for you, and hope you do the same for me as we figure out our next steps." I later heard from her daughter that Franny had taken out a huge home equity line of credit to invest and now had no way to pay the loans back. Her family was considering foreclosure and attempting to figure out where she would live if that happened.

I'll be forever grateful to the kindness of the people who were able to express some compassion in addition to their feelings of anger and worry. Their generosity gave me strength to deal with the people who understandably had only rage and fear. Over the course of the next two days, I spoke to most of the forty-five people who had invested and lost money. Each phone call required that I go through every detail of the situation and then hear their anger, disappointment, and fear. It seemed like a never-ending reliving of my own horror. I felt it was my responsibility to let each person ask questions and vent their emotions. My presence and attention were the only things I had control over and all that I could offer at that time. Of course it wasn't enough.

I also attempted to call Troy and Gregory to warn them. Even though we hadn't really spoken in a year, I understood that they were innocent victims just like my family and I. After a day of having my calls, texts, and emails ignored, I felt the only path to reach them was to call Gregory's family, who lived in Philadelphia. Prior to our fallout, I had bonded with his parents, both therapists, and knew that they lived in Philadelphia. I called information and quickly was connected. Dan, Gregory's father, answered the phone.

"Hi Dan, it's Mark, Gregory and Troy's neighbor."

There was a pause and then a cool response. "Uh, this is not a good time, Mark. We're on our way out the door to the symphony."

I spat everything out as quickly as my mouth could form the words: "Laurie's been running a Ponzi scheme and all of your investments are likely lost. I've been trying to get hold of Gregory and Troy all day to tell them."

Gregory's quiet demeanor is easy to trace to his father, who spoke calmly, "She *just* called us for a loan of $400,000, and I was planning on sending it to her later this week."

"Don't give her any money, Dan. It will all just go to paying other investors who are demanding their money. And get an attorney right away. We've all been fucked."

Dan and his family missed the performance so he could hear all the information I had to share. I told them that Laurie would likely say that other investments were in danger but that she had protected their money because they were her favorite family. By now I had woken up to her modus operandi: everyone was the most special, most beautiful, and most adored person when Laurie was talking to them. I wanted to scream from the tallest building, "Laurie has screwed everyone including you!"

A few days later, I sat in a small cubicle with Laurie, Nancy, and Matt, the Chase Bank employee who had helped Laurie set up and maintain her business accounts. Laurie and her mother sat on one side of the desk and I sat next to Matt. Laurie kept her sunglasses on and her head down. This was the first face-to-face time that I had been able to have with her since finding out the full extent of her lies. She had been maintaining a distance from me, but we were both needed to sign the paperwork to take her off the business accounts. When I saw her, I wanted to tear her heart out with my bare hands.

"Ah, I see you're still alive after all your talk of wanting to be dead," I said.

Nancy looked shocked at my venom. "Let's just try to get through this."

"Well, your criminal daughter may be interested in knowing that I called all my investors two days ago and told them she was running a Ponzi scheme, and that their money is gone."

Laurie's body shuddered. Without taking her eyes off the desk, she asked, "You called *everyone*?"

"All forty-five of them, you miserable b—"

Nancy put out her right hand in a stop motion. "Just calm down. We're here to do a task. I won't have you attacking my daughter."

I turned to the banker. "Matt, Laurie's been running a Ponzi scheme using the accounts you set up for her. You better tell Chase Bank, because the Feds are going to hear about this soon."

Matt said nothing but handed me several sheets of paper and explained that each was the signature page for a different account at the bank. The documents took Laurie off the accounts and put Nancy and me on as sole signers.

"Are these the only accounts she has here, Matt?" I asked as I signed the documents.

"This is everything," he said, awkward as he observed our interaction.

I turned to Laurie. "Show me your wallet. What other accounts do you have at other banks? I know you used to bank at Washington Mutual."

Sounding like a zombie, Laurie said, "My purse is in my car. I'll show you my wallet so you can see for yourself."

Nancy put her hand on Laurie's. "That's not necessary." Turning to me, she said, "The Chase accounts are everything. I vouch that there're no other accounts."

"Nancy, I know there are Washington Mutual accounts Laurie used."

"She closed those accounts months ago. I repeat: that I vouch that the Chase accounts are all that currently exist." She took her hand off Laurie's and pointed at me. "You and I have to find a way to work together now."

"Nancy, I don't trust either of you as far as I can throw your hideously obese daughter. Until I get a better handle on the situation of these accounts, all activity is going to stop."

Laurie interjected. "But I have pawties and janitorial supply orders. If you kill my business, how can I ever have money to pay you back?"

"I'll be checking the accounts online throughout the day, and I'm going to be in communication with you, Nancy."

For the first time, Laurie looked up at me. "She doesn't know the computer at all, so she can't get online. Email my sistah, who can tell my mothah what each message says."

"Don't look me in the eye, you sociopathic monster. At least keep pretending to feel shame for ruining so many lives." I was so angry that

I wanted to pound her face into the desk. I got up out of the chair and turned to Nancy. "I'll email you later."

I rushed home to review all the online account information. I had spoken to a friend who was an accountant and he directed me to make a log of all the deposits and withdrawals for the past six months. He said that it would be easy to trace if there were one or two accounts that Laurie was transferring money into but never received anything from. If that was the case, then I would find the magical silent partner or secret accounts that Laurie may have used to steal the money.

It took me no more than thirty minutes on that first review to figure out it was all a Ponzi scheme. First of all, none of her accounts had any money in them. Both the entertainment and janitorial companies had constant transfers of money from the accounts that were supposedly for the investments. From this I understood that the entertainment and janitorial companies were shells that looked legitimate. Laurie met new wealthy people by planning their parties or by supplying their business or apartment building with toilet paper and paper towels. She then dropped hints about her other "lucrative" ventures. I understood immediately why she'd always been so resistant to my idea of dropping Party Hearty and Scrub-A-Dub-Dub to just focus on the investments.

Even though I had no accounting background, it was easy to see that money I wired to her immediately was transferred to another investor to whom Laurie owed money. Other people's money was wired to my folks as payment on our investments. It was a sick cycle of money in and money out. There was no silent partner or secret accounts.

"How the fuck did Larry not see this if he was reviewing her account books every quarter?" I said to Louis on the phone later that day. "This explains why he told me to stop investing with her."

"When did he say that to you?"

"A few times Larry looked at me strangely and tell me I was crazy for investing with her."

"Did he give you any indication of why he'd say that?"

"Yeah, of course I'd ask him why, and he'd respond that she was crazy, and that I was crazier to trust her with my family's money."

"Didn't you think that was odd?" Louis said with more emotion than he usually used in his conversations with me about the situation.

"Everything in Laurieland was odd, Louis. I was a stranger in a very strange land. I had seen Laurie hand Larry an envelope full of cash several times, and the bookkeeper told me she had seen the same thing. Larry had been Laurie's accountant for years. I thought he meant that she was chaotic and disorganized. I always responded to his comments with the knowledge that Laurie loved me the most and would never do harm to me or my family. I had also seen the receipts that Laurie said were for the closeouts, and Betty confirmed all the meetings she had with Dick. It was all the perfect cover."

Louis urged me to continue digging through the records to find out as much as I could. My initial review was only cursory and I could have missed something. In the meantime, he promised to check with colleagues about finding the best route to go to the authorities. It seemed as though that was an obvious step since her bank accounts weren't showing us a secret account or silent partner where we could have found a pile of money. Louis wasn't sure if I should go to the local, state, or federal authorities.

"And you're going to need a criminal attorney. I'll keep advising you on the civil aspects of the case."

"But I'm a victim, too. Why would I need a criminal attorney?"

"You never walk into the state's district attorney or the FBI without counsel, to make sure you're protected. From now on every step has to be well thought out."

I took in a deep breath. "I got it. I fucked up big time."

Later that day, the last item of the house renovation, which I had ordered and paid for months before, arrived. As the vertical blinds for the sliding glass doors in the kitchen were installed, I looked around at the vast space I had reshaped and decorated over the past year. I was overwhelmed with sadness and despair.

I'd found tenants off of Craigslist to move into my unit and the basement apartment. The top two apartments were already occupied. I had only three weeks to move out. My dream of filling my home with a husband and children was obliterated. I now had a mother to support and two mortgages to pay and very little in my bank account. I put out a call to the few friends I had to help me pack up my house and to find buyers for my furniture and art. I needed to sell everything as soon as possible. Nate, who'd checked in by phone a few times, made the trek from Manhattan to pick up a few things he wanted from the house. He didn't stay to help pack.

Within a day of removing Laurie from the business accounts, I started getting calls and emails from her investors who wanted to be paid. I found out through them that Laurie was telling everyone I was the reason she couldn't make any payments; by taking her off the accounts, I was preventing the proper flow of money. She never admitted to others that she didn't have a dime or that her "investments" had been a scheme. Showing her true sociopathic self, she had made me the bad guy and admitted no guilt or responsibility in the situation.

In addition, there were several strange transactions in the accounts over the course of a week. First, I discovered a deposit of $100,000 from someone I'd never heard of before. I immediately emailed Nancy and demanded an explanation. I assumed Laurie would continue to lure people into giving her money until she was put in jail or was dead, and so I assumed this was another victim. I didn't want this transaction to take place while my name was on the account because of course then I would be implicated. I had begun to understand more and more how lethal it could be to be the nemesis of Laurie Schneider. When I demanded that the money be sent back immediately, Nancy responded.

"We asked Laurie's attorney, and he agreed that a family friend could loan Laurie money. He fully understands the situation, and it's only a loan." I didn't believe them for a second but didn't know what to do so let the money stay in the account.

Within a matter of days, there was a withdrawal of $90,000 from one of the accounts. I immediately emailed Laurie and her mother to find out what was going on. Both claimed to be completely shocked at the transaction, and Laurie seemed particularly incredulous as though these things never happened when she was in control of her accounts.

Thankfully, I was a signer on the account and could trace the transaction. It took a few days for the bank to be able to identify that the check had been written to Troy and Gregory's company. I called them to find out what had happened.

"Laurie said we should write ourselves a check off the account because she was prioritizing payment back to us and our family."

"She's pathological. You have to put the money back. I'm worried it'll look like you're in on this, when no one else is getting paid," I said.

They were distraught to begin with, and the added drama of this last move by Laurie made us all realize she could easily put us in danger.

After two weeks, I had analyzed the accounts enough to know that they showed no secret hiding place. I had also become aware of the huge amounts of money she was moving through the accounts each month. It was a mystery to me how Chase Bank, Larry, or Laurie's two bookkeepers could not easily see she was running a fraud when it was so plainly clear to me, someone with no financial training. Even though I knew Laurie was trying to provoke me with these crazy moves, I had had enough and was ready to go to the authorities. I planned on taking myself off her accounts, with Louis's permission, but not before I made copies of every document I could get my hands on in her office. I emailed Laurie to let her know I would be in the next day so she could let the staff know I'd be there.

When I arrived at her office, the only people there were workers of both Party Hearty and Scrub-A-Dub-Dub. Although I had been very friendly with all of them until I'd learned the truth, I guessed they'd now despise me. Laurie was a master of twisting the truth to put blame on others, and I assumed she'd told them lies about me stealing or taking over her company illegally. I was correct. The room went silent as I walked in and I felt cold stares from everyone. The air was filled with

again proved herself to be a genius of strategy. Whatever the outcome, the record would show that Laurie turned herself in before anyone reported her crimes.

Laurie was still the mayor of Laurieland.

Time to Pay the Piper

In the wee hours of March 1, 2009, snow began to fall as I frantically finished packing and cleaning Hazel. The new tenants would all be arriving
in a few hours and there was still work to be done. With the exception of
a few days in which Ira's sister came over to help, I had sold off or boxed
up everything that I owned by myself. Furniture and art that I had bought
only a few months before were sold at a fraction of the cost to haggling
buyers, unconcerned that my life had totally fallen apart. For most of the
week, I'd gone to bed at 4 a.m. and woke at 7, in tears. The house that I
had worked so hard to reshape and design would be a home to strangers.
I had no idea what my future would be and carried the weight of knowing
so many people I loved were going through difficult times because I had
introduced them to Laurie.

My friends Sheila and Harry, who lived on the second floor, braved
the snow to help me move the carload of clothes and boxes to the room I
had rented. Although the building was only a few blocks away, it seemed
worlds apart from Hazel and the life that I knew.

Unsure if I could find employment in New York City, I had rented a
room for two months to give myself the option of leaving town if my job
search took me there. After hugging Harry and Sheila, I closed my door
and fell into bed. Since finding out about the Ponzi, I hadn't slept more
than four hours a night, and the past few days had been full of hard work

to get the house ready. My body and mind needed to fully recharge as I slept for the next fourteen hours.

The only apartment I could afford, which cost $600 a month, was a share with four other people, all of whom were in their early twenties. I was aware of this fact but had not been told that two of the other roommates worked nights. This meant that they came home around 4 or 5 a.m. and not only took a shower together in the bathroom, which was directly next to my bedroom, but also loved to cook elaborate and loud meals in the kitchen, which was on the other side of the hallway from me. The result was that there was never a time when the kitchen or bathroom was not full of loud twenty-somethings yelling, laughing, or sometimes having sex. Although it was still better than the pressure of having to pack up my whole existence, the inability to sleep soundly during this time of stress wore me down.

When I awoke from my long slumber on that first day, I didn't have time to fret about the noise level in the apartment because there were twenty-four hours before the meeting with the FBI. In preparation of my first meeting with my criminal attorneys a few weeks before, I had created a large document that chronicled my history with Laurie and shared all the knowledge I had about the situation. Based on their feedback, I revised the document to include all emails and correspondence with Laurie to give a true history of our time together.

During these last hours before I drove to the FBI, I scoured my email inbox and boxes full of business-related documents to make sure I had included everything I knew. I had a bad feeling that I had only one chance to make an impression; otherwise the case against her might go away.

As I pulled into the FBI parking lot, I felt tired but calm. I was confident that the comprehensive summary and the hundreds of backup documents would substantiate my claim that Laurie had run a Ponzi scheme. This was finally my chance to tell someone of authority who could do something to stop her and possibly put her in jail.

I met Sam, my attorney, in the lobby of the building. Because he'd previously worked for the U.S. Attorney's office, he was familiar with the layout of the FBI building and easily walked us through security and up to the correct floor. He left me waiting in the reception room as he let the agent know we had arrived.

An attractive man in his early thirties came out and led us to the interview room. He introduced himself as Agent Ben Mumford. As we sat down, I was excited to finally begin and launched into an introduction of what I had brought.

"So I've prepared a summary document that should—"

Agent Mumford cut me off. "Hold on, sir. Let me begin by asking you whether it is true that you declared bankruptcy in 1997."

I turned to Sam with a look of confusion. He gave me no signal and said nothing.

I guessed that I was on my own. "Yes, I was twenty-seven, had $17,000 in debt, and my credit card company jacked up the interest rate to 22 percent. I couldn't afford my monthly payments and I felt I had nowhere to go. My family had no ability to help me at the time."

The agent was silent as he reviewed the folder in front of him.

Confused and annoyed, I didn't hold back. "I don't understand how that would have anything to do with why I am here, Agent Mumford. I'm trying to give you information that will help clarify the case against Laurie Schneider." I turned to Sam. "My understanding is that my attorney called ahead and explained the situation to you."

What became clear in the next few minutes is that Agent Mumford, and maybe the FBI in general, had not yet established that I was credible. In fact, the tone of the conversation led me to believe that there was suspicion that I may be a guilty party in the situation trying to cover my tracks by pointing a finger at Laurie.

"Let me be clear, Agent. Laurie Schneider committed fraud many times over, and the document in my hand explains the scheme and names of the many victims. If you'll let me give you an overview, then maybe the situation will be a bit clearer."

Mumford looked at the tome I handed him and glanced warily over at Sam, who finally said something. "He has prepared a very thorough review of the case. You're gonna find it very helpful."

I took the agent's silence as a signal to move forward. "My understanding is that Laurie has already approached the FBI. She is a master at smoke and mirrors and likely attempted to confuse the situation." I turned to Sam. "Based on my conversations with my legal advisors, it makes sense to begin with an explanation, which is on page five, of the types of fake deals Laurie created."

An hour and a half later, the agent looked overwhelmed. There were hundreds of pages of emails, all of which someone without context of the situation would take a long time to understand. He thanked me for my time and walked Sam and me to the elevator.

"At least the authorities are aware of her now and can do something about it," I said to Sam before I walked to my car. I knew there was nothing else to do on that front until I heard back from the FBI with questions.

A few days later, Sam said he had spoken to the FBI to confirm that I was not a person of interest. It seemed clear to everyone that I was a victim, as were my family and friends. He said the FBI was very appreciative of my efforts and would be contacting me as they continued to investigate the case against Laurie.

I didn't have much time to be relieved that I wasn't a suspect because tax time was fast approaching. I'd been working with Larry on the complex process of figuring out exactly how much each Collective Good investor had lost so that their tax records would be accurate. Many of these folks had already seen a huge amount of their life savings disappear into Laurie's Ponzi. Without proper tax documentation, their taxes could be screwed up, including additional IRS penalties, for years. Some could get a write-off if they could show a total loss of monies from the fraudulent investments. It was my responsibility to get them proper documentation, and that meant pushing Larry to get the job done.

Initially, I thought the process would be somewhat easy, but Larry disagreed.

"This is gonna take a *lot* of my staff's time. Can you afford to pay my firm?" Larry said with a ball of spit glistening at the corner of his mouth.

I was angry that Larry was only looking at his bottom line and not seeing the enormity of the crisis for all the Collective Good investors; I felt he was partially at fault for not catching the Ponzi during his years of doing Laurie's taxes.

"I'll get you your money, Larry, but explain what is going to take such a long time? I've been working with you each month to reconcile the Collective Good books, so isn't it just a matter of adding up all the money that people invested and lost?"

Larry looked at me with annoyance before he explained. "Any money that someone received as profit on previous investments is going to count toward their total loss. You and your amateur investors don't realize that the IRS is going to look at every penny Laurie paid you and subtract that amount from what you invested."

Since I looked confused, Larry explained: if, for example, someone had invested $10,000 and received $12,000 back a year ago and then invested another $10,000 but lost it all, the IRS would subtract the extra $2,000 the investor thought was profit from the earlier investment. The total loss would then only be $8,000. Most of my family and friends had participated in a handful of investments, so each would have received what they thought was profit along the way.

I was upset to hear this information because it felt like another way my investors would be screwed. "But people didn't know it was a Ponzi and may have sent their kids to college, or bought cars, or paid off loans. That money doesn't exist anymore."

Larry shrugged. "That's what you get for dealing with a crazy person."

"How can you be so insensitive to what is happening?" I shot back. "You're acting like you had nothing to do with this mess when you were doing her books! How could you not have known she was running a scam?"

"She had a bookkeeper doing her books. My firm only did her taxes, and I did them based on documents she gave me. As you know, she is very good at only telling you what she wants you to know." His tone was defensive.

"But the bookkeeper was a friend of yours, and you supposedly rec-onciled Laurie's books quarterly. I was there when she made appoint-ments with you." In that moment, I remembered Laurie stuffing a stack of hundreds into an envelope that she later passed to him. "What about the stash of cash that I saw Laurie give you on more than one occasion? Accountants are not usually the recipients of envelopes full of cash."

Larry was quiet for several seconds. When he responded he was not looking me in the eyes. "Well," he paused, "I loaned her some money, and that, uh, cash was repayment."

"Hmmm, so I guess if I reported what I saw to the FBI or the IRS, I'm sure you would have documentation of that loan, right? I mean, it was all on the books since you are a certified accountant." Larry looked terrified as I stood up.

"So listen carefully. You're going to prioritize getting the Collective Good tax documents in order so my family and friends don't have to suf-fer any longer than they have to. And you're going to cut the attitude."

Over the next ten days, I visited Larry's office frequently to assist on this project. Although I had previously been coming in monthly to recon-cile the books with him, somehow the system was not as well organized as he had led me to believe, and there was a lot of work to do. Using my spreadsheets and memory, I was able to fill in gaps of information that he didn't have regarding specific investments. In the course of these visits, we also would touch on my financial situation. He wanted to know what I spent on my house, how much I earned overall, and the amount I lost in the Ponzi. All of these questions made sense in the context of my speak-ing to my accountant, who would also be doing my taxes.

I was furious to hear through the grapevine that Laurie was getting information about my personal finances from Larry. I highly doubted that she had bugged Larry's office, so I assumed he was not only still in touch with her but sharing my information. All of this reinforced my belief that he had been very aware of her schemes all along.

I put in calls to the FBI and Louis. Agent Mumford thanked me for my concern and told me he assumed they would be looking into Larry. He reiterated that the federal investigation process was a long and arduous one. Louis convinced me that I needed Larry because obviously there was still work to be done to get the Collective Good investor tax records out, and he urged me to focus on that task.

I understood what Louis was saying but felt trapped in a crazy world where there was only Louis who was trustworthy. In a desperate moment, I asked Louis to draft a confidentiality agreement so Larry couldn't share any more information related to me or Collective Good.

A few days later, I walked into Larry's office and asked two of his employees who often worked on the Collective Good projects to join us.

As I pulled out the confidentiality agreement and put it in front of Larry on his desk, I began explaining. "Larry's been sharing information from our conversations with Laurie, who I think you all know is being investigated by the Feds for fraud. I'm asking him to sign this confidentiality agreement, which prohibits anyone from this firm from sharing information about me or Collective Good LLC without my written permission."

Larry stood up and slammed his fist on the desk. "Get out!"

His employees looked awkwardly down at the floor. I stood my ground and continued talking.

"I'm not going anywhere. We're stuck with each other until this mess is done. No one else has all the records I need to get my family and friends their tax documents. You just have to shut up and have some professional boundaries."

Larry looked at the paper and then back up at me like a confused child. "Oh, all right. Jesus Christ, you're all crazy," he said as he signed the form and handed it back to me.

From that point on, I heard nothing else through the grapevine about Laurie getting any information. Within a few weeks, we had the tax documents completed, and I sent them all out to the investors after working with Louis to draft an email explaining how to interpret the forms and what to tell their tax preparers.

With that Herculean task completed, I knew the only thing I could focus on now was finding work so I could continue to pay my mom's mortgage and somehow survive. Over the next weeks, I spent my days camped out in my room looking online for jobs, checking Laurie's email, and keeping in touch with other victims.

In April 2009, after almost three months of looking for work and with the funds in my bank account dwindling, I finally got a bite from an old colleague. Samantha and I had worked in the San Francisco public health system throughout the nineties. Now head of her own public health consulting company, she said that there were several projects that could use my expertise. Although it was not permanent work, it was a start, and I hoped that once I moved back to San Francisco, I could find something more permanent.

At the exact time of hearing about Laurie's Ponzi, the U.S. economy tanked. This meant a lot of people were looking for work and trying to get out of current debt such as expensive car leases, among other things. Only several months before, Larry had urged me to trade in the 1997 Honda and lease a car so that I would have a write-off for some of the profits I was expected to make in 2009. Based on his guidance, I had gotten the Prius in December 2008. Now a few months later, the monthly payment seemed exorbitant, and I made every attempt to get out of my lease, but to no avail. I was stuck with my car. So when I accepted the consulting gig, I decided to drive myself to San Francisco.

Days before leaving for San Francisco, I discovered that Laurie was still scamming others. My daily surveillance of her email occurred four to five times a day. I had recalled that she would always delete incoming emails immediately after reading them the first time. At the time, she had told me that Vince was jealous and that she was afraid he'd read her emails and texts to find out about all the other men she was seeing. But now I knew better. She had spun so many lies that she had to be vigilant about keeping all of her victims away from any kernels of truth.

I knew that I had to get to those emails before she could delete them so I could glean information about the case to pass on to the FBI.

Although I should not have been surprised, I was shocked to learn she was continuing to prey on other innocent victims.

Since being ostracized from her old friends and community, Laurie had apparently continued to meet wealthy people through her party planning. By reading her emails, I found that she simply told others that "greedy" investors and business partners were trying to take advantage of her generous nature. To these new friends, Laurie was the innocent victim.

One of these new friends was a woman named Liza Seltzer, who had hired Laurie to plan a party for her daughter's bat mitzvah. As usual in Laurieland, any wealthy person in Laurie's sphere became a friend. Soon I saw many emails between the two, mostly from Liza telling Laurie to "hang in there, it will get better soon! You're such a lovely person, and I'm sure everything will work out!"

When I typed "Liza Seltzer" into a search engine, I found a slew of articles on her brilliance as a sales and PR executive at a national financial institution. She was responsible for developing a national television ad for fiscal planning services. I wasn't surprised that Laurie's newest target was a successful businessperson who happened to have a busy life and needed some help. Laurie was a pro at saving the day.

Each time I opened up Laurie's email, acid pooled in my stomach. I hated her and felt an adrenaline rush knowing I was doing what I could to get her ass in jail. With every lie I read, I despised her more and wished the FBI would make the arrest that much quicker. When I read a new scheme that Laurie had hatched involving Liza, I thought we had finally caught her in the act:

"I am so stressed about finding another contractor to finish my kitchen renovation. You know my first one quit before finishing the job and I'm so busy with work and the family," Liza wrote like a fly walking into the black widow's spider web. "We have this trip planned, and I won't have time to find a new contractor before I go."

In typical Laurie fashion, she had an answer to every problem: "Sweetheart, I have the best contractor in the world. He built out my warehouse and renovated my second bedroom into a closet."

Liza responded right away: "Do you totally trust this guy? Can he really do it?"

I could almost feel the surge of excitement in Laurie as she responded: "He is amazing, my best and favorite male friend, and you of course are my favorite girl. He's a pro and will give you much more than he promises—just like me!"

I knew that Joey Romano had been the one to build out the warehouse and renovate her closet. But I knew he hated Laurie as much I as did and was doing his best to get his family's money back from her. I couldn't imagine that he'd have anything to do with her at this point. It didn't take long for me to see an email to Keith, Laurie's faithful partner in crime: "I'm going to email her like the bid came from you. We can make a lot of money on this and finally pay off your mortgage."

Laurie went on to explain to Keith about Liza's renovation trouble. Within a matter of days, I saw how smooth Laurie's operation was. She was telling Keith that his money troubles would be taken care of by the scam they would be doing on Liza. At the same time, she told Liza that all the stress of the renovation would be dealt with by her trusted contractor friend. Both Liza and Keith were totally taken in by her and willingly gave her carte blanche in decision making.

A day later, Laurie emailed Liza to seal the deal on the scam: "So Keith drove an hour out to see me to give me this beautiful proposal with pretty pictures and explanations, but I don't have a scanner to email it! My husband is Catholic, so I need to pretend and do the Easter thing and then go to the Islander game, so I'll summarize the proposal for you here."

The email went on to list a half-page of items and projects that went beyond the kitchen to include pool and landscaping. At the bottom of the email, Laurie wrote, "Minimum $100,000 and maximum $120,000 . . . you can have a new looking house for only $120,000—what a deal, right?"

"Your guy is definitely the cheapest, and I trust him because I trust you!" Liza gushed like a school girl.

Naïvely, I thought that catching Laurie in the act could help the FBI case against her. As soon as I had enough evidence to show the full extent of this mini-scheme, I contacted Ben, who quickly schooled me on the reality of the situation: "What you're describing wouldn't constitute a federal crime. At this time we are gathering evidence for the federal case against Laurie." Although the agent was reciting bureaucratic rules, he also spoke with some warmth and understanding. "I get that this must be very frustrating for you, but I have to focus on the investigation at hand."

"What about the drugs in their house? Her husband uses various narcotics and prescription pills all day long," I said.

"Not a federal crime. If you have more information on the fraud we initially spoke about, please keep in touch." And with that, FBI agent Mumford signed off. I remained extremely frustrated that Laurie was going to hurt another victim.

I decided to warn Liza by faxing her a letter.

The next day, I ventured to a Kinkos in Manhattan. I had purchased a Visa gift card from Walgreens so that the fax could not be traced to me. I had called her office the day before to get the fax number from her secretary. I reread the letter before I faxed it:

Ms. Seltzer,

You are about to be a victim of Laurie Schneider. The person she has told you is a contractor is in fact an ex-convict and a drug dealer. He has no experience in construction or landscaping. Laurie Schneider is planning on taking your money. She is being investigated by the FBI for fraud and running a Ponzi scheme. This is a warning to disassociate from her and this "deal" immediately. Many others have lost their life savings by trusting Laurie. You do not have to be a victim. You have been warned. It is now up to you to check out the facts.

As the fax machine beeped indicating that the transmission went through, I was deeply happy to be thwarting Laurie. I wanted her to feel restricted in the same way my life had become.

After that day, I saw no more emails from Liza Seltzer to Laurie. I hoped that meant that she received the fax and reconsidered the deal Laurie was trying to sell her.

Although Vince was a misogynistic asshole most of the time, my gut told me that he had no inkling that Laurie had been swindling everyone in her path. The same blindness that enabled him not to know about her secret apartment and the many men she had had sex with and even dated while I had known her, also served to block out the reality of her business dealings. Like everyone else in her life, Vince had been brainwashed by Laurie into being content with what she provided for him and had been trained to ask no questions and hear no lies.

I somehow thought that Vince could be our ace-in-the-hole to getting Laurie to come clean on all the nasty details of her scheme. He had a weird integrity that I wanted to use to pressure Laurie into at least telling him the truth. I had a strange faith that if Vince knew that all the claims against Laurie were true, he could get Laurie to turn herself in. While I worked for her, I witnessed Laurie going through his phone to read texts and hear his voicemail. She also read his email and got the mail before he had a chance to look it over. There was no way that I would be able to send anything to him that she wouldn't first intercept and destroy. I was also heeding Louis's advice to "stay under the radar because Laurie needs a scapegoat." I didn't want her targeting me in any way.

I remembered the previous Christmas when I had cooked Laurie's family dinner for their party. Vince's parents, Lisa and Tony, had been there. I had met both several times and had heard much from Laurie about them; they were normal working-class folks who were totally removed from the chaotic craziness that Vince and Laurie lived on a daily basis. I decided to write to them in the hope their Main Street values could help convince Vince to pressure Laurie to turn herself in.

Two years before I had naïvely entered Laurie's sick web of lies and now I had learned enough from her to understand I had to work like a spy. I needed to write the letter anonymously and be severe enough that Vince's parents would be concerned enough to get over the wall of illusion Laurie had created. After finding Lisa and Tony's address online, I emailed the final version to several friends asking them to send it from a Manhattan address to throw the scent off:

We are concerned that your daughter-in-law checks your son's mail, emails, and voicemails and filters out what she does not want him to know. Since 2002, Laurie has swindled over $15 million from "friends" of both hers and Vince's. Many innocent people just like you two have lost their retirement, college tuition money, emergency funds, and day-to-day living money due to Laurie's fraudulent schemes. The FBI is investigating her actions. Your son may not think this has anything to do with him, but he has been living in a house paid for by stolen money, works in a studio paid for by stolen money and has been financially supported by a wife who has defrauded people of millions of dollars. He benefited greatly by her schemes even if he didn't know about it.

In addition, Laurie's many romantic and sexual affairs have been uncovered through this investigation and may be publicly aired via the NY press. Her liaisons with Steven Berber, Stuart Silverman, and Matt Wielding can easily be proven by emails, security camera tape, and eyewitnesses. There are many more men she had sex or romantic affairs with who may come forward once the media frenzy gets going.

Vince's daily use of drugs and alcohol may also come out in the press. He should fully educate himself on what legal liabilities he has, know all about his wife's extramarital activities, and make an informed decision about what to do next. Trusting his wife, or her attorney, to take care of him may not prove to be the wisest thing for his future.

While I was on the road to San Francisco, Troy called to tell me some exciting new information: "Someone sent Vince's parents a hilarious letter telling them what a slut Laurie is and all about her fraud. I hear his parents told Vince to get far away from his crazy-ass wife. They've always known she was a loser, but now there's proof."

"Oh my god, I'm loving everything you're saying. So what did Vince do?"

"He ain't going anywhere, honey," Troy said with sass. "She has him by the balls because she pays for everything in his world. There is NO way he would leave her and start over in a shit apartment with no income."

I was shocked. I had naïvely thought more of Vince's morals and ethics.

"And I hear Laurie is super pissed at you because she thinks you wrote it."

"How the hell would I even know where Vince's parents live? She has so many enemies who hate her. There are lots of people who could have written that shit." I didn't trust Troy to keep my secret and certainly didn't want Laurie to involve me any further in her lies, so I tried to deflect as much as possible so Troy would pass on my feigned ignorance of the situation. "I'm just glad someone finally had the balls to do something against her."

"Amen to that, brother," Troy chimed in. "But I have much more amazing news to tell you."

"Yay! Tell me more, tell me more!" I called out as I sped down the highway.

"Joey Romano broke into Laurie's warehouse at 1 a.m. with the key she gave him when she pretended he was co-owner of her janitorial supply company. With a whole crew, he was able to move out every piece of equipment, all the janitorial supplies, and the bitch's car! And you'll never believe what she had in her backseat!"

Hearing him take a dramatic pause, I yelled out, "Don't make me wait. Tell me what was in the back of the car."

After another beat of silence Troy screamed out, "Boxes and boxes of every fucking bank account document that the witch has. She was supposedly taking them to her attorney the next day. HAHA!"

Joey's mother, Mary, had been like a surrogate mother to Laurie during the years when Nancy had stopped talking to her. Laurie had invited Mary to invest heavily in both Party Hearty and Scrub-A-Dub-Dub in addition to real estate, closeouts, and China Deals. Typical to the incestuous way we were all intertwined with Laurie, Mary brought along all of her family and friends and gave permission for Laurie to use her credit cards to lease cars and equipment for the businesses. Defiantly, Laurie had continued to drive a car and use entertainment equipment leased in Mary's name while ignoring requests for an explanation of what happened to all the investments. After months of Laurie's lies, Joey had decided to retrieve what he could.

"And he took all the computers in the office, too, and is gonna be going through them to see if he can find out where she put all the money!"

"Troy, I'm thinking that there is no secret hiding place and that she just kept recycling money back and forth from investor to investor. Like if I gave her $10,000, she would immediately use that to pay a debt off she had with you and then had to find another sucker to give her money in a few months to use to pay me."

I spent the remainder of my drive thinking through all that had happened and what my next steps were going to be. I was beginning a new life but by no means was I free from the nightmare I'd left behind in Laurieland.

Best of Times, Worst of Times

San Francisco was the oasis I had hoped it would be. Each day, I breathed in its awe-inspiring beauty as I biked or drove through the city. Driving on the upslope of a hill on the north side of town to see the deep blue of the bay literally took my breath away. Walking along the water felt like a prayer. I made the short trek to Lands End, the most northwestern point of the city where the bay meets the ocean, each day to see the Golden Gate Bridge and the beautiful brown and greens of the Marin Headlands across the bay. That piece of land was my solace and my savior.

I moved to a charming apartment in Duboce Triangle, a quaint neighborhood between the Lower Haight and the Castro. My new home was only one block from the place I lived for eleven years before moving to New York City. I also felt right at home with old friends who helped erase the memory of all the loneliness of New York. Within days of moving back, I had an instant community of friends and acquaintances clamoring to make a date and catch up with me. On a purely interpersonal level, this time spent with my community provided enormous healing.

A few weeks after I arrived in San Francisco, I received a letter from the U.S. Bankruptcy Court. It stated that Laurie had been forced into bankruptcy through a lawsuit of one of the victims. Because there was potential fraud involved, the court appointed Milton Soloman, an attorney, to be the trustee over the case. I knew from following the Bernie Madoff case that a trustee provided in-depth analysis of relevant bank accounts and assets to determine if there were secret accounts or silent partners. All of the victims were very excited by this new development. Some expected that money would be found. I simply wanted Laurie to be held accountable. Louis encouraged me to get in touch with the trustee and cooperate in every way. He was concerned about one issue.

"Understand that the trustee is on our side, but his job is to find money and return it to the victims. He gets a percentage of any money he collects, so he will be very motivated to go after 'clawbacks.'"

"I have no idea what a *clawback* is. That sounds like seafood," I said.

"If it's determined through the forensic analysis that someone who invested with Laurie received more money than they put in, the trustee will ask for that money back. If he does not get it, he will sue."

"That makes total sense. I'm not worried. Larry assures me that the Collective Good investors put in over $2 million more than they got out." I was confident in my statement. "This should not be an issue."

I immediately sent Soloman all the documents I had kept on Collective Good investors involved with Laurie.

Through luck and chutzpah, I talked my way into a three-month temporary gig working at a nonprofit at a job for which I was completely overqualified. At least it gave me a recent local job to list when applying for permanent work. The funds from selling my furniture and art were quickly dwindling. I knew that all of the other investors' lives had also changed due to the loss of money.

My cousins in Rhode Island had to sell their vacation home, which had been a place they hoped to move to in old age. Franny, the mother of my college friend, continued to struggle to pay for her mortgage but thankfully didn't go into foreclosure. Several investors who had previously retired were forced to go back to work, while others had to totally reconfigure their lifestyle to eke out enough to get by. It was a very stressful and sad time for all of us. The biggest burden was that we had taken out loans against the equity of our homes to invest with Laurie. Now that the money had disappeared, we all still owed hundreds of thousands of dollars with no extra income coming in.

Each time I heard another story of heartache and financial struggle, it felt like my heart was being ripped out. Of course, my pain didn't bring back the money or the dreams of my friends and family. Each had trusted me enough to invest, and most had put in amounts that seriously impacted their lives. Throughout all the horrible stress of the first months after finding out about the scheme, I had been in total survival mode, which had in some ways protected me. I likely had been in a kind of shock for six months; now that I was safe in my new home in San Francisco, all the emotions surrounding this horrible chapter came crashing down.

By the fall of 2009, Laurie had stopped using the AOL email account, but I knew she was living freely and likely still scamming others. My family and friends were suffering, and many held me responsible while others just thought I was a total schmuck.

My mother seemed more and more panicked knowing that I didn't have a job and soon wouldn't be able to pay her mortgage. My brothers were doing what they could to help her out, but it was a difficult time for everyone. Out of desperation, I asked for a small loan from a cousin to get me through the beginning of the new year. When I received his check, something clicked within me, and I began to think about the life insurance policy I had bought a few years before.

At the time, my brother Zack was a new insurance agent and had recently opened up his own shop near my hometown in Virginia. I wanted to support him in every way I could, and so I switched over my home insurance and also bought a $2 million life insurance policy. I remember reading over the paperwork before signing it and asking him about the suicide clause, which I had been surprised to see.

"The policy stipulates that it will not pay out the balance if someone kills themselves within two years of signing the policy. However, at two years and one day, the policy will pay in full for that reason."

Out of guilt and desperation to help my family and friends, I made a pact with myself that if I didn't have some way of making money by

February 2010, then I would kill myself, which would leave enough money to the investors to almost cover the amount they all initially invested.

Each day when I walked the beach at Lands End, I began to think of the details of how I could execute my plan in the least intrusive way to my family. I would overdose in my apartment and ask to be cremated with my ashes scattered by Land's End. I'd pack everything and leave letters for my family and a will so that there would be no more cleaning up my mess. In my most desperate moments, I focused on the $2 million that I hoped would help alleviate some fear and suffering of my family and friends. At night in bed, worry about the future and my continuing rage at Laurie kept me awake. I planned my suicide down to the last detail in the wee hours of each morning.

During this time, I had several phone conversations and email exchanges with the trustee, Soloman, who was very interested in my knowledge of Laurie and her world.

One day he surprised me with an out-of-the-blue comment: "You gonna sue Larry the accountant? Because he sure didn't do right by you and probably knew more about what she was doing than he is telling anyone."

I was taken aback by his directness.

"Yeah, I know, he's scum. I literally have no money, and my investors lost so much with Laurie, so we're gonna wait for the criminal case to be completed, so we can let the FBI do the investigating."

I heard from Troy that because of her bankruptcy Laurie had lost use of all of her businesses and had gone to work for an established entertainment company in Long Island. She had begun to use her husband's name ever since her local community became aware she was under investigation by the FBI.

I emailed a letter to a friend in Manhattan and asked her to mail it to Laurie's new employer notifying them of the various cases against Laurie. Weeks later I was surprised to hear that they hadn't paid any attention and had kept her on staff. When I spoke to Troy, he provided some clarification. "You remember Miguel who ran Laurie's warehouse? He's now working for another entertainment company and heard that she and the owner of the company are running some type of pyramid scam with clients of the agency. That bitch will never stop her evil ways."

I was furious to hear the news. "Did you call the FBI and tell them what you heard?"

"No, the FBI never called me, so I have nothing to do with them."

"Are you on crack? The FBI didn't call me either. I contacted them. If you want Laurie to go to jail, we all gotta do our part and pass along any information to the FBI."

Very matter-a-factly, Troy said, "Gregory's dad's taking care of all of that. We're just trying to survive." He sounded deflated.

I shot an email to Agent Mumford right away with the news of a possible new scheme.

All I got back was "Thanks. I'll follow up on this." When I didn't hear anything more back from him, I assumed the case was one of many that he had on his desk. There was no way for me to know if Laurie's scheme was a priority or was even being taken seriously. All this led me to feeling even more powerless.

It felt strange to spend time with friends whom I loved dearly and to keep my suicide plan from them.

In October 2009, I was called into an interview with the Department of Public Health for a position in public health administration. By sheer luck, the person who interviewed me was someone I'd known through my professional community for more than fifteen years. During the interview process he enthusiastically declared, "You'll be perfect in this job!" and within a few weeks, I received an offer. The pay was generous but because it was only part-time, I still wouldn't be able to support myself, and I decided to keep on schedule with my February 2010 decision.

I started work in November 2009. During those first weeks, I was in a trance. My inner life was so torn up and focused on Laurie and the cases against her that it felt was like an out-of-body experience to report to a job where I was supposed to do other things. I managed to get my ass to work on time and made sure I did everything within my power to please my supervisors. Luckily, I was able to meet my goal: they were happy and my job seemed secure. I frantically applied to every part-time job that I could, hoping to bring in the extra few thousand dollars a month I needed to meet my basic expenses.

Around that time, Soloman sent me an email that stated the information it contained was strictly confidential and could not be shared with anyone. I was being asked to verify the amounts of each of the Collective Good LLC investors including myself as part of the forensic accounting investigation. Soloman had a tight deadline for me to return the document, and so I worked tirelessly every night after work pouring over the Collective Good accounting books, my spreadsheets, and reams of bank records to make sure the numbers the trustee had were correct. He had separated the figures into two categories. One showed every deposit made into Laurie's accounts. The other was every dollar Laurie sent to each of the investors. His goal was to show who actually put in more money than they got back to make sure the list of victims was correct.

I found a lot of errors in his data including an extra $75,000 transferred from Laurie to Collective Good LLC. A month later when I sent him the corrected spreadsheets, I felt great thinking that I was helping prosecute the civil case against Laurie.

It had already been six months since the FBI got involved and they hadn't yet arrested her, although the newspapers showed people arrested for similar crimes all over the country. The other victims and I were upset and frustrated. They communicated their anger to me and expected me to do something about it. My mother also freely shared biting remarks she heard from family and friends. In their minds, I was the one responsible for getting them into this mess. Conversations with my mother solidified my feeling that the only way to make amends was to kill myself and leave everyone the money. I remained in friendly ongoing contact with Agent Mumford, who assured me that he was continuing to work on the case and that it simply was a slow process.

When I lived in New York City, I read the *New York Times* and *New York Post* every day to get the liberal and conservative and perspectives on life in the Big Apple. As I fumed about the delay in Laurie's arrest, I had a brainstorm about how to drum up media attention and put public pressure on the FBI. When I approached Louis about it, he was clear in his opinion: "Absolutely not. You are in no way to draw attention to yourself. Laurie is sly and will take any opportunity to place blame. If she sees your name or knows you're out in the front on this issue, she'll target you."

I also consulted the FBI. Agent Mumford's answer was succinct: "We prefer that no one involved in the case speak to the press because it could compromise their ability to provide testimony at a later date."

From my frustration grew a new plan. I created a new screen name on my AOL account and contacted several newspapers and local Long Island TV news programs with a summary of the story. I emphasized Laurie's charisma and highlighted the drama of her bizarre life. I didn't give any details that would interfere with the case. Within twenty-four hours, I had interest from a *New York Post* reporter who wanted to speak to me on the phone to confirm I was a real person. He wanted me to identify myself and tell him more about my relationship with Laurie. I heeded Louis's warning and remained anonymous by blocking my cell number before calling him. I gave the reporter as much general information as I could without giving away my identity. Prior to calling him, I had decided to call her "The Ponzi Princess," hoping the nickname would sensationalize the story and get some attention. Luckily, he liked it.

A few days later, *the New York Post* published an article titled "LI Biz Gal a Ponzi Princess." I was ecstatic that the paper decided to include a photo. I had given them the contact information for the photographer who took her wedding pictures. Laurie's face was now all over the greater New York metro area.

"She can't hide or pretend none of this is happening!" my mom yelled over the phone when I sent her the link. "I hope she rots in hell for what she has done to you, Mark."

"Well, hell or not, I think this warns others who know her to watch their backs and certainly keep their money away from her."

I played dumb when Troy contacted me because I didn't want anyone to know I had planted the story.

"I bet that crazy bitch is gonna try to hide her face all day long," he said in between loud laughs. "I am going to call that reporter and tell him what I know. The public needs to see the face of the victims!"

"I totally agree and understand your feelings, but just check with your lawyer first, because mine said the FBI probably doesn't want any potential witnesses telling their story to the press before a trial."

"Damn, you're probably right."

I sent the link of the article to Agent Mumford as though I had been told of the article by other investors. He didn't respond immediately, but a few weeks later, he emailed me asking to be in touch with other investors.

"Can you connect us to a few of your family and friends who lost money with Laurie as individuals before you started Collective Good? In building our case, it helps to have as many victims listed as possible, and because Collective Good is considered one big group we are looking for more individual victims. With the addition of each person, we can add years to the possible sentence."

I was excited. "Does this mean you're moving forward with pressing charges?"

He responded like any FBI agent should. "We always intended on pressing charges. This is just a step in the process."

I reached out to several of the people I had brought in who had initially invested as individuals before I started Collective Good. I got a resounding "No way" from most I contacted. When I spoke to Derek, my old college friend who had been an early investor, he seemed terrified. He spoke softly into the phone like a little boy. I could almost hear him shaking as he said, "I'm sorry, Mark. Please don't be disappointed, but I just can't talk to the FBI. Thank you for all you're doing, though." I hung up feeling so sad for him and full of remorse for ever bringing Laurie into his life. My call to him reminded me that many people felt incredible shame for having lost money, while others were traumatized. Thankfully, my Mom and a childhood friend agreed to share their stories with the FBI.

The conversation with Derek helped me understand the level of fear many people had. Most were attempting to simply not think about the pain of the situation. All of this helped motivate me to keep planning my death down to the last detail.

The apartment I had moved into was only one block from Ira's. The close proximity to my first boyfriend allowed us to see each other frequently for dinner and to share stories about guys we met. It had been more than ten years since we had dated, and we had since become more like brothers. During all this stress, I had found that eating copious amounts of sugar and having regular sex helped me to gather the strength to wake up each day. I continued the practice I began in New York of using online hook-up sites to find a few regular playmates. This did not quiet the desperation I felt to find another job, to put Laurie in jail, and to somehow make things right with my family and friends.

During one of our dinners, I begged Ira, a doctor in the San Francisco public health system, to ask around to see if any of his friends knew of jobs. Miracle upon miracles, he texted me the next week that someone I had worked with ten years before was looking for a project director of a University of California study focusing on HIV-positive inmates in the local jails. Prior to moving to New York, I had been the medical social worker and then briefly the director of the unit that served the HIV-positive jail population and therefore knew the local system like the back of my hand.

Ira had come through at my most desperate hour! After a few informal conversations with the principal investigator of the study, I was hired and began my second job in March 2010. Somehow, the universe was telling me that I was going to survive. Although the job was meant to be full-time, my new boss valued me enough to let me cut down the hours knowing that I'd do the work necessary to get the study on track. No one at the time knew that this second job literally saved my life.

The afternoon that I was hired for the study, I drove out to Lands End. It was a sunny day and few people were around because it was the middle of the week. I had paradise to myself for a few moments. I sat quietly, tears streaming down my face, as I thought about all that had happened during the past year and the many dreams lost along the way.

"I'm gonna get through this now," I said to myself.

The plan to kill myself was certainly a way to raise money to pay back the Collective Good investors, but it was also an escape from all my pain—and failure. I had given the universe my life, and I was given a second chance. Now it was time to rebuild my life.

Within a few months, I began telling those who were closest to me of what I had been planning and how I would never again put my life on the line. I received loving support from the family and friends with whom I shared my secret. I also told my brother that I wouldn't be renewing the life insurance policy. There would be no need to have that as an option ever again.

Soon after starting my second job, I received news from the FBI that Laurie would soon be arrested. I immediately contacted the *New York Post* reporter to let him know of the impending arrest. I also anonymously contacted all the local Long Island news stations. People in Long Island loved a sensational storyline, and I attempted to highlight the sex and lies in Laurie's melodrama as part of the impending scandal.

On April 13, 2010, all of her victims were very pleased to see that several New York newspapers and local television stations ran stories on her arrest that morning. Out of what I considered misplaced courtesy, the U.S. Attorney, who would be using evidence collected by the FBI to try the case, allowed Laurie to turn herself in rather than being arrested at her home.

News footage of the event shows an extra-bloated Laurie walking out of the courthouse with Beatty, the attorney I had met the night I found out the full truth about her scheme. She wore huge Jackie O glasses and looked as if she had her hair blown out for the occasion. In addition to the uncharacteristic blazer she had on to cover her cleavage, she wore a comfortable smile on her face as though this was all part of her plan. After all, she had simply walked in, been booked, paid bail, and left an hour later.

Walking from the opposite end of the parking lot to greet her daughter was Nancy, who looked Kardasian-coiffed in her signature white pantsuit. Plastered on her face was a creepy grin that gave away her discomfort and fear. Most surprisingly, Nancy was surrounded by three huge linebacker-sized men who walked in stride with her every step to provide protection from a crowd of expected onlookers. As the camera pulled away from a close-up of Laurie's mother, it was clear the parking lot was totally empty, making her look even more bizarre.

"When can we expect the trial to begin?" I naïvely asked Agent Mumford later that week. I thought an arrest meant that things were finally moving.

"Be patient, it'll be awhile. We're waiting to get a final amount of the fraud from the trustee and continue our investigation."

Disappointed, I didn't want to lose the opportunity to find out all I could, knowing the investors would soon be asking me for an update. "Why did you use wire fraud as the charge instead of the Ponzi scheme?"

"We're still investigating the situation and may add other charges."

Out of desperation, I put in a call to Betty, Laurie's assistant, to see if I could glean any helpful information from her that I could pass along to the FBI. I had heard that although she and her boyfriend had lost a substantial amount of money, she had chosen to keep working with Laurie out of loyalty and in hopes that Laurie would find a way to pay her back. It took Betty a few days to call me back after I texted her to check in. When the phone rang, I was out for a walk on a hill close to my apartment.

"Hi, Mawk. How you doin'?" she said in her characteristic sweet voice. "How's your mom's health these days?" We made small talk for a while before I asked her more pointed questions about Laurie. "How can you still work with her after all you know she has done to everyone?"

Her tone was blunt. "I don't ask questions. I just believe that she's gonna take care of me in the end."

Her words enraged me but I didn't want to lash out because she was a close tie to Laurie.

"You know, I'm in a really bad place and am trying to figure out all that happened. All those times you told everyone that you had been down to the docks with Laurie in the early morning and all those meetings with Dick that you supposedly went to with Laurie—what was that all about?"

There was a brief silence. "I nevah got out of the car at the docks. She sometimes called me at four or five in the morning to go down but probably only like three or four times total. I would sit in the car, and she would get out and go into a building."

"But, Betty, you told everyone that you were with her when she bought the closeouts and even made jokes about how all the Jewish men in black hats would stare at you. Remember all the times we all talked about that?"

"Laurie's the one who told me to say those things, so I did." She quickly added, "I didn't know nothing was wrong with what I was saying. I thought Laurie was just keeping her . . . you know, trade secrets about the closeouts."

From the hill I was standing on, I could see the whole city of San Francisco below me. It helped remind me that I was safe and this gave me strength.

"What about all the meetings with Dick that you went to with Laurie? At least two times a week you two went to his office to get a check or discuss new deals." I paused then remembered a little tidbit. "Oh yeah, wasn't Dick trying to hook you up with someone he knew so he and Laurie could double-date with you?"

There was an uncomfortable pause. "I never went into the office. I stayed in the reception place while Laurie went in with Dick. He never had anyone to fix me up with. All that was just Laurie telling stories."

"But so many times when Laurie was discussing the specifics about a meeting with Dick, you'd back her up."

"Yeah, Laurie told me stuff to say." There was another pause. "I'm gettin' uncomfortable with all of this. I like you, Mawk, but Laurie hasn't done all you said she did. She was just trying to help us all make money. We was greedy and got too caught up in everything."

When she hung up the phone with me, I just stood frozen for a little time while all the new information seeped in. Then I screamed at the top of my lungs, "Fuck you, Laurie Schneider."

Six weeks later, I heard news from Troy that turned my stomach sour.

"The bitch is pregnant!"

My first question was a logical one for anyone who actually knew Laurie. "Who's the father?"

He laughed. "Supposedly Vince. What a putz to keep fucking her even when she has been such a horrible person to him."

"Jesus, do you know how many abortions she told me she's had? She was always adamant that she never wanted to actually carry a baby. Vince told me himself that he never wanted to be a father especially with Laurie, who he thought would be the worst mother in the world."

Troy sounded despondent on the other end of the line. "Can you believe this?

"She got pregnant a month after she was arrested so she could get sympathy from the judge. Who wants to put a pregnant lady or a mom with a newborn in prison? She's so fucking good at manipulating everything!"

I didn't have much time to adjust to the news of her pregnancy before I received two large envelopes from the trustee. The pit in my stomach gave me warning before I opened the mail. Soloman, who had asked for my help in determining the correct amounts of deposits to and payments from Laurie, was suing me personally for $500,000 and Collective Good for $5,000,000. Louis had been correct in fearing that Soloman would sue for clawbacks.

From all the stress of the past year, I was used to living with panic, but seeing the huge amounts took the wind out of me and I sat down to review the full documents. The suits used the exact numbers I had provided Soloman a few months earlier.

"What a fucking prick!" I said to no one. "And I walked right into his trap."

The lawsuits demanded repayment for every cent that had been paid out of Laurie's accounts to me and Collective Good, regardless of the amount that was originally invested.

I immediately emailed Louis, who got back to me right away with a message to call him as soon as possible.

"The suit does not take into account any of the money that we put into Laurie's accounts as investments. It's like Soloman's totally forgetting that we all invested money with Laurie in order for her to pay us back. "

"This is what I was afraid of but had no idea he would go about it this way."

"How do I deal with this? This is too much for you to advise me on. I need another attorney, right?"

"Yes, someone who specializes in bankruptcy law." Louis was always consistent in his tone.

"But I don't want to declare bankruptcy. I want to fight this. It makes no sense."

"I know this is upsetting, Mark, but you have to focus. This suit is filed in the U.S. Bankruptcy Court. You need an attorney with expertise in that area. He or she can advise you on a strategy. I will of course be here for you."

"Jeez, this never ends. I mean she's out there enjoying her life and probably scamming someone right now, but we have to prove to the courts that we didn't take advantage of her and basically steal money from her estate? SHE is the con artist!"

It turned out that anyone who had invested individually with Laurie had been sued by the trustee. The suits didn't take into account the losses that people had through Collective Good. Soloman had ignored the fact that many people had initially made money as individuals investing directly with Laurie, but had then reinvested and lost it all through the investments made by Collective Good. The amounts of the suits ranged from a few thousand dollars to millions; it all depended on how much the individual had invested and gotten back over time.

My family and friends who had been sued were extremely upset. Like me, most had never been sued before and wanted to take care of the situation as soon as possible. Because the case had been filed in New York, it made sense to get a local attorney. Luckily, a friend named in the suit found a qualified attorney in Brooklyn. Sarah Goldman was someone about my age with twenty years of bankruptcy experience. After she took my friend's case, I called her to see about taking mine.

The first words out of her mouth were not what I wanted to hear: "I recommend you declare bankruptcy so the lawsuit can be discharged and you'll owe nothing."

I shot back, "Don't you want to hear anything about my actual situation before steering me in that direction?"

"Yes, of course, but please understand that no matter what direction you take, my initial retainer is $5,000, and my hourly rate is $350."

I was furious that Laurie continued living free while I was forced to use credit cards to pay an attorney to defend Collective Good and myself. The attorney had one final statement as part of her sales pitch.

"I want to add that I know the trustee well. We've worked together before, and in fact he sometimes uses my office space when he needs to do business in Brooklyn. I'll be able to speak to him on your behalf aside from formal correspondence."

With that bit of information, I hired Sarah Goldman and began to tell my side of the story. Within a short amount of time, she spoke to the trustee to get a sense of his take on my cases.

"Because of your close relationship with Laurie, Soloman considers you an 'insider' or someone who should have known what was going on. I don't see that he is going to be willing to negotiate on either case." This logic was incredibly confusing because the FBI considered me a key witness for the prosecution in the criminal case. It seemed very unfair that the trustee had a whole other set of rules that he used to judge for the civic case.

Although I pushed Sarah to explore every legal option, during the next six months her initial statements to me proved to be true. Soloman somehow thought of me, out of all the people sued, as a villain, and it seemed all of our earlier conversations were just a ruse for him to pick my brain and get information he needed from me. Unfortunately, the generous bonus Laurie had given me from the first China Deal was the cause for the lawsuit against me.

In the end, the only way out of my personal case was to declare bankruptcy. Fortunately, the plummeting housing market had left Hazel and my mom's house with almost no value. When I thought Laurie's investments were real, I had taken out $300,000 in home equity loans to give her. Legally, I was still only 25 percent owner of Hazel and had not paid off Joe or Nate, so that extra debt kept my holdings in the house at a low value. All of this helped me keep both properties after the bankruptcy proceedings.

By the time I stood before the Bankruptcy Court judge to discuss my personal case, I had adjusted to the idea of letting go of this particular fight. Unlike most of the people in the courtroom whose faces showed that this was an all-time low point in their lives, I actually felt a certain kind of freedom. I had been struggling to survive and fighting to get justice for two years. It turned out the legal system had a direct and simple way for me to move on with my life.

With my urging, Sarah negotiated a special deal with Soloman for the Collective Good case that enabled it to end. The agreement enabled Collective Good investors to state in the final document that we didn't agree with the suit or believe that the surrender clause indicated guilt in any way. It was simply a lack of finances that prevented me from fighting that case for the years it would take to possibly win. A $5 million judgment remains open against Collective Good, LLC.

In January 2012, when my personal bankruptcy was finally approved, it signified a new beginning for me. Although I had been current on all my debt, I now had bad credit for years to come thanks to my involvement with

Laurie, who delivered a boy in 2011 and from what I heard from Troy, continued living a comfortable lifestyle. During a phone conversation, he told me a funny story about Leah, who had worked for Laurie in Party Hearty as a manager and had invested both her family's money in the China Deals.

"One night Leah's husband, Bill, dropped off their daughter at a bat mitzvah party, and as he walked her in, he saw Laurie, who was the event planner, across the room. She took one look at him and ran the hell away. He followed her through the kitchen and then let her go when he saw her run to her car, lock the door, and start the engine."

I laughed out loud. "Oh my God, that is funny. I can't picture her being that scared, after all the harm she's done to so many people."

"He said she looked terrified. All he expected to do was talk, but she acted like he was trying to murder her. Can you picture that *fat* ass jiggling as she ran through the building? Someone should shoot the evil bitch," Troy spat out in his raspy voice.

"I've thought the same thing so many times over the years, but I'm glad to know at least she lives in fear. She's gonna get punished, Troy. The Feds can't just drop a case that they've said all along is ironclad."

"It's just not fucking fair that the monster gets to live her life as though nothing is gonna happen to her."

After I hung up, I thought about that night in San Francisco a few years before when I still thought Laurie's deals were real and I was contemplating my next step in life—as though I actually had any control over what was about to happen to me and my family. I had woken myself up with a powerful message to *write it all down.*

I sat looking out my window, letting the whole story of Laurie Schneider go through my mind. I realized it was finally time to put the story down on paper. Of course, I wanted to warn other people so there would be no more victims. The less altruistic motivation is that I wanted justice. Almost four years had passed and all Laurie had gotten was a metaphorical slap on the wrist. Through her lies, she had been a devastating force that destroyed my hopes and dreams along with those of so many people I cared deeply about.

With a fire in my belly and a million thoughts going through my mind, I walked over to my dining table, flipped open the laptop, took a deep breath, and began to finally tell the tale of the Ponzi Princess. If the courts didn't get it right, I wanted the truth about this horrible chapter in my life to be told.

Preparing for Trial

At the beginning of January 2014, I emailed Ben Mumford to check the status of the case. He had told me in the fall of 2013 to contact him in early in the New Year because they anticipated having a date for the trial.

I had sold Hazel in December 2013 due to costs of maintaining the property which I could no longer afford. After paying what I owed to Nate and Joe for their shares in the house, I had barely enough to pay off the loans I had taken out to invest with Laurie. Through the nightmare process of getting my tenants to move out and realizing this was just another failure in a long list of failures, I maintained hope that 2014 would bring an end to this horrible chapter. The new year would bring a trial that would result in Laurie going to prison. I kept my thoughts positive when I sent the email to the FBI agent.

"Hi, Ben, it's been FIVE years since Schneider told me about the Ponzi. What's happening with the case? Can't believe she is still free and unpunished after all this time."

He responded within the hour. "Great timing. I wanted to ask whether you would be willing to give the U.S. Attorneys a lesson about the details of Schneider's scheme. We plan on going to trial on March 17th."

I was thrilled that there was movement in the case. I emailed him back right away: "Sounds great! You know I'll do anything I can to put her behind bars. Just let me know what you need from me."

It took a few weeks of our emailing back and forth to find a date and time that worked for everyone. It turned out there were two U.S. Attorneys working on the case and two FBI agents who were familiar with the facts. My understanding was that I would be providing background information to the team so everyone had a thorough understanding of the case.

The morning of the call, I woke up excited and a little nervous. After the bankruptcy trustee had lured me into a trusting relationship, then used everything I shared with him against me in two ludicrously huge lawsuits, I was extremely wary of all those involved in this case. I also remembered Louis repeatedly telling me to be careful. I knew a trial would mean that I would be able to present all the substantial facts about the case, but that I would also be scrutinized heavily under cross-examination. Even though I had nothing to hide, I assumed Laurie and her lawyers would try to discredit me any way they could. I didn't trust that the U.S. Attorneys or FBI would do anything to protect me, so I wanted to figure out a way to take care of myself. I decided to record my end of the phone call using a digital recorder. This would ensure that I could verify everything I said for future reference—in case things got complicated with my relationship with the attorneys or the FBI.

I sat gazing out of my apartment window overlooking the bucolic park across the street. The sun was shining brightly on the San Francisco chilly day. The phone rang a few minutes after our agreed-upon time of eleven in the morning. Each of the four people introduced themselves: Stephen Donaldson and Sheila Stevens were the U.S. Attorneys on the case; Ben Mumford and Frederick Lopez were the FBI agents. Before we began, I asked for some clarity on their expectations of me.

"Could someone let me know if I am training you all on the facts of the case, or am I being tutored to be a witness—because how I interact with you on each of these situations would be very different."

Ms. Stevens authoritatively called out, "Don't worry about all of that. Just tell us the story of you and Laurie Schneider."

I paused for a second, not sure how to proceed. They had not given me clear direction. I decided that since the FBI agent had initially said I was there to provide training for them, I'd tell them everything I knew. I launched into how Laurie and I met at Gregory's birthday party in November 2005 and continued the story. Several times, I checked in with the group to ask, "Is this what you are looking for—I mean, is this helpful?" Everyone assured me that the information was useful to them and that I should continue.

About fifteen minutes into my story, when I began getting questions that made no sense, I realized the group held very little knowledge of the case.

"So Schneider's husband was the source of the real estate that she was flipping?" asked Donaldson.

His statement was ludicrous. Vince wasn't at all involved with Laurie's real estate schemes. "No, Schneider's husband had nothing to do with anything with FlippingMax Real Estate. She told us that it was her two Latina housekeepers who introduced her to poor people from their churches who were on the verge of foreclosure. Floyd Durgin was the guy she said was her real estate mentor."

Later, when I mentioned the bankruptcy trustee, the attorneys seemed to have no context of what I meant. "You mean you had to declare bankruptcy?" Ms. Stevens asked.

"Yes, in response to being sued by the bankruptcy trustee, I declared bankruptcy because I had no money to pay back what they said I owed."

Donaldson jumped in. "You mean a trustee was assigned to your bankruptcy case?"

I responded as evenly as possible, even though I was getting annoyed with their lack of knowledge. "No, a trustee was assigned to Schneider's bankruptcy case after an investor sued her and forced her into bankruptcy." I went on to explain the process of clawbacks because they seemed to have no knowledge of the civil court process that had been operating parallel with their efforts for the past five years. It was infuriating to me that they seemed to have no relationship with the civil court or understanding of the deep forensic analysis of Schneider's bank accounts, which should have yielded important evidence for the criminal case.

The next range of questions from Donaldson led to a very uncomfortable exchange. As I was explaining the trajectory of my relationship with Schneider and her deals in which I was investing, Donaldson kept asking, "Didn't you know something was suspicious about these deals?"

I responded quickly, "No, we all believed everything was real until we found out it wasn't. Remember, my neighbors had been investing with her for years and doing well. Then I met other people in her sphere who also had been making money with her; these included her former accountant and other high-level business people . . . and she showed us falsified financial statements and invoices." I continued to explain the details of each type of investment and how Laurie convinced me to open up Collective Good LLC.

"Didn't you know something was suspicious about these deals at THAT point?" he spat out.

I paused. I was very annoyed. After five years, it seemed the attorney in charge of prosecuting Laurie didn't know the basic timeline of the case. "I'm hoping by now that all of you understand that no one knew anything was wrong until January 2009 when Laurie told me some of the deals were fake and stopped paying everyone." I knew I had an edge in my voice as I continued to explain that the summary document I prepared for the FBI in 2009 explained all the dates. "So I hope you won't ask me again when I knew it was a Ponzi." I had not filtered my annoyance in my choice or words or tone.

Donaldson made a grunt then yelled, "Look, you can answer the questions voluntarily, or I can subpoena you and fly you out here! Understand?"

I couldn't believe he was being such a prick when I was trying to help them. I tried to remain calm; this was a deputy U.S. Attorney. "Yes I understand. And hopefully you get that I've been waiting five years for this case to go to trial, and the way I responded was appropriate to all the emotion related to this situation for me."

My response infuriated Donaldson. "Cut the attitude. Don't you understand that I work for the federal court system and can force you to cooperate?"

I wanted to placate him. "Yes, I do, Mr. Donaldson. I respect the court system and hope to be helpful in putting Laurie Schneider behind bars. If you look at your files, you'll see I've made substantial contributions to your evidence and strategy. I've been waiting a long time for this opportunity."

He kept yelling. "You're here to assist us, not the other way around!" His ranting at me continued. I was surprised no one on his end intervened or helped mediate the situation. This went on for a few minutes. Finally, I had had enough. I spoke calmly but with authority. "Mr. Donaldson, I have forty-five minutes before I have to be back at work. Let's be productive and move on." There was silence on the other end of the phone for a few seconds, and then thankfully the other attorney began another line of questioning. We proceeded discussing the case for another twenty minutes.

A few minutes after I hung up, I received a call from Ben, the FBI agent who had been on the call.

"That was intense, wasn't it?" he said in a friendly way. "But listen, you have to be prepared for handling your emotions better when you are on the stand during trial."

"I'm really frustrated. I specifically asked at the beginning of the call whether I was being trained to be a witness or there to help train everyone on the facts of the case," I said quickly in response.

"Yeah, you are right," he conceded.

"And Donaldson was a total asshole to me . . . sorry for my language."

Ben laughed. "No, you're right. He was really after you. I'm not sure what was going on with him today."

I knew that part of Donaldson's frustration is that he was never supposed to try this case. It had been left to him to babysit by another deputy U.S. Attorney who had chosen another assignment for a year. When that attorney never came back, Donaldson was responsible for moving the case forward. I'd been dealing with Ben since March 2009; we had a better rapport. He explained that a few days before the trial, they would fly me out to Long Island to prepare me for testifying. "The pretrial session will probably be two full days. You're a key witness, so we'll bring you on the stand early."

Over the next six weeks, I was excited to finally have the case move to court. I was not looking forward to the cross-examination and having Laurie's lawyers try to tear me apart, but it was worth it to put her ass in jail. I was actually getting hopeful that this nightmare would end soon.

Two weeks before the trial date, I emailed Ben to check in about plans for me to be flown out for the preparation work.

I received his response in a few minutes. "Great timing. We just found out she's going to enter a guilty plea. So no trial. The hearing should be February 28th."

At first I was elated—finally an end was in sight! Ben made it clear that because she was entering a plea bargain, she would be officially charged for only one of the seven charges against her.

"What does that mean for her sentence?" I wrote him.

"She won't do the maximum sentence of twenty years attached to all the charges. Her time will be reduced to something like five to seven years."

I sat looking at his words. The time didn't seem long enough to punish her for all she'd done, but it was still substantial and that made me happy. I went online to book my flight and make hotel arrangements. I notified Ben that I'd be coming in for the hearing.

A few weeks later I got on a plane feeling calm and confident. All the frustration and misery of the past five years would be coming to a close soon. I'd done my part in putting her in jail. I looked forward to hearing her say the word, "Guilty."

The hearing would take place at the Central Islip federal courthouse in the heart of Long Island. As I drove the rental car, I was aware I had not been back to Long Island since 2009 during the worst of the nightmare. I chose to take the same route to Long Island that I used to drive when I worked for Laurie. It felt weird to be returning back to a place that held such misery for me.

The courthouse is a stately, white modern building in the midst of several acres of trees. Walking up its long stairway to the entrance, I felt dwarfed by its size and hopeful that the system would finally bring justice to my situation. After going through a rigorous security screening, I walked down a long hallway filled with floor-to-ceiling windows with magnificent views of the acres of land around the building. The courtroom was at the end of the majestic hallway. I chose a seat across the aisle from where I assumed Laurie would be sitting. I sat alone taking in the formality of the room and getting ready for what was about to happen.

The room looked like something off the set of a legal-drama television show. Its walls were covered in warm wood paneling. There was a waist-high wooden wall separating the area where the public sat from the judge, attorneys, and others involved in the case. Beyond the wall were two desks to the left and right, where opposing attorneys sat with their clients. In between the desks was a podium where witnesses gave testimony. On the wall opposite from the public entrance was the judge's impressive dais, which spanned a huge portion of the width of the room. I sat on one of the ten wooden benches on the right side of the room and waited quietly. The security guards had taken my phone so I had no distraction from staying present.

A few minutes later, the U.S. Attorney and FBI agent entered. I stood and shook Ben's hand. It was nice to see him again after five years of emailing and a few phone calls. The greeting between the U.S. Attorney and me was much more awkward. Neither of us made an effort to shake hands but both said a brief hello. The two men kept walking forward and put the folders they were carrying on the wooden desk in front of them.

Rick Beatty, Laurie's attorney, entered a minute later. Dressed in a finely tailored suit, he looked the same as when I last saw him—the day he insinuated that Laurie had been running a Ponzi. I took in a deep breath and let it out as I remembered that horrible day and the aftermath that led us to this hearing. He briskly walked in and put his papers on the desk to the left and went over to Donaldson to offer his hand.

"So which one of the seven charges is she pleading to again?" Beatty asked Donaldson.

"Number two . . . the one where Morewitz was victim," Donaldson responded.

"Ah . . . the ever-present Mr. Morewitz," said Beatty, and both men let out a laugh. Neither of the men liked me. I was a thorn in the side of Laurie's case—the one always nudging the FBI and U.S. Attorney to move forward. And of course, Donaldson and I had not had a good start with the training conference call earlier in the year.

I stood up and cleared my throat loud enough for the two men to notice. My strategy worked. Both men looked over at me and stopped laughing, then separated and went back to their respective desks. *"They may not like me, but there is no fucking way they're going to disrespect me after all I've done to push the case to this courtroom,"* I thought as I took my seat. I took another deep breath and let it out.

A few minutes later, a small group of people huddled close together walked in. In the midst of the entourage, I saw Laurie, much heavier and without the glamorous image. Her hair was now shoulder length and her natural dark color. She was wearing a long black sweater that covered her heft like something Bea Arthur would have worn in her heavier *Maude* days.

As she sat down, I felt my eyes turn into a laser beam focused on the woman who had taken so much from me. She had caused me so much heartache and pain. For the past five years, I had endured on my own to push the legal system to punish her. During that time, I had lost many family and friends who no longer wanted anything to do with me. I had been forced into bankruptcy and had let go of many hopes and dreams of what I thought my life would be. I couldn't take my eyes off her as I let all these experiences and feelings wash over me. I could see she was aware of me but didn't look over. True to her nature, she was instead seductively making small talk with one of her attorney's staff. From across the room I could hear her call the man "sweetheart" and reach over to touch his hand and arm. It was typical Laurie Schneider, Seduction 101. I could see that he was under her spell even though all the facts of the case clearly showed she was guilty of defrauding so many of us.

My attention was diverted as Judge Dennis Hurley entered the room. He was an older white gentleman with a tired-sounding raspy voice—of course with a Long Island accent. He asked us all to sit down. As he began to talk, I felt my eyes go back to staring at Laurie, and several of her entourage immediately turned to look back at me. I ignored them as I let my gaze continue to be on her, all the while keeping my ears focused on the trial proceedings. Her attorneys and members of the group who accompanied her turned their heads toward me, somehow disturbed that I was staring so intently at her. I ignored the reaction of others and let my process continue. I hadn't planned it, but somehow I was letting go and transferring all the misery I'd been carrying for five years to the monster across the room. It felt incredibly healing.

The judge spent some time going over logistics with the U.S. Attorney and Schneider's lawyer. He asked Donaldson to verify which charge would be put forth for Schneider to plead; he then confirmed with her lawyer if he was in agreement with the specific charge for the plea. After ten minutes of logistical conversation with the lawyers, he turned his attention to Laurie.

In a warm tone that sounded as if he were talking to someone he deeply cared about, the judge began speaking to the monster who had destroyed my life. "Ms. Schneider, it's my understanding that you may be changing your plea today. Before we move forward, I want to make sure you are aware of all the options you have. Do you understand that if you choose to go to trial, you could win the case and not have to plead guilty?"

Laurie moved her face close to the microphone and in a deep, gravelly voice said, "Yes."

Continuing in a paternalistic tone that made my stomach ache from anger, the judge spent the next *forty-five* minutes going through a litany of issues that he made sure Laurie understood before making her choice to plead guilty: she'd lose her right to vote; she may be sentenced to prison; she would have to pay restitution to victims. It felt as though he was encouraging her not to plead guilty and to have hope that she would have a chance at a trial.

Finally, when the judge had exhausted his list of things to discuss, he asked if she was ready to change her plea. A huge smile crept across my face as my eyes continued to bore a hole in her soul.

She turned to her attorney for affirmation. He nodded and silently pointed to the microphone. "Yes, Your Honor," she said softy.

"For the charge of wire fraud against John Doe number two in the amount of $200,000 committed in October of 2007, what do you say, Ms. Schneider?"

"Guilty." She had barely been able to spit out the word, but it was audible enough for us to hear. She had finally admitted guilt and it was to my charge! In that moment I felt a huge weight lift from me. I stopped staring at her and closed my eyes. I felt whole and elated.

The judge gave a sentencing hearing date of May 28th and dismissed the hearing. The FBI agent came right over to congratulate me.

"That went well, although I've never seen the judge spend so much time going through the list he talked about today," the agent said.

"Yeah, what was that about?" I responded. "That part didn't give me confidence that the judge was impartial."

The U.S. Attorney walked up at that moment and responded to my statement. "The judge is a very fair man and was just making sure Schneider understood what she was doing before pleading. Not a big deal at all."

The FBI agent spoke next. "Listen, don't get a plane ticket for the May hearing yet. It's likely to be delayed. A parole officer is assigned to do a report and make sentencing recommendations."

As he reached out to shake my hand, Laurie quietly scooted past him and out the door. I didn't take my focus from the FBI agent; I had spent enough time and attention on the monster for the day.

I walked to the elevator and heard Laurie's attorney speaking to one of the men in her entourage who had seemed most upset by me staring. They became silent as I walked up to the elevator. When the door opened, I walked in ahead of them and stood in the back. The entourage man kept turning to look at me angrily, but he only made me smile. Laurie Schneider had just pled guilty to a charge that carried a prison sentence. No one was going to rain on my parade!

A few weeks later, I emailed the U.S. Attorney's Victim Notification Unit to get the contact information for Nate Silverman, the parole officer who had been assigned to the case. Mr. Silverman responded to my introductory voicemail within a day. He was warm and freely gave a brief explanation of what his role was in the sentencing process.

"I'll interview Ms. Schneider and all the victims to get a sense of the situation so I can make recommendations to the judge regarding Ms. Schneider's sentence."

I didn't understand why more investigation had to happen. "The FBI's been investigating the case for five years. Are you saying that you have to start over again with each victim? I'm not quite sure what the actual process is."

Mr. Silverman explained that because Laurie had already pled guilty, his role was not to investigate but to get a sense from the victims how extensive the impact of her crime was on each person. Through that process, he would develop sentencing recommendations. Although the procedure seemed like overkill, it was good to know what to expect.

After our phone call, I sent him a long email explaining my history with Laurie and a document listing all the Collective Good losses. He thanked me for my information and ended his email by saying, "I'm so sorry this happened to you and your family. It sounds devastating." It felt good to finally have someone working on the case who seemed to have empathy for the victims.

In the beginning of May, I reached out to Mr. Silverman again to see if the May sentencing hearing was going to be delayed. I was horrified at what he said in his response. "I've not been able to interview Schneider because she is having a complicated high-risk pregnancy. She's isn't supposed to leave her house until she has the baby in September."

I sat looking at the words in his email. She'd gotten pregnant with her second child soon after having her son. Now she was carrying her third. My bet was that she wanted the judge to have sympathy for a mother of a newborn and toddlers. "Mr. Silverman, she's lying to you and will continue to lie about everything you ask her until she goes to prison. I encourage you to get two doctors to verify her high-risk pregnancy. I am confident she is leaving the house to continue to work and scam others. And if she cannot come to you, please consider going to her home to interview her. This is a scheme to delay the sentencing." Silverman thanked me and said he'd look into getting verification but reiterated that the sentencing would not take place in May.

I called Donaldson and found out he was supportive of the hearing delay. "Of course I agreed to the delay. She should have time to have her child."

"The parole officer said he had verified her claim that she's under doctor's orders to not leave her home. Did you verify anything with her doctors?" I said, trying not to get too reactive and start a fight.

"Listen, I know her attorney. Like me, he is a member of the Bar, and I trust he would not do anything outside the realm of ethical behavior."

I let out an audible sigh, "For the record, you are allowing her to manipulate you and the court. She is a liar and her attorney is helping her. But I guess we victims have no power in this decision, so I'll see you whenever the hearing takes place."

Within a few days, I received notice from the U.S. Attorney's Victim Notification Unit noting that the May sentencing date had been postponed until September 26th. The parole officer told me that she was supposed to deliver her baby the week before.

In early September, I wrote a letter to the judge, copying the U.S. Attorney and the parole officer in an attempt to preempt Laurie's next move. The judge had scheduled the hearing on the second day of Rosh Hashanah and a week after she was due to give birth. It was almost like he was spoonfeeding her ideas for her next delay request.

Dear Judge Hurley,

I write to request that you reject any request by Laurie Schneider's attorneys to delay her sentencing date; there are no valid reasons to delay her sentencing any further. It has taken almost six years for the justice system to sentence Schneider; she has already been able to negotiate (via plea bargain) down from seven felony charges to just one. You previously gave her several months' delay in the sentencing date to allow her to have her baby in the community. There is no reason for further leniency for Schneider, who has already pled guilty to her crime.

Schneider is not observant and would not normally observe the holiday, especially the second day, which most American Jews do not observe. Additionally, she will have counsel present; it does not matter that a co-counsel will not be in court. Her legal rights will be protected.

If for some reason, you do decide to delay the sentencing, please reschedule for the soonest date possible—and check the Jewish calendar before you set a new date. There is no legitimate reason to delay her sentencing for any significant period of time.

When you do sentence this criminal, please remember that she devastated our lives through her crimes and deserves the most severe punishment the law will allow.

Thank you.

Mark Morewitz

I received word from the parole officer that Schneider had requested a delay due to her "observance of the Jewish High Holy Day." I wasn't surprised but was still infuriated that she was given the chance to use this excuse, because I knew it was difficult for the court to refuse. I called Donaldson and was surprised that he was frustrated too.

"She's just using this as an excuse," he said.

"Yeah, I tried telling you that about her pregnancy. Trust me, her next thing will be her children's health and maybe postpartum depression. You

guys should know better than to trust someone you know is a sociopath."
I offered to round up some victims to write the judge so he would feel
some pressure from the victims' side. I emailed the Collective Good folks,
and about a dozen people agreed to contact the U.S. Attorney or write
the judge directly. When I heard back from Donaldson a few days later,
he said that the judge had taken notice of the other victims' letters but
felt he had to honor the delay request because it was a religious holiday.
The new date of the hearing would be October 3rd, which was only a week
later. I was happy to hear that the judge also stated that he would accept
no more requests for hearing delays from Laurie's attorney.

I was also pleased that finally the court and the justice system were
recognizing Laurie as a pathetic liar. Because I only had a week to make
travel arrangements, the trip would cost me almost fifteen hundred dollars, but I still felt it was worth it to drain my bank account to see this stage
of the process firsthand.

The week of the new hearing date, I heard from the parole officer
that the judge turned down another request to delay because Laurie's
children were supposedly sick. I could feel her desperation through the
last pathetic excuse, and I loved thinking of her as a caged animal with
nowhere to run.

The morning of the hearing, I woke up in my Manhattan hotel room. I
had planned to take the train this time, and before I jumped in the shower
to get ready I checked my phone for messages. There was a voicemail
from the Victim Notification Unit and one from Donaldson. Both said that
something had happened and they needed to speak to me immediately.

My first thought was that Laurie had killed herself. I sat on the bed
looking out the window letting that sink in for a minute. It felt good. It felt
right. I knew she would only cause more destruction, and I hoped that her
kids would be better off without being raised by a crazy person.

However, my assumption was just a fantasy. When I called the U.S.
Victim Unit back, I was told that the judge had a "personal emergency"
and the hearing was postponed. I very much appreciated the courtesy
and respect that Donaldson showed by calling me personally. The Victim

Unit staff member told me that Donaldson even offered to meet me at the courthouse if I wanted to talk about anything to do with the case or show him the statement I planned to read. I was highly suspicious that the judge had found his own reason to postpone the hearing to give Laurie more time with her children. However, I knew that—like lightning striking twice in the same place—it was quite unlikely that the hearing would be delayed further and so looked forward to November 7th, the new hearing date.

In the month in between, I rewrote the statement I planned to read. My previous version was full of vitriol. As the date of the new hearing approached, my internal tone shifted. I simply wanted to be effective in helping the judge to understand that Laurie's crime was not one simply about stolen money but also about the twisted way that she enmeshed herself with all her victims' lives, leaving us all broke and deeply betrayed. I also realized that for the first time since February 2009, I'd be face to face with her when I walked up to read the statement. In my private moments, I felt the sadness that was underneath all the anger I had for her, the bankruptcy trustee, and everyone involved in the criminal proceedings. Although I was still eager to attend the hearing, my feelings were now mixed, and I was feeling vulnerable—not a good place to be in when the Ponzi Princess is around.

The Perp Walks the Plank

On November 7, 2014, I felt quiet inside. I didn't know what to expect and so kept in touch with my curiosity, doing my best to protect my heart. As I walked into the courtroom, I wasn't surprised to be alone. I expected a repeat of the last hearing where there was no one present in the audience but me. I was proven wrong a few minutes later as a dozen of Laurie's family and supporters walked in huddled around her. I stood to get a look at who was in the group. Betty was next to Nancy and Rachel, Laurie's sister. The two other women in the group looked like her two older half-sisters I recognized from photos Laurie had shown me years ago. The posse completely ignored me as they filled the first two pews. Laurie waddled to the desk next to her two attorneys. She had gained substantial weight with her pregnancy. The man in her legal team who had seemed so upset with my staring at the last hearing walked over and sat in the seat in front of me. Every few minutes he'd turn around to flare his nostrils at me.

Troy walked in soon after Laurie's group sat down. He was dressed in a gray velvet sports jacket, colorful patterned shirt, and tailored pants—and was definitely the best dressed gay man in the room. I had worn simple brown pants and a black wool blazer looking typically Banana Republic business casual. I stood and gave him a hug.

As he looked around, Troy mumbled, "I'm not sure where to sit."

I pointed to the section where Laurie's entourage was and quietly said, "The crazies are over there. Come sit next to me."

The man from her entourage who had sat in front of me immediately stood up and approached the bailiff, who in turn walked over to the U.S. Attorney. Donaldson was soon standing over me.

"Mr. Morewitz, we can have no disruptive behavior or the bailiff will ask you to leave," Donaldson said. The man in front of me was now flashing a wide smile at me.

"*What a pathetic dick*," I thought, but I knew I may have done the same thing when I was under her spell.

"Mark didn't say anything loud or disruptive, but we'll make sure we stay quiet," Troy said. His statement satisfied Donaldson, who walked away. I explained the situation to Troy, who was confused about why the guy in front of us would have lied to the bailiff. It was just the beginning of a very bizarre two hours.

"Oh my God! Look at how *huge* the monster got," Troy spat out as we both looked at Laurie. Her back was wide like a football player. She looked tired and haggard in her dark blue blazer. Unlike the flirtatious behavior from the last meeting, she was instead rocking back and forth with the added effect of ringing her hands while looking down at the table. She was either very scared or putting on a good act; knowing her, I assumed the latter.

I glanced over at the group of her supporters. Betty looked heavier and every one of her fifty-five years but still had the gorgeous mane of Christie Brinkley blonde hair. Nancy must have just gotten a full face lift. Her tight skin was covered in far too much makeup. Newly applied filler puffed up her ridiculous looking cheeks and lips. From the side view, she looked like a mannequin made to look as though she was puckering up for a kiss.

"Where's her father?" Troy whispered in his raspy voice.

"He died this summer," I said. "Sometimes when I can't sleep late at night, I cyber-spy on Laurie on Facebook. Her sister posted about their dad's death in June. There are also pictures of Laurie's first two toddlers."

"Who's the father?" Troy asked sarcastically. "'Cause we know it may not be Vince!"

I laughed. "They look just like him, though, so maybe they are his. Can you believe he kept having sex with her after all he knew about what she'd done?"

Troy didn't hesitate in his response. "He knows who takes care of him. She's his sugar momma and keeps him stocked with drugs and booze."

I thought about what he was saying for a moment. It was still shocking that Vince stayed with Laurie and kept getting her pregnant. He had loudly pronounced many times in my presence that he never wanted kids, but in the end he had three children with a woman who was sure to be going to prison. It didn't make any sense, but then again nothing did in Laurieland.

As the judge entered the room I checked in with myself. I didn't feel confident the way I did at the hearing in February when Laurie pled guilty. I was aware that the judge might decide to let Laurie off with community service. My hope was that she'd get at least two solid years in prison, which felt like enough time for her life to be severely impacted. I took a deep breath as the final chapter in this nightmare began.

"Mr. Dentoni, I am honored to have you in my court. Your reputation precedes you," the judge called out to the attorney on Laurie's team whom I had not met. The man looked like he was in his late sixties with thick silver hair and was dressed in a very expensive suit.

He stood and with the bravado of a superstar said, "Thank you, Your Honor, pleasure to meet you."

Troy turned his head and gave me a look that said, "What the fuck was that!"

I silently shook my head back and forth knowing this was a sign that Laurie had power in the courtroom today.

After the judge formally announced that the purpose of the hearing was to determine the length of the sentence for Schneider, he immediately launched into a lengthy discussion regarding whether to accept the sentencing guidelines of fifty-one to seventy-two months offered by the probation offer.

"I'm in agreement with the guidelines, Your Honor, and think they are appropriate for this case," said Donaldson. I was impressed with his professional persona.

Beatty stood up and pointed to a phonebook-sized document on the table. "Your Honor, we sent the court a report yesterday by a pediatric psychologist stating that Ms. Schneider's middle child, Sheila, is on the autism scale and is already having some severe behavioral issues." He went on to claim that the psychologist felt the consistent presence of her parent was vital to her healthy development and growth. "Dr. Goldberg is here in the courtroom but must be home by 4:37 p.m. today in order to properly observe the Jewish Sabbath, so she may answer any questions you may have for her."

I let out an audible groan as Troy said under his breath, "This is bullshit." We victims who knew Laurie best expected her legal team to use the children to gain sympathy from the court. In fact, we suspected this was a major contributing factor in her having three kids since she was arrested in 2010. Claiming that one of her children is autistic a few days before the sentencing seemed like such an obvious ploy, but I feared the judge didn't see things my way.

"I think the report stands for itself, but thank you for the offer, Mr. Beatty," Judge Hurley stated. "Mr. Donaldson, do you have an opinion on the report?"

Donaldson stood up and buttoned his jacket. "The report seems clear and the U.S. Attorney's office does not refute the possible diagnosis of Ms. Schneider's daughter with autism. We do not see the assessment as having relevance on the court's decision to honor the sentencing guidelines put forth by the probation officer."

I looked over at Laurie's posse in the peanut gallery to get a read on her crowd, but I saw no register of emotion.

"Your Honor, in the case of the United States against Williamson, the court ruled that the status of the defendant's family would be detrimentally impacted if a prison sentence was served," said Beatty. "We offer this as precedent for your decision on whether to adhere to the sentencing guidelines."

Donaldson shot up to speak. "Your Honor, that was my case and the circumstances were completely different. I can give you details of the situation if necessary, but the decision of that case should have no relevance on Ms. Schneider's sentencing. We strongly believe the sentencing guidelines are fair to use for this case."

Again, I was impressed by Donaldson for stepping up to the plate. I could see how he would be a skilled trial attorney, maybe just not so great with preparing witnesses.

The judge looked at Donaldson then back at Beatty. Silently he leafed through some papers on his desk. I reflected that Laurie would have faced twenty years had she not pled guilty. Now she was only facing three to five years, the final recommendation from the parole officer. It seemed that her attorneys had a lot of nerve asking for a larger reduction, especially when we all know she was guilty of the crime.

Dentoni stood up and walked around his chair. It was clear he was getting ready to perform for his courtroom audience. "Judge Hurley, Laurie Schneider is just a single parent trying to raise a family. Sure, she made some mistakes, but her children shouldn't have to pay for what she's done."

The hearing had only been going on for thirty minutes, but it was already a circus with Laurie's attorneys running the show. Thankfully, the judge saw through the charismatic attorney and with a wave of his hand dismissed the drama.

"Thank you, Mr. Dentoni, but I have to agree with Mr. Donaldson. I'm comfortable sticking to the sentencing guidelines for today. Let's move on."

Dentoni, clearly looking dejected, walked back to his chair.

I was doing a happy dance inside my head. Maybe today wouldn't be so bad after all. I looked over at Laurie's posse and saw the same empty expressions on their faces.

Judge Hurley then asked each side to present closing arguments in a final effort to persuade him. He let the U.S. Attorney go first.

Donaldson stood up, buttoned his jacket, and quickly looked down at his notes before launching into his pitch.

"Laurie Schneider pled guilty to a charge of wire fraud in February of this year. The facts clearly show that this fraud was related to running a Ponzi scheme in the amount of almost $7 million. Ms. Schneider used shell companies that included FlippingMax and Janitorial Closeout City to lure unsuspecting people to invest in completely fraudulent schemes."

I was blown away at how much authority Donaldson carried in his voice as he passionately made a case to put Laurie in prison.

Donaldson continued: "Ms. Schneider told people that she had connections to factories in China that make industrial construction equipment and could arrange for buyers to purchase this equipment, making huge profits for investors. She called these 'China Deals' and solicited millions of dollars from investors. In fact, Schneider had no connections to China. She simply took people's money using this lie."

I looked over at Laurie. She continued rocking back and forth with her forehead touching the palms of her hands. She played the part of a frightened and remorseful defendant well.

I shot a glance at the judge and saw he was totally engaged by Donaldson's words. I remained hopeful and felt my palms sweaty from anxiety as he continued his presentation.

"Ms. Schneider also lured investors into real estate schemes involving flipping residential homes. She claimed to have bought and sold many properties, making investors money on the resale of these homes. As the facts clearly show, Schneider never purchased any property. This was simply another example of her fraud."

Donaldson spent another ten minutes going through the details of Laurie's various schemes and ended his speech by stating that she had profited from her Ponzi scheme. He gave examples of her purchase of a boat, leasing of expensive cars, living on waterfront property, and membership to a country club as proof.

During Donaldson's last statement, Dentoni stood up, pointed at Donaldson, and yelled, "Not True! The boat that you refer to was a small motorboat and the home she lives in is modest and now in foreclosure. She's living off of $1,200 a month. How is that profiting from a Ponzi scheme?!"

Donaldson responded by restating that Laurie had run a $7 million Ponzi, and records clearly show she made money.

I was flabbergasted at how Dentoni was taking over the proceedings. I also wondered how Laurie had enough money to pay these two high-end attorneys for six years.

Dentoni continued to yell for a few minutes about how Laurie didn't profit from her "mistakes" and in fact suffered greatly due to the stress of attempting to support her family since she was arrested. Although it was clear to everyone in the courtroom we were there for a sentencing of someone who already admitted her guilt, this guy was so good—he effectively made it seem that Laurie was a victim.

Finally, Judge Hurley asked for Dentoni to be quiet while Donaldson finished discussing the impact of Laurie's crime on her victims. Donaldson noted that many of our lives had been devastated, both financially and emotionally due to the deep betrayal of trust and fraud. As he sat down, I was grateful that he had done a great job at presenting the case. He had some facts wrong about how the China Deals actually worked, but he had gotten the basic message across.

A feeling of dread filled me as Dentoni stood up to present closing remarks on behalf of Laurie. I had seen enough to know he would be brilliant and very convincing.

"Yes, Laurie Schneider made mistakes. She was a young businesswoman with enormous charisma trying to survive in a cutthroat world. As we all know, she made some errors in judgment. She's pled guilty, and as you will hear from her later is incredibly remorseful for the suffering she's caused."

He paused for dramatic effect.

"Ms. Schneider is now a single mother raising three young children all under the age of four. She has a newborn child and one just diagnosed with autism. These children are the *real* victims of the situation."

I felt myself tense up. Troy and I looked at each other. "Here comes the bullshit," said Troy.

"Ms. Schneider will soon be divorced. Her husband left due to the pressure and publicity of her situation," Dentoni continued. "He's been completely out of the picture for months and has no interest in the care of his children."

I knew this was a lie. Vince had recently put up pictures of his children on his Facebook profile. I shifted in my seat and gave an involuntary grunt.

Donaldson stood up quickly. "Your Honor, if I may. The psychological report, which was submitted by Ms. Schneider's legal team, clearly states that at two of the three assessment sessions of their daughter Ms. Schneider's husband was present. For the other, the nanny was there in place of either parent. All these sessions took place in the past six weeks."

Dentoni quickly retorted, "The husband has *nothing* to do with these children. Ms. Schneider is sole parent. Her seventy-year-old mother works full-time and must tend to her ailing ninety-one-year-old mother. She is too old and burdened to take care of these children."

The judge interrupted. "I believe Ms. Schneider's mother is sixty-six and I'm well aware of her need to work at her party supply store."

I glanced over at Laurie's mother who looked like an old street whore. She still showed no expression or any emotion, even when the court was discussing the welfare of her grandchildren.

Dentoni went on with the passion of someone campaigning for office. "The *true* victims of this situation are these pure and innocent children who've done nothing to deserve having their mother be taken away during the most important years of their lives. What will little Sheila do without her mother? This young girl has just been given a devastating diagnosis and will need her mother in the next years."

I felt nauseous. My worst fears were coming true. Laurie's legal team was using her children in an attempt to gain sympathy from the judge.

For the next *forty minutes*, the discussion focused on who could take care of Laurie's children if she were sentenced. Most of the time, the bantering back and forth pertained to whether Laurie's husband was active in the children's lives. Donaldson continuously brought up the fact that Vince had been at the psychological assessment only a few months before, but because Donaldson had not used the FBI to gather any information to help substantiate Vince's involvement or even where Vince was living, the question remained unanswered.

I sat seething with anger. Donaldson should have anticipated this issue, especially when Laurie's legal team submitted the psychological assessment. It seemed to be a reflection of Donaldson's lack of focus on the case, not a lack of skill. He had not done his research, and this would impact the length of any sentence Laurie received.

As the discussion continued, I wanted to pass a note to Donaldson saying things like "Check Vince's Facebook page!" and "Laurie's three sisters could be candidates to take the kids!" but knew I could have been thrown out of court, so I just sat stewing in my frustration.

Finally, the judge determined that with the limited information presented, it was not possible for him to determine the involvement of Vince as a parent. He then asked Laurie if she would like to address the court.

As he walked to his seat, Dentoni called out, "We didn't help her write her statement at all . . . every word is her own!"

Laurie pulled out a sheet of paper and paused before beginning to read. I imagined that she was thinking of her dead father, dead puppies, prison, and anything sad so she could conjure up some emotion to seem as though she cared about what she had done to us. She spoke in a tone much deeper than her normal voice. It was an attempt to sound emotional.

"I have thought deeply about the events that have led me to this day and I am very regretful. I took money from business associates, friends, and even my family. I know what I have done was wrong, and I wish I could take back all that I did. I know I have hurt many people including people

I love dearly. I want to thank my mothah for her support. Even though I took money from her, too."

She made an audible sigh and continued with her litany of things she had learned about since getting caught.

"People trusted me with their money, and many people lost amounts that have impacted their lives. I know what I did was wrong and will continue to do what I can to make the situation right."

I looked over at Laurie's posse and saw the same blank faces. I wondered if they had any idea what she'd actually done.

When Laurie's voice rose, her kids were the next topic. "I ask not for me but for my children to please let me continue to be with them for the sake of their well-being. Please—" At this juncture, she paused to fake cry and lay her head on the desk as she put her arms out in front of her—prostrating herself before the court as she begged for mercy.

She lifted her head to speak. "Please don't let my children suffah for the mistakes I've made. I'm a good mothah. I love my children dearly and want the best for them. I know in my heart that I need to stay with my children especially my dawtah who needs her mothah right now. Please, please, please have mercy on my children." She then pretended to cry again.

I looked up to see how the judge was reacting and saw that he was shuffling papers and avoiding looking at Laurie, who was obviously making a play for his sympathy.

After her performance was over and she continued to fake-sob as her body rocked back and forth, the judge thanked Laurie and asked Mr. Donaldson if there were any victims who wished to speak.

Donaldson stood up and told the judge that there were two victims present who had statements and that he would be reading them. He had told me prior to the hearing that it would be best if he read my statement to minimize potential drama in the court. Now that I had seen Dentoni, I understood better what he had anticipated. He moved to the center podium and began to read:

My name is Mark Morewitz. I am a victim of Laurie Schneider and am listed as John Doe #2 in the charge that you will sentence her for today. I represent forty-four of my family and friends who lost $2.2 million in her scam.

We victims are concerned that since this case was not tried, the court may not fully understand the extent to which Laurie Schneider viciously manipulated her mostly very middle-class victims out of almost $7 million.

Please do not mistake the situation as a crime in which Schneider only defrauded victims out of money or be fooled into thinking Schneider did not realize what she was doing. We victims know firsthand that Laurie Schneider consciously wove a deep web of lies and manipulated everyone around her for years in order to successfully operate her fraudulent schemes. She constructed elaborate plans that involved falsifying financial documents, bribing people, and paying off business associates to lie to victims in order to further her schemes. She fabricated social relationships to swindle unsuspecting victims into investing in her Ponzi. She seduced all of us and became embedded in our lives while stealing every cent we had.

One simple example is that she claimed Dick Goldstein, listed as John Doe #4 in the charges she pled guilty to, was the person who ran the China Deal investments. She used the fact that he is a business mogul to lure her victims into giving her our life savings and even encouraged us to take out huge home loans to invest. As Schneider's attorney John Beatty told me in February 2009, she in fact never transferred any of her victims' investment funds to Dick Goldstein. She was actually borrowing money from him on an ongoing basis to pay back her investors. Goldstein thought he was lending money to someone he was romantically involved with—Schneider was even planning to get pregnant with his child—but in fact she was using all of us to get what she wanted, which was money and power.

Schneider has shown no remorse during the almost six years since she was caught and in fact blames her victims for being greedy. She destroyed the life I had, left me bankrupt, and caused me to lose the precious trust of all my family and friends, who blame me for losing their life savings.

After almost six years, we victims have lost faith in the federal justice system. When I approached the FBI in March 2009 with all the evidence needed for the case, we already knew that she had been running a Ponzi scheme. However, we disappointedly watched as hundreds of other similar cases moved toward sentencing while Schneider lived free, continued to manipulate the justice system, and gave birth to three children in three years.

Judge Hurley, today you have the opportunity to finally deliver justice to this admitted criminal who destroyed our dreams. We consider your sentence of Laurie Schneider a final legacy you will leave for this case.

We request that Schneider receive a sentence no shorter than a full five years. This is substantially shorter than the twenty-year sentence she may have received if there had been a trial.

We also request that she be remanded into custody no more than one week from today. She has had plenty of time to live free in the community. Now it is time for her to serve her sentence for the crimes she committed against us. As a sociopath *and someone who has admitted to postpartum depression, once knowing her sentence Schneider will be a high risk for suicide. This is another reason to remand her as soon as possible; we victims do not want her to have any more easy escapes from her deserved punishment.*

We hope you agree with us that every day that Laurie Schneider spends in jail makes the world a safer place.

I watched Laurie as my words were read aloud. When Donaldson read the sentence about Dick and Laurie being romantically involved, she stopped ringing her hands and acting distraught. The expression in her face showed deep tension. She whispered something in Beatty's ear. It was clear that she was angry and on the offensive.

I was happy the judge could see how she maneuvered from her pretend agony to anger so quickly.

I was stunned a moment later when Beatty stood up and began railing against me. "Judge, there were people who were victimized by Ms. Schneider, but Mark Morewitz was not one of them. He worked in Ms. Schneider's office and was well aware of what was happening. He is no victim."

I fought the rage to stand up and say something to defend myself.

Beatty continued his tirade by explaining that the first wave of Laurie's victims invested and received small returns. The second wave of people were brought in at the very end when she was desperately trying to find cash to pay out her existing investments. Beatty ended his speech by saying a third group of people *victimized Laurie* by demanding returns of up to 60 percent of what they invested.

The ferociousness to which Beatty attacked my statement and my character took my breath away. Since there was no trial, there was no place to challenge all the letters I'd written or the evidence I had supplied. This was his one shot, and he did a devastatingly good job even though everything he said was completely wrong

I sat feeling a range of emotions as Donaldson read a statement by another victim who was present but whom I'd never met. Laurie had recruited him late in her scam after I had stopped working in the office, so I wasn't familiar with his situation. His statement was wrenching. Laurie had gotten him to invest in late 2008 when she already knew she was losing money. She siphoned his entire life savings and he lost everything. In his statement, he discussed how he has been unable to assist his ailing parents due to struggling to support his wife and kids. It was heartbreaking to hear someone else's pain.

Finally, we were at the juncture where the judge began discussing his decision regarding a sentence. It would have been perfect if the judge had been able to spit out the sentence in the first minute of his speech. To my dismay, he seesawed back and forth for the next twenty minutes.

"Ms. Schneider, the crime you committed hurt many people, and I appreciate that you understand the impact of your actions. Really, your crime was not very different from holding a gun to someone and asking for their money. For example, taking investors on a drive to look at properties to buy and potentially flip, then taking their money for that purpose but never buying any property was heinous."

Troy and I turned and smiled at each other. So far this was going well.

"But I have received letters from some of your supporters, even Ms. Betty Descio, a former employee, who lost money with you. All these people say you are the first to help a friend when someone is in need."

His words felt like a slap in the face. *"Why would a seasoned judge pay attention to letters from Laurie's supporters?"* I thought.

The judge kept going back and forth stating something horrendous Laurie did, then mentioning something positive that in his mind balanced out the negative. It was incredibly frustrating because he was taking us all on a rollercoaster ride through his thought process. He also stated his concern for the well-being of her children.

"Even though you chose to have these children after being arrested, and you should consider yourself fully responsible for that decision, the court must take into consideration their well-being. And of course we are unsure of the actual status of your husband in the care planning for the children."

I still didn't understand why no one had subpoenaed Vince to attend the hearing or get a sworn statement regarding the status of their marriage and his involvement with the kids. After almost six years, couldn't someone have taken care of that detail?

Finally, the judge got to the point and said what we all wanted to hear, "Ms. Schneider I sentence you to thirty-six months in federal prison. After release you will be responsible for paying restitution to the victims as determined by the justice system."

My heart sank. Three years didn't seem like a substantial enough time for all the destruction she had caused. In that moment, it felt like Laurie had won. Dentoni shot a huge smile to the guy sitting in front of Troy and me.

The judge then stated that it would take time to assign Laurie to a prison, so he would not be remanding her into custody for a few months until that was decided.

Beatty stood up to speak. "Your Honor, we request Danbury Federal Prison due to the close proximity of Ms. Schneider's family. And we request that she have six months to complete breastfeeding of her youngest child."

My first thought was that Martha Stewart was sent to the same prison: it looked like summer camp from all the media reports of her stay there.

"Six fucking months for breastfeeding?" Troy muttered to me.

Thankfully, Donaldson stood up in a mild protest. "We request that amount be reduced to four months, Your Honor."

"Wow, what a substantial reduction," I quietly muttered sarcastically.

The judge thanked Donaldson and started leafing through his calendar. "So that puts us at March 27, 2015, as the date Ms. Schneider is to report to prison . . . likely Danbury Prison."

As he adjourned the hearing, Laurie's entourage crowded around her with joyful adulation. In the center of a circle of her supporters, Laurie

looked stunned but wore a smile on her face. She and her posse immediately left the courtroom.

I walked directly to Donaldson's desk, furious. "That was horrible. Why
didn't anyone know whether Vince and Laurie are getting a divorce or if
he's going to be involved with the kids when she's in prison?" Donaldson
had no answer for me.

"How long will she actually serve?" I spat out.

"She will likely do thirty months on a thirty-six-month sentence,"
Donaldson answered.

I gave him no time to pause. "And when she doesn't show up to
prison on
March 27, 2015, what will be done?"

Donaldson looked at me with a confused look. "If she doesn't report
to prison, then a warrant will be put out for her arrest."

"And then what?" I said accusingly, then didn't let him finish. "Here's
the deal: she's not going to show up. She's going to have a family crisis
or health emergency and her attorneys are going to put in a request for
a delay." I realized I was railing at him. Although he had presented well,
he hadn't done his homework and his lack of thoroughness may have reduced her sentence by a few years.

Before he could answer, I shouted out my next question. "And is there
a mechanism in place to make sure she claims all the money she makes
so she is paying as much restitution as possible once she is released?"

"We'll make sure that she is paying a percentage of what she earns
to victims," he said, trying to remain calm. I could see in his eyes that he
wanted to say to me, "*Let it go. It's over.*"

"But today, her attorney said she is currently earning only $1,200 a
month, yet she's supporting her three kids, likely her husband, and has
several nannies. Don't you see that she gets paid in cash for her party
planning? She's already scamming the system."

I quickly continued. "Look, I know I'm being harsh here, but you're
aware that I don't think this case was handled appropriately by you or
your office. I do very much appreciate that you stayed in touch with me

and realize you didn't have to do that during the last year. Thank you for that courtesy."

After finishing my tirade and realizing I had a lot of emotion to tend to that did not relate to Donaldson, I left with Troy. He offered me a ride home so we could both process the hearing.

Caught in traffic, we spent the next two hours going over everything we had experienced during the day. I hadn't had a peer, someone who had also been victimized directly by Laurie, to talk to since I moved from Brooklyn in 2009. It was both cathartic and toxic, because neither of us could provide comfort to the other. Each time one of us told a horrendous story, the other had a similar one to offer.

I told him I was writing a book and it would include a lot about our interactions.

As we slowly moved in traffic, he turned to me. "You know she told me you had AIDS and to have nothing to do with your sick ass, right? She wanted to make sure you and I stayed far apart so neither would figure out how much the other was investing with her."

Troy's words stung deeply. I do not have HIV, nor did Laurie ever think I did. Even after all the work I had done getting Laurie in prison, I still held on to some fantasy that she and I had some tiny connection that was real—that somehow back in those days there had been a component of friendship. My mind turned to the moment when she put her hand on my shoulder at my father's gravesite after driving eight hours to bring me my favorite desserts from New York. It was still difficult to understand that all of that was part of her manipulation. Troy's comment reminded me that she is a heartless sociopath without regard or feeling for any of us. She had used me in any way she could to get money and power. In court, we witnessed the degree to which she would go to save herself.

Over the next weeks, I let all the feelings from the hearing wash over me again and again. I visited Lands End frequently and was thankful I had allowed myself to live to see each and every day. I tried my best not to overwhelm the people in my present life with the haunting feelings I had about my past. Seeing Laurie and her team actively manipulate the court had retriggered the trauma I had been through and highlighted the fractured relationships I now have with many family members and friends. As time passed, I could finally celebrate that this tumultuous chapter was over.

The Ponzi Princess has been dethroned. Laurieland no longer exists, and Laurie Schneider will soon rot in prison for a miserable nine hundred days.

UPDATE:

Schneider was granted a three month extension by Judge Dennis Hurley so that she can attend to her children's needs. In his decision, he stated that no more delays would be granted. The new date for her to report to prison is June 15, 2015.

Epilogue

Before Laurie entered my life, greed seemed like something other people experienced. The green monster motivated huge corporations to tear down vast acres of rain forest to make a quick buck or fueled Dickensian slumlords to force the poorest of people to live in squalid living conditions.

I've since learned that there is a multitude of ways that greed can enter and take over our lives. Nate and I wanted to have more money to renovate our house and possibly raise kids one day. Most of my family and friends also had simple and specific goals for money made through what we all thought were legitimate business ventures. A relative put new gutters on her house; another installed replacement windows. Friends saved money for their son's college education, and others were able to increase the amount of childcare they had for their two sons. We thought we were improving our lives through investments that were obviously unusual but that seemed real. And our desire to improve our lives blinded us, especially me, to the realities of Laurie and her world.

Many successful businesspeople, unassociated with me, invested huge sums of money with Laurie. Everyone entered Laurieland with the appropriate level of skepticism but none was prepared to deal with a sociopath. As each one of us walked into her door, she assessed what we needed to hear in order to be convinced to hand over our money.

A friend recently commented that this situation had all the makings of a cult. We were blinded by her charisma.

Laurie of course recognized our greed even though we were all naively unaware of it. She created a world of deceit to keep us in the dark. For example, she instructed Larry the accountant to create false financial documents showing huge profits to woo new investors, but the profits never existed. She bribed an administrator of a large nonprofit in Brooklyn to vouch that the organization, which runs most of the homeless shelters in the outer boroughs, used Laurie's janitorial supply company to stock their many sites. And of course she had staff and friends tell blatant lies in her effort to create the mirage of success in her businesses and investments. Her bookkeeper, who worked in her offices every day, was fooled so much that she invested $40,000 of her own money into Laurie's sham deals through Collective Good LLC.

Laurie accomplished her scheme through a combination of incredible skill at reading people, expertise in telling lies, and an ability to juggle many separate fictitious lives to hundreds of people. Except for the brief moments on the evening that she first told me of the fake closeouts, Laurie has shown no remorse and in fact seems to be increasingly angry at everyone who lost money. We are the reality that shattered her fantasy world.

None of this takes away the monumental amount of pain and suffering brought to those I love and care about. Writing this book, I found myself in awe of my ongoing stupidity and lack of awareness in regard to Laurie Schneider. My desire of a better life for my family and me overrode my intuition, which was clearly telling me to get as far away from her as I could. Yet I stayed so that my inner circle and I could continue to make money, which seemed to expand our life choices and thus make our lives better. It's pathetically that simple.

When people thought I was helping them make money, they put me high on a pedestal. After the truth about Laurie's scheme came out, I fell far below dignity in their eyes. This book is meant to give a narrative to explain how this horrible episode in our lives could and did happen. I will forever regret the pain caused by introducing anyone to Laurie Schneider and her world.

My friends and family continue to adjust to the dramatic loss of income. There has of course been a substantial change in the dynamic between most of the people I introduced to Laurie and me; this group represents almost all my family and friends. The faith and trust most intuitively had in me are now only a faint memory. My contact with most of the folks who invested through Collective Good is limited to periodic updates I send on both the civic and criminal cases. The loss of familial relationships and lifelong friendships continues to leave a gaping hole in my soul.

People continue to ask me whether I think Laurie consciously planned the Ponzi scheme and if she actually cared for me at all. These questions are not easily answered. Laurie clearly has sociopathic qualities. For years, she was able to lie to every person, every day, about all aspects of her life. My assumption is that whatever connection and friendship I felt on my end were sheer manipulation by her. There is no way for me to ever know her true motivation for anything that happened. I don't want to give her the benefit of the doubt in regard to how the Ponzi scheme unfolded. What I know is that she swindled huge sums of money from my family and friends, using me as the bait. The steps that led to her doing so and her genuine intentions are of little interest to me. I assume she wouldn't be able to truthfully answer these questions anyway, because she only knows how to lie and manipulate.

I will always despise her.

Laurie may have taken our money and destroyed the trust between me and those I love, but she didn't take my heart or my strength, both of which served as a guiding light to get me through this dark episode and helped me build a new life. I'm grateful to live happily in San Francisco. I enjoy my work and am in a wonderfully balanced relationship with an amazing man who treats me with enormous respect. His love and support have helped me continue to heal. I'm the luckiest guy in the world for finding such a sweet, nurturing man at this stage of my life.

Amen to that.

Mark Morewitz
May 2015

Author's note: A portion of the profits from this book will be shared with Schneider's victims who are my family and friends.

Acknowledgments

Brian, thank you for your huge heart and ongoing support. Waking up to your smiling face every day makes me the happiest guy on the planet.

With enormous gratitude, I thank Frances Culp, Kim Martin, Rich Aranow, Joseph Cecere, Becky Packard, Susan Williams, Shanna Williams, Bill Glenn, Sean Cavanaugh, and Katrina Kaiser for giving me feedback on early drafts of the book and for being such supportive friends during this dark period in my life. Elaina Costa Ford and Rani Marx, thank you both for your ongoing interest in the book.

A huge shout-out to my big brother Steve for lovingly taking the time to suggest a few final edits on the book.

Thank you to Julia Scheeres and Tony Dushane for teaching me how to write a book. Louisa Castner, my editor, thank you for helping me round out the sharp edges.

My deep gratitude to Sally and Steve Seltzer for being there in my most desperate hour.

Robert Bloch, thank you for your courage and integrity.

Glossary

Alterkocher   Old man

Bridge and Tunnel   People from the suburbs

Mensch   A good person

Mishegoss   Craziness

Mitzvah   Good deed

Oy   "Oh my"

Schmuck   Someone stupid of foolish

Shvartza   A derogatory way of saying African American

Yente   Busybody

Made in the USA
Charleston, SC
25 June 2015